C000178998

A FEW GOOD MEN
THE BRIGHTON & HOVE ALBION DREAM TEAM

First published in Great Britain in 2007 by

The Breedon Books Publishing Company Limited

Breedon House, 3 The Parker Centre,

Derby, DE21 4SZ.

© Spencer Vignes 2007

All Rights Reserved. No part of this publication may be reproduced,
stored in a retrieval system, or transmitted in any form, or by any
means, electronic, mechanical, photocopying, recording or otherwise
without the prior permission in writing of the copyright holders, nor
be otherwise circulated in any form or binding or cover other than in
which it is published and without a similar condition being imposed
on the subsequent publisher.

ISBN 978-1-85983-573-9

Printed and bound by Cromwell Press,
Trowbridge, Wiltshire.

A FEW GOOD MEN

THE BRIGHTON & HOVE ALBION DREAM TEAM

SPENCER VIGNES

For Sally Vignes, admirer of Steve Foster (and his thighs)

Contents

Introduction

It will never win any prizes for being the wittiest football chant ever, but it still makes me smile even after all these years. Sung by fans of Brighton & Hove Albion to the tune of *Yellow Submarine* by The Beatles, the lyrics of the song go like this:

Number one was Peter Ward
Number two was Peter Ward
Number three was Peter Ward
Number four was Peter Ward
Number five was Peter Ward
Number six was Peter Ward
Number seven was Peter Ward
Number eight was Peter Ward
Number nine was Peter Ward
Number ten was Peter Ward
Number eleven was Peter Ward

We all live in a Wardy wonderland, a Wardy wonderland, a Wardy wonderland (repeat)

Trust me, it sounds a darned sight better when sung than it looks on paper.

Now, for the benefit of any non-Brighton & Hove Albion fans reading this, I had better explain who Peter Ward is. Between the years 1976 and 1980 this son of Staffordshire scored 92 goals as the club rose from the old Third Division to the top flight of English football, the first of which arrived just 50 seconds into his debut. During the 1977–78 season he came third in a national poll to find the country's favourite football player and scored a hat-trick for England's Under-21s against Norway in September 1977 at, of all places, the Goldstone Ground, Albion's home from 1902 to 1997. Ask any Brighton supporter between the ages of nine and 90 to name the greatest player ever to have worn the club's blue and white colours, and the chances are they will say Peter Ward.

I cannot remember exactly when it first started, but at some point a few years ago a rendition of the *Wardy Wonderland* song at a Brighton match did get me thinking about which players would in fact make up my Albion dream team. Peter Ward had to be in there, but what about the other 10? This conundrum was taken a step further following a conversation with Steve Caron at Breedon Books, who expressed an interest in publishing a book on the subject should I have the time and inspiration to write it. Finding the time was a problem. Finding the inspiration was not. And so one night, armed with a bottle of red wine, I sat down and wrote out a list of 46 names. Reducing that to a final 11 was surprisingly easy, although deciding who would play where in defence and which two from three would occupy central-midfield did involve the opening of a second bottle of wine. Needs must, you understand.

The chosen few were selected not just for their skill levels, but because of what I felt they had contributed as players to Brighton & Hove Albion. Joe Corrigan, Dennis Mortimer and Dean Saunders probably have more silverware dotted around their houses than Buckingham Palace, but in the average football fan's mind they will always be Manchester City, Aston Villa and – in Dean's case – just about everywhere other than Brighton, so they failed to make the final cut. There was also no room for sentiment. Stuart Storer, for example, scored the last ever goal at the Goldstone Ground, helping to safeguard the club's then extremely precarious position in the Football League in the process. But, let's face it, he was not the finest right-winger the Albion has ever had. Stuart would probably tell you that himself.

Agree or disagree with my choice, there is one thing you cannot deny. These 11 players at some stage gave their all for the Albion and made the lives of supporters such as myself all the better for it. For that they deserve our eternal gratitude. As Peter Ward said himself of the ones selected, 'That's not a bad team, is it? That would do okay in the Premier League. It wouldn't win it, but it would do okay.'

My thanks go to the 11 who all willingly gave up their time to be interviewed. One former Albion player, on learning that he had not made the XI, did refuse to have anything to do with the project and is not quoted in the pages that follow. However, countless others were only too happy to co-operate by sharing their memories, for which I am extremely grateful. A big tip of the hat also goes to Tim Carder for his support and helping to source photographs, together with Bennett Dean, Sarah Watts, Bob Herrick, Paul Hazlewood and, last but not least, my old friend Ron Chakraborty at BBC Sport.

Spencer Vignes
2007

Chapter One
Accidents Will Happen

Here's a dilemma for you: you are one of England's most promising young goalkeepers, and for the first time in your career you have been selected as the number-one stopper at your club for the forthcoming season. Your side are favourites to win the League, so expectations are high. One Sunday morning you notice that the large hedge separating your back garden from next door could do with a bit of attention. It is a job that's going to involve an electric trimmer and a stepladder. Bearing in mind you have a reputation for being a tad accident prone, do you:

a) Employ someone to come round and do it for you.

b) Ignore it, put the kettle on and hope the thing will burn down.

c) Tend to it yourself.

Now you do not need to be a brain surgeon to work out that the vast majority of goalkeepers, precious in the extreme of their hands, would probably have gone for a or b. Then again, Graham Moseley was not like most other 'keepers. Mistakes, there were a few – enough for him to be dropped more times than a bungee rope during his nine years on Brighton's books. Career-threatening injuries? Plenty of them, including the

above scenario which nearly cost him a finger, a fight with a plate glass window resulting in more blood than the shower scene from *Psycho*, and the horrific car accident that eventually did for his livelihood (and his marriage).

That said, when Graham was good there were few, in my extremely humble opinion, who could touch him. His record on penalties was second to none. When Sheffield Wednesday were doing their level best to deny Albion a first appearance at Wembley during the 1983 FA Cup semi-final, it was Graham who perhaps did more than anyone to keep them at bay. His form during the 1984–85 season, when no team managed to put more than two goals past him in 42 straight League games, still defies all logic. So I think we can forgive him the odd domestic mishap.

When it came to deciding who I would interview first for this book, Graham was always the clear favourite. And not just because the two of us now live only 30 miles apart in South Wales. Tradition has it that the goalkeeper's name is always first on a team sheet, the number one. However, I had also worked out that he had starred alongside more members of my dream XI than any other player. We

Graham Moseley, Chepstow, 2006.

had spoken before on several occasions over the phone, and I knew he trusted me. Chances were he would come up with some gems from the memory banks about the others. After a week of speaking to our respective answering machines, we finally arranged to meet one lunchtime in late September at the Boat Inn in Chepstow, Graham's home town for over 15 years. It is a bit quiet compared with the hubbub of Brighton, but, in the words of the man himself, 'excellent for pubs…there just seems to be a lot of them here, which you can't help but like.'

Graham Moseley was born in 1953 in the Manchester suburb of Stretford. He grew up as a Manchester United fan and used to support the Reds from the famous Stretford End at Old Trafford. I had heard tell he even made it to Wembley for United's famous European Cup Final triumph over Benfica in 1968. 'Even better than that, I used to live in a terraced house that overlooked the Manchester Ship Canal Recreation Ground, which United always used to use for pre-season training,' says Graham, who still looks pretty much like Graham Moseley circa 1985, only with greying locks. 'They had two wonderful football pitches which local kids weren't allowed to go on as such, but we'd bend the iron rails back and squeeze through and get five minutes in there before the groundsman came and kicked us off. That was the time of Law, Best, Charlton, that era. Afterwards I'd

stand at the entrance with my autograph book, and they would come up in their Mark One Jaguars. Sometimes they would stop and you'd get the occasional autograph.' So did he get Best's signature? 'Oh yeah. But I haven't got it anymore. That is one thing I really regret. Probably my younger brother took it off somewhere when I left home.'

Graham's father, Charles Albert Moseley, had been a decent Rugby League player for Salford until an injury forced him to retire and take up running the lines. Moseley junior would often accompany his dad to matches in exotic-sounding places such as Barrow and St Helens, getting an early taste for 'that dressing-room experience, the feeling and the smell of liniment, all those sort of things.' As a kid he played centre-forward for his junior school, a team that tended to concede more goals than Graham could score. So, being the tallest lad in the side, he was switched to goalkeeper. At 15 years old he was spotted playing for Stretford Boys against Liverpool Boys by a scout called – no sniggering please – Neil Diamond. After the match Diamond paid a visit to the Moseley household, only for Graham to panic and disappear out of the back door. The youngster returned two hours later to discover he had been asked to try out for the Lancashire county side at Blackburn Rovers. This time he saw sense and refused to bolt. His performance was good enough to win him an apprenticeship at Ewood Park.

Graham spent the next couple of years cutting his teeth in the B team at Blackburn. Eventually he was promoted to the reserve side for an away match at Derby County, then in the extremely capable hands of Brian Clough and his coaching sidekick Peter Taylor. 'I must have impressed them because Jimmy Gordon, who used to be the coach and went everywhere Brian Clough went, came into the dressing room afterwards and enquired about myself, and it went from there. Derby had just got promotion to the First Division, and I ended up playing for their reserves all year. We won the Central League against the Manchester Uniteds and Liverpools and that got me sent to the England Youth trials with three or four other goalkeepers who had all made it into their first teams. I got into that youth-team side under Gordon Milne, who went on to manage Coventry, and we won a mini World Cup tournament in Spain, and I didn't let a goal in all the way through the tournament. We did have a good side, though – Kevin Beattie, Trevor Francis, players of that kind of standing. It was a great experience.'

Despite the plaudits, Graham was finding it virtually impossible to break into Derby's first team, such was the outstanding form of regular goalkeeper Colin Boulton. A break of sorts finally

came in November 1973 following the departure of Clough and Taylor to, of all places, Brighton. Keen to stamp his authority on the side, new manager Dave Mackay decided to give Graham the opportunity to show what he could do. He made only 44 appearances over the following four years, but it was a start. One of those matches was an FA Cup semi-final defeat to his boyhood heroes, Manchester United, at Hillsborough. Afterwards, Graham was so distraught he made a pact with himself: 'I swore that if an opportunity like that came my way again, I would lay down my life to make sure it didn't slip through my fingers.' Seven years later an opportunity would arise, but more about that later.

The summer of 1977 saw Mackay replaced at the Baseball Ground by Tommy Docherty, who the previous year had guided Manchester United to that FA Cup victory over Derby. Straight away Docherty told both Graham and Colin Boulton that if an offer came in for either one of them they would be on their way. It is at this point that Albion manager Alan Mullery arrives on the scene. 'I don't know exactly how it came about,' says Graham. 'It could've been because Alan and Dave Mackay, who of course had been pals from their old Tottenham days, had spoken to each other. But we had played Brighton in a League Cup game, and I was in the side that drew at the

Goldstone, so it might have been something to do with that.'

If truth be told, Graham did not want to join Brighton. Sure, he had walked along the promenade prior to that Cup game at the Goldstone and quite liked what he saw, but there was an alternative offer on the table to play for Vancouver Whitecaps in the showbiz surroundings of the North American Soccer League. George Best, Franz Beckenbauer, Pele – they were all heading west for a piece of the action, not to mention the dollars, and Graham wanted to join them. So why didn't he? 'I was all keen to go, but my wife at the time was the one who had the common sense. We had children, and she said "I don't want to take them across to Canada. If you go there and something goes wrong, are you going to find it difficult to get back into the League over here? You haven't proved yourself yet." And she was right. Brighton were going well at the time. They had just had a promotion and were signing players like Mark Lawrenson and Gary Williams. They were being tipped to do things. So she said "Let's go there." And we did.'

I've only got one thing to say about that. God bless you Graham's ex, God bless you.

By the time he arrived in Sussex in November 1977, Albion had already entered what are still fondly remembered today as the club's 'glory years'. With ambitious chairman Mike Bamber at the ship's helm and Mullery in charge of team affairs, Brighton had just secured promotion from the old Third Division and set their sights on achieving a place in the top flight for the first time. Whereas attendances at football grounds across the country continued to fall, a victim of poor facilities and rife hooliganism, crowds at the Goldstone regularly topped 30,000. The enthusiasm was infectious, helping to persuade the new arrival that he had made the right decision after all.

'The whole county, not just Brighton, seemed to live and breathe the club. It was the focal point of everything that went on. I think what helped was that the players went out and mixed with the fans. We all ate and drank together in restaurants and pubs alongside the supporters. We'd talk to them, and they felt they could talk to us. We would also go out to these little villages all over the place to do promotional things like the draws for the Seagull Lottery. It was like one huge family, thousands of us.'

One big part of this happy family was regular first-team goalkeeper Eric Steele, a crowd favourite who had come into the side during the closing stages of the 1976–77 Third Division promotion year. Eric's form throughout the following season meant it was five months before Graham got to make his Albion debut away against Bristol Rovers. He held on to the jersey for the final match of the campaign at home to Blackpool, a game

Albion won only to then discover they had been pipped to promotion to Division One by Southampton and Spurs, both teams somewhat conveniently playing out a 0–0 draw against each other at The Dell. After the final whistle, Mullery took to the Goldstone's public address system and promised that the club would go up next time around. To many people's surprise, Graham was chosen above Eric as goalkeeper for the first game of that 1978–79 season. And then the hedge went and intervened.

'I'd just done the last stroke and was standing on the high step ladder admiring it when for some reason I let go of the trimmer,' remembers Graham. 'It came down by my side and caught the little finger on my left hand. Luckily it caught me on the way down rather than across, because if it had been across it probably would have taken the top of my little finger off. But it cut through my nail down to the first joint on my little finger, and that was me out for the next few weeks.'

With Eric back between the sticks, Albion's form during the opening two months of the 1978–79 season was patchy. The weight of expectations around the Goldstone together with the anti-climatic end to the previous campaign seemed to be taking its toll. Following a 3–1 away defeat to Crystal Palace on 7 October, a fit again Graham was reinstated to a side that over the

winter months would at last find its groove. A record of seven clean sheets during November and December speaks for itself.

On 3 February 1979 goals by Teddy Maybank, Peter Sayer and Peter Ward were enough to see off Leicester City and send Albion to the top of the Second Division. As a reward for their excellent run, the first team were sent on a three-day break to Jersey. One night, after several beers, Graham and around half a dozen other players got together in private for a card school. At one point Maybank lost a sizeable amount of money prompting Graham, who, until then, had been sat on the edge of a bed, to roll laughing from his perch straight through a plate glass window. Goodbye card game, hello hospital, where doctors inserted 14 stitches in the goalkeeper's lacerated left arm. On returning to England Mullery refused to say a word about the incident to Graham, leaving the goalkeeper in no doubt as to what he thought about yet another self-inflected injury.

That card school cost Graham his place in the side for the rest of the season, Eric playing in the final 14 games including the historic 3–1 win at Newcastle on 5 May that clinched promotion to Division One. Three games into the following season Graham was then caught by Mullery breaking a Friday night curfew along with new signing Steve Foster before an away match against Manchester City. Neither player had been selected for the final 12 (only one substitute was allowed in those days) yet both feared severe reprimands, or, in Graham's case, the transfer list. 'We were sent home the next morning on the train in shame, the two naughty boys. And we were like "Why are they picking on us?", which I can see now is daft because, although we weren't playing, if someone had got ill we would've had to play, wouldn't we? Anyway, we lost 3–2. The following week we were playing Cambridge in the League Cup, and Fozzie and I were both chosen to start. That made our minds boggle. Why that happened, I don't know. We thought we were out in the cold.'

Two months later Mullery would show his less forgiving side after a League match against Manchester United at Old Trafford, only this time it was Eric who would pay the price. During the game Steele had clashed with Albion left-back Gary Williams, the two indulging in a spot of fisticuffs before being separated by teammates. The goalkeeper was immediately transfer-listed and within a fortnight had been sold to Watford. The rivalry between Eric and Graham was over – at least it was until I told Eric which one of them I had selected for my dream team.

'There's no animosity between us, but maybe I should have tried to stay and battle it out rather than go to Watford, then you'd have me in your team instead

of him,' says Eric, who now works as a goalkeeping coach. 'He's a nice lad, but I never seriously saw him as a threat. You look at my record between 1977 and 1979 and tell me it's better than his, because it's not. He had the bigger physical presence and was much more of a natural 'keeper, whereas I had to work hard at it, a bit like [Peter] Shilton. He [Graham] didn't. He never wanted to work at his game.'

Far from disagreeing, it's an assessment Graham is partly ready to acknowledge. 'He [Eric] was very dedicated, much more so than I ever was. He would train every day after everybody else had finished. He'd go through his routines whereas I was just relying on my natural ability. That's my big regret. If I had worked much harder, I probably could have gone a lot further. I know I could have done.'

There is an interesting post-script to Eric's moment of madness at Old Trafford. In November 1995 Blackburn teammates David Batty and Graeme Le Saux also came to blows during a Champions League match in Moscow. Two days afterwards, the *Daily Mail* published a list of similar flair-ups between players supposedly on the same side including the Manchester United versus Brighton incident from October 1979. Right place, right date, but – unfortunately for whoever wrote the piece – wrong players, the journalist confusing Eric Steele with Graham

Moseley and Gary Williams with left-back Graham Pearce, who didn't become a Seagull until 1982. When Graham heard that Pearce had complained to the newspaper about the error and received some compensation, he decided to do likewise. Cue one cheque for £1,500, enough to pay the deposit on a flat he had seen in Brighton and fancied as an investment. He still owns the flat today.

Anyway, back to the 1979–80 season. Without Eric's constant shadow looming over him, Graham's form seemed to flourish during the remainder of the campaign as Albion transformed themselves from relegation certainties in November to comfortable survivors come May. Two of his 12 clean sheets came in stunning victories over Brian Clough's all-powerful Nottingham Forest side, the reigning European Cup champions who would go on to win the trophy once again in 1980. Graham's performance at the City Ground, which included a penalty save from Scottish international John Robertson just before half-time, has to go down as one of the finest of his career.

Despite finishing well clear of relegation, Albion's form during the opening three months of the 1980–81 season was once again cause for concern. Bottom of Division One in early November, the boo boys began to get to Graham following a series of errors, the worst of which came at home against Birmingham – a simple shot slipping

through his fingers to give the visitors a draw they scarcely deserved. 'I was the first to hold up my hands and say I wasn't playing well, but it was a horrible time. My confidence was shattered and confidence is everything to a goalkeeper. I found it particularly hard that Mullers didn't speak to me about it. I'm not blaming him – sometimes, at the end of the day, you have to sort your own game out. But at no time did he come to me and say "You're having a bad time, what's the problem? How can we help you?" You've got to remember that back then we didn't have goalkeeping coaches to help us with our game. Myself and Eric used to just go over the park opposite the Goldstone and throw balls at each other among all the dog shit. That's how basic it was.'

A run of four wins from five games during December gave Albion renewed hope going into 1981, but it wasn't enough to prevent Mullery from dropping Graham in favour of his new £150,000 signing from Fulham, the wonderfully-named Perry Digweed. Very much the boy about town, with his dandy dress sense and coiffured hair, Perry looked more like one of Adam's Ants than a goalkeeper. Yet his presence had a steadying effect on a side that still only managed to stay up by the skin of their teeth, winning the last four League games of the season to remain in Division One for another year.

In terms of goalkeeping styles, it was

clear from day one that Perry and Graham came from opposite ends of the spectrum. Like Eric Steele, Perry was an excellent shot-stopper, while Graham got the vote when it came to all-round ability including kicking and coming for crosses. But that didn't stop the two new rivals from getting on famously. 'With Eric it had been very much a professional relationship,' remembers Graham. 'We'd come in and get on with our jobs. He'd never really say much about his personal life or anything like that, but Perry was a single boy who still lived in London and would tell you all about his conquests the previous night. He was a great lad and a lot of fun to be with.'

Perry's arrival seemed to have a galvanising effect on Graham, as, too, did Mullery's decision to quit as manager during the summer of 1981 following a disagreement with chairman Mike Bamber over the sale of Mark Lawrenson to Liverpool. His replacement, Mike Bailey, recognised Graham's improved work ethic immediately and selected him as his first-choice goalkeeper for the start of the 1981–82 season. The Stretford lad would go on to play in 36 League and Cup matches that year as Albion threatened to qualify for Europe. Alas, a dreadful run of form following a 1–0 away win against Liverpool at the beginning of March saw Bailey's side fall away into 13th place, still the highest League finish in the club's history.

Unfortunately, Albion were unable to arrest their nosedive during the opening weeks of the 1982–83 season, resulting in Bailey's dismissal in December with the club once again back among the relegation places. By this time Graham and Perry were exchanging the goalkeeper's shirt approximately every eight or nine games, back to back defeats perhaps leading to the other one getting a turn between the sticks. This pattern continued under the joint acting-managerial team of George Aitken and Jimmy Melia, the latter finally given the job full-time on the strength of the club's surprise run in the FA Cup semi-finals.

Exactly why Albion performed so well in the FA Cup that year, while struggling for any kind of form in the League, is anyone's guess. Graham's opinion goes along the following lines: 'When you go into a Cup match you don't have to worry about your League position, or whether a side is 34 points ahead of you with a vastly superior goal difference. You just go in there, put in 100 percent and everybody knows shocks can happen. It's like anything in life, if the odds are against you, you try that much harder and hope things can happen. Newcastle were like that against us; so were Sheffield Wednesday.'

Newcastle had been Albion's opponents in the third round, with Graham in goal for the first game at the Goldstone (a 1–1 draw) and a somewhat fortuitous win in the replay on Tyneside when Barnsley referee Trelford Mills disallowed two late United goals. He had kept his place for the 4–0 home win over Manchester City in round four but made way for Perry on Sunday 20 February, the day Albion did the unthinkable by winning at Anfield against a Liverpool side undefeated at home for 63 Cup ties. By the time the quarter-final against Norwich City came round, Graham was back in again, Jimmy Case's second-half goal sending Melia's side through to a semi-final showdown against Sheffield Wednesday at Highbury. Now very much the man in form, Graham got the nod for what would prove to be one of the games of his life.

Yet another strike by Case – a free-kick this time and his fourth in consecutive FA Cup ties – put Albion 1–0 up in the first period, a lead they held until the 56th minute when Ante Mirocevic equalised for the Owls. Graham, for one, thinks their goal should never have stood. 'I've got photographs at home of Mick Lyons [Wednesday's captain] going right through me in the build up with his boot and catching me on the thigh. What I was trying to do was punch clear rather than catch it, but the ball hit somebody's shoulder, ricocheted back towards goal and was knocked in. When the game restarted I went down in agony – well, so-called agony, just to waste a bit of time and take some of the wind from their sails

– but it did hurt and it was bleeding. I missed our next game because of it.'

As Wednesday piled on the pressure, so Graham began to earn his wages – and then some. Two saves in particular stand out. One came from a header by Lyons, the other a long-range volley by Pat Heard. 'You get remembered for certain things in life, and that was my 15 minutes I suppose. That first one started with a free-kick floated into the box. I couldn't come for it because it was never going to reach me, and luckily the header was above me, and I was able to arch up and knock it over the bar.' And the second? 'That was hit from outside the area. Originally it was going higher than the crossbar, but it was dipping fast. I was lucky, though, because I normally came off my line when the ball was that far out, but this time I hadn't. I often wonder whether I could have wandered across and knocked it over without diving!'

Although Michael Robinson grabbed the lion's share of the headlines with his late winner, it was Graham who many fans felt had done more than anyone that afternoon to take Albion to Wembley for their first and, so far, only FA Cup Final. 'As I said before to you, there was no way I wanted to lose that semi-final, not after the way I had felt when Derby lost to Manchester United. I don't really think I ever thought I'd get the opportunity to get that close to Wembley again, so when that game at Highbury came along…well, I was going to do everything possible to make sure they didn't score.'

In 2006 Graham managed to get hold of a rare DVD containing highlights from that semi-final, a man in New Zealand having advertised it on ebay. He's also got several pictures for posterity taken on FA Cup Final day itself. Some are of his own doing, such as the shots taken as the team flew into Wembley in a helicopter (well, the team were sponsored by an airline at the time). Others were taken from the sidelines by Perry, who had lost out on a Cup Final place but 'still enjoyed the day, judging by the number of pictures he took on my camera of girls in the crowd!'

Albion, whose relegation from the First Division had been confirmed two weeks previously, started out as massive underdogs against Manchester United in the Final. Never mind that the Seagulls had taken four points off the Red Devils during the League season. The common consensus outside Sussex was that United's side – brimming, as ever, with stars such as Bryan Robson, Frank Stapleton and Norman Whiteside – would sweep Melia's team aside in their quest for their first trophy in six years. This fuelled a school of thought among media pundits that the pressure would be off Brighton because nobody expected them to do anything. So was the pressure off among the team? 'No, not at all. It's a prime-time television spectacular,

probably even more so then than it is now. You are carrying the hopes of a town, or a county in our case, as well as your own reputation. We had done relatively well against them in the League games, but our form up until that Cup Final had been pretty dire. I, for one, had a terrible night's sleep the night before. I think being a goalkeeper you feel it a bit more. You're in such a vital position. If the ball goes past you then it's probably going to be a goal, and we were playing a side that could score a lot of goals if they were on song. Still, we'd had a good Cup run and you live in fantasy land where dreams can come true.'

Brighton's fantasy land reached a new plane 14 minutes into the game when the young Irish midfielder Gary Howlett floated a cross from the right into the blind spot between United centre-backs Gordon McQueen and Kevin Moran, Gordon Smith ghosting into the gap to score with a header. It was a lead they held until early in the second half when the game swung United's way following a dreadful foul on Albion right-back Chris Ramsey by Whiteside. When the game restarted, United attacked immediately down the right with Mike Duxbury's cross being flicked on by Whiteside to Stapleton, who scored. It didn't matter that Whiteside shouldn't have been on the pitch (even by 1983 standards the challenge was shocking) or that a fit rather than a hobbling Ramsey would've

Graham Moseley adorns the front of Albion's matchday programme for the final game of the 1984–85 campaign, the year he won Player of the Season.

been there to clear the ball before it reached Stapleton – United were level.

With 16 minutes remaining, Albion fell behind when Ray Wilkins, brother of future Albion midfielder and manager Dean Wilkins, decided to shoot from outside the area instead of delivering one of his trademark sideways passes. It was a good goal, but there's always been the sneaking suspicion that perhaps Graham invited the United player to have a go by being too far off his line. 'At that time we were going through the Bruce Grobbelaar thing of goalkeepers "sweeping" on the edge of the box,' he says in his defence. 'I was on the edge of the box when the ball was played across from the left-hand side, and I couldn't get to it. So when I went back into my goal I was probably a little bit too far out. I got back into my six-yard box, where I always used to try and check my angles, but didn't go a step and a half back, which maybe I should have done by the time he hit the ball. Whether I would have got to it, I don't know.'

Albion equalised through Gary Stevens in the 87th minute and then wasted a glorious opportunity to wrap the game up 22 seconds from the end of extra-time (trust me, I've timed it), the unmarked Smith famously seeing his close-range shot blocked by the legs of United goalkeeper Gary Bailey, having been set up by Michael Robinson. 'It was a long way away from where I was standing, but at that stage we were very confident. It

had gone to 2–2, we were in extra-time, and I don't remember them having any chances at all. The pitch was in an awful condition and extremely heavy, and they were tired. In those days you were only allowed one substitute so you weren't able to change sides around to liven it up. Even to this day I wish Robbo had shot himself. We all thought at the time, especially having seen it on television, that that's what he should've done because he was more central than Gordon. Maybe Gordon should've hit it harder, I don't know. Hindsight is a wonderful thing.'

Graham's voice tails off at the memory of 'that' miss and the resulting replay, a 4–0 win by United five days later on what was Sir Matt Busby's 74th birthday. I tell him that I didn't think he was at fault for any of United's goals that night, and he agrees. 'They were too good for us. You get your one shot and we were the inferior side in the replay, even though we had more shots on goal than we had done in the first game. It was odds on that they would win it second time around, and they won it quite emphatically.'

The months immediately after the 1983 FA Cup Final proved to be a massive anti-climax for everyone connected with the Albion, except perhaps Gary Stevens and Michael Robinson, whose performances at Wembley helped net them big-money transfers to Tottenham and Liverpool respectively. Far from setting Division Two alight, Brighton lost their opening three League games of the 1983–84 season, each one with a different goalkeeper in the side (Graham, Perry and 19-year-old rookie Simon Steele). For Graham the gloom deepened in September when Melia signed yet another goalkeeper. Not just any old one mind you. Joe Corrigan had been generally regarded as the third-best stopper in England, behind Peter Shilton and Ray Clemence. At 34 the former Manchester City player was still in fantastic shape and immediately went into the first team. He remained there even after Melia was replaced as manager in October by Chris Cattlin, a veteran of Alan Mullery's promotion-winning sides from 1977 and 1979. Within the space of four months Graham had gone from Wembley to being the number-three 'keeper behind Joe and Perry.

'It was a crazy situation, and to be honest I don't really know what happened other than Jimmy clearly didn't fancy myself or Perry. But entertainment wise Joe was terrific value, probably having come from the old Manchester City school of [Mike] Summerbee and that lot. He would go out and drink pints of champagne, then come in the next morning with a bag over his body under his top to sweat it all out. And he would work his socks off. Me being such a laid back lazy sod would stand there and think "Why can't I be like that?"

'The strange thing was that when I'd

been at Derby I remember Joe doing one of those question and answer pieces in a football magazine. He had been asked who he rated as a player for the future, and he had said my name. I never mentioned that to him, but Joe did tell me that when Jimmy had asked him to sign for Brighton, he'd said "But why on earth do you want me? You've already got a good goalkeeper." Still, I suppose Joe wanted to come back to England from Seattle where he'd been playing and that was his big opportunity.'

Joe Corrigan played in all bar one of Albion's remaining games that season, becoming a popular figure with the fans as the side recovered from their awful start to finish ninth. Yet within weeks what Graham now laughingly refers to as 'our little charade of goalkeepers' had started all over again. Despite his good form, Joe found himself out of favour during the 1984–85 pre-season, with Perry pencilled in to wear the goalkeeper's shirt. That all changed when the flamboyant Londoner broke his foot, leaving Cattlin with a straight choice between Joe and Graham. 'There was around three weeks to go before our first fixture, and we had a game against Arsenal. Joe played one half and I played the other. It was made clear to us beforehand that whoever played the better half would get in the side. Joe let in a goal and I didn't, so I got the shirt. The whole thing was bizarre. Bare in mind I'd played just a couple of reserve games in a year and felt completely off the pace. To be totally honest I didn't know what I was doing. It was like picking somebody off the street.'

It certainly didn't look that way, as Albion – with Danny Wilson, Steve Penney and the much travelled Frank Worthington forming a formidable creative trio in midfield – won four of their opening five League games to become Second Division pace-setters. Although the goals dried up during the autumn, Cattlin's side remained in touch with the promotion pack simply by nicking points here and there courtesy of a defence tighter than the London Symphony Orchestra. With the exception of Aldershot in the League Cup, no team managed to put more than two goals past Graham throughout the entire season, a truly astonishing achievement.

'That side had a great understanding of the duties we were all supposed to perform,' says Gary O'Reilly, one of the key performers in a defence that more often than not included Chris Hutchings, Graham Pearce, Eric Young and towards the end of the campaign, a young Martin Keown on loan from Arsenal. 'If you don't concede many goals what you find is that the whole team works well, because confidence grows from the back. Danny Wilson could get on with his job, Terry Connor could get on with his job, Steve Penney could get on with his job, and so on. As for Mose? He would pull off the

kind of saves where you would think "I don't know how he did that." He was a very dominant 'keeper as well. He was good in the six-yard box, in the area, on his reflexes, everything really. He would get on with his business and that made our lives all the easier.'

One of my own abiding memories of that season is a home game against Carlisle on 5 February 1985. Albion won 4–1, but the match was a lot closer than the scoreline suggests. At 3–1 and with 25 minutes still to go, the Cumbrians got a penalty. Graham saved David McAughtrie's initial kick, only for referee Keith Miller to order a retake. Up stepped McAughtrie, once more placing his shot towards the bottom right-hand corner, only for Graham to guess correctly again.

'I don't think I really became aware of it until quite close to the end of the season,' says Graham of his two goals or less record over the 42-game fixture list. 'I do remember Blackburn scoring a third against me which was disallowed and thinking "Phew!" But just as important to me was being ever present in the team all the way through, because I'd never done that before and I wanted to do it once in my career before it was over. That was a big objective for me.'

Graham achieved his ever-present objective, winning the Player of the Season award in the process, but his outstanding efforts weren't enough to help Albion to promotion. The final day of the campaign saw other results go against the Seagulls, a 1–0 home victory over Sheffield United meaning Cattlin's side finished a disappointing sixth. Two games into the 1985–86 season, Graham conceded three goals for the first time in a League match since 22 January 1983 and was promptly dropped. I ask you, who would want to be a goalkeeper?

Once again the baton had been passed to Perry, who ran with it until Cattlin recalled Graham in the wake of a 5–3 home defeat by Charlton on 19 October 1985. Despite back to back 4–0 away thrashings at the hands of Oldham and Liverpool, 'Mose' kept his place over the next few weeks, yet something clearly wasn't right. The man who exuded confidence the previous season had made way for a nervy, inconsistent impostor. In a home game against Barnsley on 7 December he let a soft header by David Hirst squirm beneath his body in front of the North Stand for the only goal of the game. Frustrated by his own form, Graham decided it was time to confide in his manager about something. 'My wife had had an abnormal cancer smear and I went to "Cat" to tell him it was playing on my mind and would he leave me out of the side. So he left me out of the side, which was great, because that's exactly what I needed.' Little did he know that the Barnsley game would be his 224th and last for the club.

Perry remained in goal for the rest of the season as the Seagulls reached the quarter-finals of the FA Cup and pushed hard for promotion back to Division One. But a dreadful run of eight defeats from the final 10 League matches saw Albion fall away to finish in mid-table, Cattlin paying the price for the slump with his job. In a bid to revive memories of better times, the man brought in to replace him in May 1986 was none other than Alan Mullery. However, the Goldstone Ground of the mid to late 80s was a very different animal to the one it had been less than a decade earlier. Crowds were dwindling and financially the club was teetering on complete collapse. In his 2006 autobiography Mullery claims he was brought in specifically to do one big hatchet job, namely removing the club's highest earners (including Graham, Alan Biley and Justin Fashanu) from the payroll. In that he was successful. Come August Graham would join Cardiff City on a free transfer. The following May Albion were relegated to the Third Division, Mullery having been sacked in January supposedly for not moving closer to Brighton from his home in Surrey – the very same home he had lived in during the promotion years of the late 70s.

'The way I remember it is that I left because Mullers and me hadn't got on that well when he'd been at the club previously,' says Graham. 'There were times when he hadn't been speaking to me and he'd been criticising people a lot in the press, which I thought was wrong. I was playing in the reserves at the time, and I went to him and said it might be better if I was to leave, because we hadn't really seen eye to eye. He said alright. I asked if there was any chance of a testimonial because they were worth a lot of money in those days. He said no but that the club would give me a benefit game instead. My name was circulated, and I spoke to Cardiff who seemed to be the best option. To be perfectly honest I was bitterly heartbroken because I still felt I was a reasonable asset to the club. I wasn't that old. I didn't leave under a cloud but the circumstances could certainly have been better.'

Graham helped Cardiff win promotion from the Fourth Division the following May before a broken arm cost him his place in the side at the start of the 1987–88 season. One evening shortly after resuming training, he was travelling through the Welsh capital in the passenger seat of a Mini when it was hit at speed by a car load of Chinese tourists on their way to the city's casino. When Graham regained consciousness in hospital he discovered the arm – not to mention other parts of his body – had been broken again. To make matters worse, the woman driving the car hadn't been Graham's wife but his girlfriend. When the local press got wind of this they had a field day. His marriage and his career were over.

'It was in all the papers and the manager was trying to make excuses for my behaviour, but of course there were none. I remember my wife storming into the hospital and giving me the kind of abuse you would expect, with me lying there unable to move with my arm propped up on a pillow and my leg stretched out. She said she wasn't going to let me back in the house when I was discharged. In the end she did, but it was like torture and eventually we split up.'

Graham later married Sheila, the woman who had been driving the car that fateful night, and after a brief spell in Devon the couple returned to Wales to live in Chepstow. He worked as an estate agent until the slump of the early 90s kicked in and then became a postman, something he continues on a part-time basis today. As with so many other ex-footballers, Civvy Street initially came as something of a rude awakening to the system. 'I thought to myself "I can't do this. This is real life. This is not like football, being mollycoddled with everybody doing everything for you." To actually have to graft at something was a shock, especially when you're getting up at half past four every morning. I was never a grafter. We [footballers] talk a good game, but we don't really know what we're on about.'

Besides the postal work, Graham survives today on his footballer's pension together with the income he receives from three flats in Brighton bought as investments once his playing days had ended. He was recently diagnosed with arthritis of the spine and 'gets quite a lot of pain when I stay in one position for too long, but it's okay through the day.' He still follows Albion's results and travelled to Wembley and Cardiff for the Play-off Final games in 1991 and 2004 respectively. In 1990 he even returned to the Goldstone one last time for that benefit game, the FA Cup Final side of 1983 reuniting to face Tottenham.

'I thank my lucky stars that I was fortunate enough to become a footballer,' he says as we prepared to go our separate ways after the kind of four-hour lunch any supporter would dream of. 'Yeah, I could've worked harder on my game I suppose, but I can't think of one thing I would want to change, good or bad. They are all life-building experiences that make a man out of you and help you stand on your own two feet, from leaving home for the first time to negotiating your own contracts, which you had to do in those days. And I'm glad I got the opportunity to experience them at Brighton, a place I loved. Remember, I came from an old industrial area, so coming down to Sussex with its lovely clean air and grazing cows and those views of the coastline when you climbed up onto the Downs was like a dream come true. I tell you, I thought I'd died and gone to heaven.'

Chapter Two
Grease

And so to the first of my two major headaches when it came to team selection – who would play where in defence?

My choice of centre-backs means some of you may disagree with the decision to name Gary Stevens at number two. He did, after all, make more appearances in the middle of defence than at right-back. On being told what position I had him down for in my Seagulls XI, Gary's initial reaction was 'I bet John Gregory's over the moon about that.' But I ask you, how could I omit one of the most gifted and graceful players ever to have appeared in an Albion shirt? His versatility meant he was able to play pretty much anywhere in midfield or at the back. John Gregory might have a few quibbles about my selection, but I do not.

'Graceful' was a word often used during the 80s to describe Gary Stevens, along with other tags such as 'cultured' and 'refined'. The suggestion was that despite being a gifted, easy on the eye player, Gary lacked a bit of bite. That, in my humble opinion, is what you might call a load of old pony. Yes, he was a graceful player with better ball control than your average defender, but he could also be a bit of a bastard when necessary. He would not have survived almost a decade in the old First Division had he not been.

Gary Stevens scores Albion's second goal versus Manchester United in the 1983 FA Cup Final.

Here is an example of one of Gary's 'thug' moments, the memory of which still makes me grin today. Two minutes from the end of normal time in the 1983 FA Cup Final (the first game rather than the replay) Manchester United went on the attack looking for a winning goal, Gary having just scored Brighton's equaliser to make it 2–2. Mike Duxbury passed to the 18-year-old Norman Whiteside, who managed to turn his marker only with the assistance of an illegal arm. Referee Alf Grey whistled for a foul, but the young Irishman continued his run into the penalty area. A little over half-an-hour earlier a ridiculously late challenge by Whiteside on Chris Ramsey had left Albion's right-back writhing in agony on the Wembley turf and out of the game. Showing the kind of contempt that Jonah Lomu would in future reserve for English rugby players, Gary smashed into Whiteside in a revenge 'tackle', sending him halfway back to Manchester.

'I knew the whistle had gone and that maybe I could take a liberty, so I did,' Gary told me in an interview I did with him many years later. 'I was angry because it was a bad tackle that could seriously have hurt a player. In fact, it did seriously hurt a player. I'd remonstrated with the referee to do something at the time and he hadn't done a thing. In fact, I think he gave a throw to them! So that was my way of letting him [Whiteside] know that we weren't happy.'

'He could look after himself alright, even though he was a young lad,' adds Graham Moseley. 'I think he tried to model himself to an extent on "Fozzie" [Steve Foster] in that "I don't want you coming at me showing your skills – take that!" way. And it worked for him. There was far more to his game that just being comfortable on the ball.'

Gary was born in March 1962 just a short drive away from Wembley in Hillingdon. At the age of six his mum and dad, Mike and Shirley Stevens, upped sticks and moved the family to a small Suffolk village just outside Bury St Edmunds called Great Livermere. It was about as rural as you could get – a Post Office and two or three streets surrounded by fields full of cows, one of which was situated at the end of the Stevens's garden. Great Livermere's small band of youngsters used this field to play football. Most of the other lads were at least three years Gary's senior but 'I held my own', something that would prove advantageous when the time came to play against children his own age.

Mike Stevens was (and remains), for his sins, a Chelsea supporter, albeit one actually raised in Chelsea rather than, say, Taunton, like so many of the new breed of Blues fans. He had been a decent amateur goalkeeper for the likes of Slough Town and Hillingdon Borough, continuing to play for a club called Elmswell after the move to Suffolk. A self-confessed football nut, Mike encouraged his son to appreciate and participate in the sport. When he was 10, Gary started turning out for White Lions in Bury St Edmunds, a team consisting of 13-year-olds, before switching allegiances to Bury North End. Despite being a 'little titch', Gary made up for lack of height with speed and skill. In his second year at Ixworth Primary School he had tested for the senior relay team and beaten every other boy out of sight. Football was not on the timetable at Ixworth Middle School but dad Mike ensured Gary kept his hand in by playing for North End, which in turn led to appearances for a League representative side, West Suffolk Schools and then Suffolk Schools.

'It was a very humble background,' says Gary, as we sit over breakfast at his house in Tunbridge Wells. 'Dad worked and mum kept the house. I can remember wearing these white cotton shorts when I was at Bury North End. They were actually my dad's but my mum had turned them in and stitched them up so I could wear them. They were fabulous. Another time one of the boys was selling a pair of really nice Puma boots which were size nine and a half. I was only size six at the time, but dad bought them and we made these cotton wool pads that sat inside the boot at the front by the toes. The ironic thing is when I was at Tottenham I was still only wearing size eight and a half!'

When Gary was 12 Mike Stevens decided it was high time his son got on nodding terms with a professional club. One of his old football pals from London was a man called Ken Craggs, later to become Alan Mullery's right-hand man at the Goldstone but who in 1974 was in charge of the youth team set-up at Fulham. One Saturday Craggs brought Fulham's youngsters up to Suffolk to face Ipswich Town. Mike and Gary Stevens went along to watch. Afterwards Craggs asked his opposite number at Ipswich what the deal was for promising local kids who wanted to make it at Portman Road. He was told the club ran a weekly Thursday night session for talented teenagers. Gary started attending.

'It was great because occasionally a senior player would come down and train with us. One night Kevin Beattie was there. Another time it was Allan Hunter. I'll never forget one Thursday this giant of a fella turned up from Lowestoft with a huge left foot on him. He looked like he was an adult, but he was only a kid. He came on trial and within no time they had signed him, then he was in the reserves, then he was in the first team. His name was Terry Butcher.'

Gary signed schoolboy forms with Ipswich when he was 14. Two years later came decision time – would he pursue football or carry on with his education? 'I worked really hard at school. I wasn't naturally bright. I struggled with my reading and struggled with my spelling. I don't read much now, but I left school with nine O levels. I got English Language at grade C, English Literature at B and both Maths and Technical Drawing at A so that was more my area. At 16 it was a case of the career's master saying "You must stay on and do your A levels." And there was me going "Well actually, I must leave because I think I've got a chance somewhere in football." So I left.'

There was only one catch. With the likes of Kevin Beattie, Allan Hunter, Russell Osman, Terry Butcher and George Burley occupying Town's defensive positions, opportunities around Portman Road for Gary were always going to be limited. Ipswich had just won the FA Cup, defeating Arsenal 1–0 at Wembley thanks to a Roger Osborne goal. Under the guidance of future England manager Bobby Robson the place was buzzing during pre-season training for the 1978–79 campaign. Gary loved the atmosphere, but that did not alter the fact that his future remained uncertain.

'Strictly speaking they [Ipswich] were in the wrong because they were supposed to notify you three months in advance of your 16th birthday if they were taking you on. I'd left school at 16 and was in pre-season training not knowing what was happening. They were still umming and aarghing over what to do because I was a borderline case. When they eventually turfed me out Bobby [Robson]

called me into his office and said "We don't think it's going to work out for you here, but we like you and things might change. Why not get a job locally, keep on training with us and play in the youth team on Saturdays?" They didn't really want to lose me, but they weren't prepared to commit to me either.'

Over the next couple of weeks Gary had an interview for a job as a draftsman in Ipswich. He also went to meet the army. 'Will I see action in Northern Ireland?' asked Gary. 'Yes,' said the man from the army. 'Bye bye,' said Gary, and he walked out. Mike Stevens had another word with his friend Ken Craggs, now part of the furniture at the Goldstone. Would Brighton be interested in taking a look at Gary? The result was a two-week no-promises trial on the south coast. One Saturday in early August 1978, Gary played for Ipswich Town's youth team against West Ham at Chadwell Heath. That night he returned home to Bury St Edmunds, packed his bags and the following morning caught the train to London and beyond to Brighton. He spent his first night in lodgings at 175 Manor Hall Road in Southwick, home of Maureen and Geoff Waller. It would be Gary's home for the next two and a half years, until 30 March 1981 to be exact (the day of his 19th birthday) when he moved into his first house in Mile Oak near Brighton.

'Compared to Bury St Edmunds Brighton was a big town. I remember arriving at the station and thinking how huge that seemed as well. I'd actually got to know the south coast a little bit before then. My dad's father, Jack Stevens, had a house in Brighton and we used to come down in the summer and spend a week with him. That was our summer holiday. Later on he moved to Middleton-on-Sea near Bognor Regis, so we'd go there for a week instead. But Brighton just seemed this busy place.'

Gary completed his fortnight trial only to be told Albion were still in two minds about whether to take him on or not. Could he do another fortnight? So he did two more weeks, at the end of which he was offered an apprenticeship. 'I really thought I'd cracked it. Sixteen pounds a week and your lodgings paid for! Of course that's only the beginning, but I didn't really appreciate that at the time. You're just happy to get your first step on the ladder. You're on your way.'

Every weekday morning Gary would catch the bus from Mile Oak along the Old Shoreham Road, alighting outside the Goldstone ready for training in Hove Park. Sometimes everyone took part – the first team, reserves, apprentices – and other times the number would be smaller depending on who wanted to work on what, away fixtures etc. Those first few mornings Gary probed the other players to find out more about the club. 'They were saying "We struggle a bit with facilities but it's alright." I asked about the

first home game and what kind of crowd it would be, and they said, "Oh, 30,000, maybe a few more." And I laughed, I actually laughed. I said "You are joking?" I kept on throwing into the conversation that I'd come from Ipswich who had just won the FA Cup, as you would. Ipswich struggled to get anything like that. Of course, I got there on the Saturday and the place was rammed out. I was flabbergasted.'

At the time Albion's youth team was under the watchful eye of John Shepherd, who had played 45 times for the first XI as a forward during the late 1950s. He quickly let it be known that, in his opinion, the club had picked up a gem in Gary. The boy from Suffolk was soon promoted to the reserves. His positive attitude towards the daily chores around the Goldstone certainly helped get his face noticed. He cleaned the changing rooms, swept the terraces and tended to the pitch quicker than the other apprentices. Coach George Aitken even started asking him to work with the first team. 'Once George wanted me to do a little bit of work with Peter Ward. I remember Wardy saying "Be careful, don't kick me." On a couple of occasions I got a little bit too competitive, and he went "Steady on Grease, give me a chance! I'm trying to build my confidence here!" So I was quickly rubbing shoulders with the senior players and seemed to be holding my own.'

Gary continued to impress in the youth team, reserves and during training throughout the 1978–79 season, as Albion's first XI won promotion to the old Division One. Never before had Brighton played in the top flight. Pre-season training during the summer of 1979 saw Gary fitter than ever. The 'little titch' from Bury St Edmunds, while still hardly Arnold Schwarzenegger, had grown physically and now stood six-foot tall. He continued with his apprentice chores (which included cleaning the boots of Mark Lawrenson, Peter Sayer and Peter Ward), but in manager Alan Mullery's mind the player was fast approaching the stage when he would be ready for first-team duty.

On the morning of 8 September 1979 Gary played in a youth-team friendly for Albion in West London against a Queen's Park Rangers side that included a young Dean Wilkins in its ranks. After the game the entire squad jumped on a bus bound for White Hart Lane to watch the first team in action against Spurs. 'We stood behind the goal at the Park Lane End, which is where all the Brighton supporters had congregated,' says Gary. 'Just in front of me was the goal. I can't remember exactly when it happened but at some point Mark Lawrenson went down injured on the edge of the penalty area and had to leave the field of play. My immediate thought was "Oh crikey! That's bad news. He's our best player." It

didn't cross my mind at any point that I might be the one brought in to replace him. I think I just presumed that someone like Andy Rollings or Graham Winstanley would come in.'

Two days later Gary reported for training as usual. After the session Alan Mullery informed the 17-year-old that he would be playing on Saturday, Lawrenson having damaged his ankle ligaments. 'I said "Who's that against then?" I was wondering where the reserves were playing. And he said "Ipswich, first team." I was just gobsmacked. Typical Mullers. I think he then said "Now go and get those boots cleaned", because I was still doing all the apprentice jobs. That continued even when I was in the first team. I was cleaning the toilets, sweeping the terraces and doing the boots. I kept doing those jobs and stayed on £20 per week until I finally signed a professional contract.'

Ipswich Town had suffered a poor start to the 1979–80 season. Then again, so had the Albion. However, goals by Paul Clark and substitute Gerry Ryan gave the Seagulls a vital win, only their second so far at the highest level. And as for Gary's performance? 'I remember my first touch that never was. I went to control the ball with my right foot and it went straight underneath. They always say "get a good first touch and you're in the game". There was a bit of a groan from the crowd, but I dug myself out of a hole. From what I recall I went on to acquit myself really well.'

Gary was paid a £65 crowd bonus for his debut based on the match attendance of 23,608, well over double his weekly wage at the time. He still has the pay slip, handwritten by club secretary Ken Calver, in a file at home. In fact, Gary still has all his Albion pay slips, including the one from the 1983 FA Cup Final, kept for the sake of posterity.

For Gary the Ipswich game vindicated his decision to stick it out at the club through one or two dark days that had occurred shortly after his arrival from Suffolk. 'When I first went to Brighton there were a couple of trainees who I guess felt threatened by me because I was this young kid who had come from Ipswich Football Club. Once, after all the players had gone, we were tidying up at the Goldstone and one of them asked me to get some rubbish out of the sauna which was off the visiting changing room. As soon as I walked in there the door was deliberately slammed shut, trapping me, and the thing turned on. I'm thinking "Ha ha, very funny." Three hours later I'm still in there lying on the floor with my nose against the bottom of the door where there was a bit of breeze. I went through a panicky stage but just realised I had to try and stay calm. Glen Wilson found me in the end, pretty dehydrated.

'On another occasion we were having a big pot of tea and four or five cups got poured out. I was given one and I started drinking. I got about halfway through

and there was all this sniggering so I twigged that something had happened. One of the lads had actually peed in the teapot. I can remember being almost in tears on the phone to my mum and dad in the evening saying "This is hard going, I think I might be coming home." But I hung in there.'

With Mark Lawrenson sidelined for two months Gary went on to keep his place in the first team, which, despite the win against Ipswich, continued to struggle near the foot of the table. The arrival of central-defender Peter Suddaby from Blackpool, along with the return from injury of regular right-back John Gregory, meant Gary was demoted from the starting XI during the opening weeks of 1980, yet he still made regular appearances as a substitute throughout the remainder of the season. One such outing came at Portman Road, Ipswich, on 2 February 1980. It led to his first goal in professional football, one laced with an element of controversy.

'I'd come on late, got the ball on the edge of the box, controlled it with my left and hit it with my right into the net. The following day it hit the papers that I had run towards the directors' box in celebration and stuck two fingers up in the air, supposedly because the club had let me go. I went into training on the Monday and all the lads were taking the mickey out of me sticking two fingers up at Bobby Robson. I don't remember doing that at all. It's not in my nature to do something like that anyway. I've not seen any photographic evidence that I did, and I doubt there were any TV cameras there either.

'That period was quite a blur for me really. Suddenly you are in the paper, reporters want to talk to you, people are recognising you in the street, things like that. I can understand how it's all way too much for somebody who hits the big time in football these days, what with the increased media coverage and the money. I thought I'd made it on £16 a week! It really is another world and not everybody today manages to adapt to it.'

The months spanning September 1979 to May 1980 represented one giant learning curve for Gary. Besides the media there were canny professionals out to exploit his inexperience, plus in Alan Mullery he had a manager with a reputation for not suffering fools gladly. Throughout the first half of an away game at Coventry City, Gary had continually shaped to knock passes down the right-hand touchline before cutting inside at the last minute. On each occasion City's Tommy Hutchinson, wise to Gary's ploy, had dispossessed him. At half-time Mullery pinned Gary against a wall and said that if he did it again he would punch him in the face. A few weeks later, following a 5–1 defeat at Southampton, the first team were made to watch a video of the mauling along with the trainees. Mullery instructed each trainee to monitor a particular Albion player, then award them a mark out of 10 for their performance. Gary, who had not even been on the bench at The Dell, was told to rate Peter Ward. 'The players were basically looking at us as if to say "If you give me a bad mark, I'm going to thump you!" And Mullers was looking at us as if to say "If you don't give him a bad mark, you're out of this club son." It put us in an impossible situation. Those types of methods to some extent maybe carry on now, but it was a very different environment then compared to football today.'

Eventually the time came for Gary to sign his full professional contract. The negotiations involved Alan Mullery, Mike Stevens and his son, with Mullery playing the part of ringmaster. 'He [Mullery] asked my dad how much he earned. My dad said "I can't tell you that in front of my son", so Mullers had a guess at it and my dad said "You might be about right." Mullers goes "I'm offering your son more to play football than you're earning in 40 hours work at a factory! Tell your son to sign!" So my dad told me to sign and I did. This was all before agents really existed so Brighton got me on the cheap. He's a bully, Mullers, and he still is, but I've got a lot of time for him, and I love being in his company, even now. He did well at the club. He got them results.'

Gary Stevens, 2007, complete with his 1983 FA Cup runners'-up medal and the BBC 1983 FA Cup Final Man of the Match award.

Gary Stevens in the 1983 FA Cup Final.

The following couple of years saw 'Grease' (a nickname bestowed on Gary by club kit man Glen Wilson due to his passing likeness to John Travolta) establish himself as a regular in the Albion side, developing a reputation for being composed on the ball and, yes, 'graceful'. He made 36 starts under Mullery during the 1980–81 season and 26 with Mike Bailey in charge during

1981–82, playing at centre-back, right-back and midfield along the way. Bailey's reign, as covered elsewhere in this book, was not to everyone's taste from the perspective of some fans and players. However, Gary for one rated him highly. 'Unfortunately he was a bit dour with the media and the fans, but as a coach he was a real football man. He always used to explain exactly how we were going to play from the first minute to the 90th. It was all mapped out because he believed that would give us the results we needed across the course of a season. Yes, occasionally you're two goals down with five minutes to go so you stick a centre-half up front and smash it forward, but we had a way of playing and we pretty much stuck to that. When people ask me about the managers and coaches that I've played under, I always say one of the best was Mike Bailey. Other players probably wouldn't say that, but I would.'

It is somehow ironic that Gary's best year at the Goldstone, the one that saw him crowned Player of the Season by the supporters, coincided with the club sliding out of the old First Division. He missed just one of the 42 League games during 1982–83 and appeared in all eight of Albion's FA Cup ties. The second of those saw him come in for criticism from some national newspapers plus one or two regionals based in north-east England for his alleged heavy-handed treatment of Kevin Keegan during a third-round replay against Newcastle United at St James' Park. 'They said I kicked him all over the park, which just wasn't my style,' says Gary. 'Keegan was the victim of some dubious tackling throughout, particularly from Stevens, who was fortunate not to be cautioned for a second-minute tackle that left him writhing in pain,' wrote the correspondent from *The Times*. Opinions, opinions. At least, for once, the ubiquitous 'graceful', 'cultured' and 'refined' were nowhere to be seen.

'I always thought of him as being very versatile, "Mr Consistent" in everything he did,' says Graham Pearce, who partnered Gary in defence on 17 occasions that season. 'He was good to play with. If I have one criticism it's that he was a very honest guy, probably too honest. Being like that in football means you don't always get your just rewards. He could have been nastier. Then again he probably wouldn't have become the player he was if he had been.'

'It was one hell of a strange season,' says Gary. 'There we were, trying to stay in the First Division, but at the same time there was this growing belief that we had the chance to do something truly unique. I for one don't think that it (Albion's FA Cup run) detracted from our League performances, but it did make up for the fact that we were struggling and ultimately got relegated. Jimmy Melia was in charge by then, and it was just bizarre after a couple of rounds how we would sit round the radio at lunchtimes, more or less say who we wanted to play next, and they were coming out of the hat. It was like "Sheffield Wednesday in the semis, it would probably be at Highbury, that would be the one to get." And there it is – "Brighton will play Sheffield Wednesday at Highbury." Nobody talks about Brighton getting relegated in '83. They all talk about the Cup Final. It had never happened before, and it will probably never happen again.'

A yellow card picked up in a League fixture at Notts County on 30 April 1983 had resulted in a two-match suspension for Albion captain Steve Foster, ruling him out of the FA Cup Final three Saturdays later. That meant Gary would be partnered by Steve Gatting in the centre of defence against Manchester United at Wembley. 'Steve Foster not being in the team meant we were weaker as a unit because he was a huge character and a huge player,' says Gary. 'But I actually think what happened was that the XI who went out there all assumed more responsibility because he wasn't there. It gave me some room to breathe. Suddenly there was some space there for Gary Stevens to blossom a little bit.'

Gordon Smith agrees. 'I think having "Fozzie" unavailable actually helped Gary because he had to come into his own. Fozzie used to be quite hard on him in terms of his positioning. Now he didn't

have Steve telling him what to do so he had to act on instinct. That FA Cup Final was the making of him, definitely. His performance took him to another level.'

Up until 1983 a typical FA Cup Final day for Gary Stevens involved sitting in front of a television from 9am watching all the traditional pre-match build up, then taking in the game (and extra-time if needed) plus the presentation of the trophy. Now the roles had been reversed. 'Suddenly I was on the TV. There we are outside the Selsdon Park Hotel hitting golf balls for the cameras. There we are going from Selsdon to a local school playing field to board the helicopter to fly to Wembley. There we are landing in a field near Wembley and getting the coach up Wembley Way to the stadium with people everywhere. You're the one who's living it and, yeah, it's a marvellous experience.'

Gordon Smith was right. The 1983 FA Cup Final would be the making of Gary Stevens. It was a while before he got his first touch – 'an attempted through ball which I pulled down with my right foot, then went through and won the tackle' – but from that moment on he became a tower of strength in the face of United's formidable midfield and front line. That said, it was the Mancunians, 2–1 ahead having been 1–0 down to Smith's goal at the break, who looked odds on to lift the Cup going into the closing stages.

With three minutes left on the clock,

Albion won a corner on the right. Gary looked over to the Brighton bench to see manager Jimmy Melia and Steve Foster both frantically waving him forward. Jimmy Case delivered a low ball in the direction of Tony Grealish standing just outside United's penalty area. Grealish hit an abysmal shot towards goal, one that rolled into a Titanic-sized hole that had opened up between Mike Duxbury and Frank Stapleton.

'We knew at some stage that the likelihood was they [United] were going to score, because they were a good side. That Ray Wilkins goal was a great goal. So we're 2–1 down, it's getting towards the end and we win this corner. My main thought was to follow Tony's shot in looking for any rebounds, and it ended up landing right at my feet. Then it was just a matter of head down, keep it below the bar and in it goes.'

Five years earlier Roger Osborne, a man of Suffolk like Gary, had been substituted after scoring Ipswich Town's winning goal against Arsenal in the FA Cup Final. The moment had simply been too much for the striker, rendering him unable to play any further part in the game. Gary looked slightly bemused in the immediate aftermath of his equaliser but thankfully did not suffer an attack of the Osbornes. It was only the third goal of his Albion career. It would also be his last.

Towards the end of extra-time, with the scoreline still finely balanced at 2–2, the BBC's co-commentator on the game, Jimmy Hill, was moved to say this about Gary: 'That Stevens is remarkable. He's managed three or four times, when it looked as if United were through and had just the final blow to drive home, to get a foot or a leg or a chest or something in front of it. A remarkable game.' Of course Hill, no stranger to controversy, then had to go and put his patronising foot in it by adding 'There's obviously a player not only interesting maybe to the better clubs but interesting to England as well.' Thanks Jimmy. Impartial to the end.

If it is any consolation to Gordon Smith, Gary refuses to blame him for failing to wrap the game up during the dying seconds of extra-time in the first match. 'I didn't see it as being a big miss. I actually give credit to Gary Bailey. He was one of my England teammates for a while and he was a good goalkeeper. That was a good save.'

With Steve Foster available for the replay five days later, Steve Gatting reverted to right-back in the absence of the injured Chris Ramsey with Fozzie once again partnering Gary as he had throughout most of the 1982–83 season. Although Albion lost 4–0, BBC viewers still chose Gary as their Man of the Match, despite him conceding the 62nd-minute penalty which led to United's fourth goal. 'I for one would not argue' said John Motson, in announcing the decision. As

Gary collected his losers' medal at the end of the game, he was captured mouthing the words 'Thanks very much' to the global TV audience, something he has absolutely no recollection of today.

There is one tragic postscript to the BBC's Man of the Match Award for the 1983 FA Cup Final. Gary's main rival for the honour proved to be United's young right-winger Alan Davies, a late replacement for the injured Steve Coppell, who had walked out of the Wembley tunnel side by side with 'Grease' before both games. Whereas Gary's career went into the ascendancy following May 1983, Davies struggled to live up to his 15 minutes of fame during subsequent spells with Newcastle United, Bradford City and Swansea City. On the afternoon of 4 February 1992 his dead body was found slumped over the steering wheel of his Vauxhall Cavalier near Port Eynon Bay on the Gower Peninsula in Wales, a length of hose leading from the driver's side window to the car's exhaust pipe. A suicide note had been placed on the passenger seat. Davies left behind a pregnant wife and a four-year-old daughter.

Gary was inundated with mail from across Britain and further afield after his Man of the Match performances. They came from Brighton supporters, United fans, armchair enthusiasts of the game, even people he had been to school with but not seen for years. 'One was from a lad called Robert Smith who I'd known back in Bury. He had gone into the church and was saying how ideally placed I was to spread the word of the Lord. I just wrote back to say thanks for your letter but that's not really my cup of tea.'

Gary knew he had played well at Wembley. The size of his post bag merely confirmed that. What he was not prepared for was what happened next to his career. 'I'd been at home going through all these letters and after a while decided to go back up to mum and dad's in Suffolk. While I was there the phone rang and it was Jimmy Melia. He said "Listen Gary, we've agreed to sell you to Tottenham. Do you want to go and have a chat with them?" I said "You've agreed to sell me to Tottenham? Don't you think you should've consulted me first?" I was in the throes of buying a house in Shirley Drive in Hove. The people I was buying off had said "Aren't you likely to be transferred?" I'd said "Absolutely no way – I won't be pulling out of this." I was thinking "Why do they want to sell me?" I thought the plan was to keep the squad together in Division Two in order to get back into the top flight. That shows you how naïve I was.

'I said "Why are you selling me Jimmy?" He said "Well the club has made the decision. I've told them (Tottenham) what you earn, but I've told them twice as much, so I've done you a right favour there." I said "Well if you've agreed to sell me then you don't want me, do you?" Jimmy said "It's not that we don't want you. It's a club business decision. What do you want to do?" I said "Well I'd better go and see them then." It was only after that that I started to get excited, thinking if I go then I'm going to be playing in the First Division next season. Jimmy had given me the contact numbers for Peter Shreeves, who was Keith Burkinshaw's [Tottenham manager] assistant. I chatted to my mum and dad about it and then phoned Peter. He said "When can you come and see us?" I said "I'll come tomorrow if you want." So I went to meet Shreevesy and spoke on the phone to Keith Burkinshaw, who was away on holiday at the time. Peter said "Listen, I want you to keep this quiet. I don't want it going out to the press because suddenly there'll be an auction for you." Manchester United and Liverpool were supposedly also interested in me. I say supposedly, because I actually believed I was staying at Brighton, and I would've happily done so. At that stage in my career I didn't feel like I needed to move on. I was 21 and a season or two in the old Second Division wouldn't have done me any harm whatsoever.'

Financially Gary cost Brighton nothing. He started out on £16 a week. By May 1983 that figure had risen to £350, peanuts by today's standards and small change compared to what some Albion players were earning at the time. Gary reckons his wages over five years amounted to no more than £70,000, if that. 'I played however many games for them, helped get them to the Cup Final and they got £300,000 for me. All I did was make money for Brighton Football Club. They'll square me up one day I'm sure. Maybe they'll name a stand after me at the new stadium!'

Gary's first season at White Hart Lane finished with him collecting a UEFA Cup-winners' medal, yet it was several months before he won over sections of the notoriously hard to please Spurs crowd. 'The boo boys really went to town on me, justifiably perhaps. I think I got a little bit ahead of my status, started to believe I was better than I was. I was taking liberties, trying to be too clever, and I was being caught out.'

It was Alan Mullery who helped him wake up to reality. 'He'd been to a Spurs match and he called me up the following day and just said "Keep it simple. It looks like every time you get the ball you're out to impress. Well don't. Do the basic things well – head it away, tackle, pass it – and the rest will come." And, of course, he was right.'

Gary's improved form during the early part of the 1984–85 season led to him winning his first full England cap at Wembley against Finland in October 1984, coming on as a substitute for Manchester United right-back Mike

Duxbury. If Gary really had stuck two fingers up at the Ipswich Town directors' box after scoring his first professional goal in February 1980, then Bobby Robson – now England's manager – had clearly forgiven him. He went on to appear a further six times in an international shirt, although five were as a substitute. The exception came in a qualifying match for the 1986 World Cup Finals against Northern Ireland in Belfast, Gary stepping into the midfield shoes of injured captain Bryan Robson. Towards the end of a tight 1–0 win a bomb went off in a neighbouring street. Gary remembers hearing the thud as it exploded. 'I didn't feel comfy the whole time we were out there to be honest with you,' he confesses now. 'The security was so tight.'

By comparison Mexico, home to the 1986 World Cup Finals, proved to be a breeze, despite the high altitude. However, issues did arise for Gary during the tournament, most notably from within his own team. The first involved what he describes as the 'old pals' act within the England squad, in other words those players with multiple caps to their name assured of a regular start. In their opening two games Bobby Robson's side lost 1–0 and drew 0–0 against Portugal and Morocco respectively, Gary coming on as a substitute for Mark Hateley during the latter after Ray Wilkins had been sent off for throwing the ball at the referee. Game three saw England progress to the second round, thanks to a 3–0 win over Poland, where they met Paraguay.

'I came on as a substitute for Peter Reid in that Paraguay match. We won it comfortably and after the game were having our debrief when Peter Shilton started going on about how we had lost our shape when 'Reidy' went off, careering forward and what have you. I looked at him and said "Shilts, what you're saying is that when I came on we lost our shape." And he was going "No, no, when Reidy came off." I said "Yeah, but I came on. You're having a pop at me." That was the old pals act. It was done to some extent to guarantee that Peter Reid played in the next match against Argentina, which he did.'

That in turn brings us round to issue number two. Gary roomed with the defender Terry Fenwick during the tournament, who was struggling with a groin strain but keeping it secret from the England management. In Gary's opinion Peter Reid was also masking the true extent of his injury, the one that had forced him to come off against Paraguay. Should perennial substitute Gary spill the beans for his own benefit, or stay tight-lipped? 'It's a tough one, isn't it? The management were asking Terry if he was okay, but he was treating it with ice packs behind their backs in our room. He wasn't fit to play against Argentina, Peter Reid wasn't fit to play against Argentina, and look who got left in Maradona's wake when he set off for their second goal. Bobby Robson asked me leading up to the game if I had ever done a man-to-man marking job because they were considering it with Maradona. All I could say was the nearest I'd come to that was Kevin Keegan playing for Brighton against Newcastle in the third round of the FA Cup. But I was fit and could get about the park all day. I feel I should've played actually, I really feel I should have played. I was right on top of my game around then.'

Maradona scored twice in the quarter-finals – the 'hand of God' plus a quite brilliant solo effort – to send England out of the competition. Fenwick lasted the course, but Reid had to be replaced by Chris Waddle after Maradona's second goal. Yet Gary's not bitter. By and large he enjoyed the whole experience, especially the Paraguay game. 'I think that's the only time I've ever had to pinch myself, coming on at the Aztec Stadium in front of around 113,000 people. You go "Right, you're not dreaming here, you actually have a job to do, get on and do it." But it was unreal.'

Over the next couple of years Gary continued to be one of Tottenham's more reliable performers, collecting another FA Cup runners'-up medal in 1987 following Coventry's 3–2 win at Wembley. Then, towards the end of 1988 his career was turned upside down thanks to a high-profile incident involving Vinnie Jones,

the former hod carrier turned professional footballer who, at the time, was playing for Wimbledon.

'I'll tell you what actually happened. During our previous game against Wimbledon I'd been stretchered off unconscious with a fractured collarbone. There was a bit of a defensive mix-up between myself and Ray Clemence, the ball spun up in the air and (John) Fashanu came in to head it. I've got a standing jump, he's got a running jump. I've got a photograph showing his elbow on the end of my chin. I was unconscious in the air and fell awkwardly. So the next game we're playing Wimbledon at White Hart Lane. "Fash" has got the ball out wide. It's right on the touchline and I've got a chance of winning the tackle and putting the ball in the stand and maybe giving him a bit of a clump at the same time. He's there, I'm there, the ball is there and we've all gone to ground. I'm trying to get up and he's half on my back keeping me pressed to the ground with the ball right at my feet. I didn't see who was coming, but it turned out to be Vinnie Jones. He just went through the ball and me. Instantly his knee hit the outside of my knee and forced it inwards. All my weight was on that leg. There's nowhere for anything to go so something has to give.

'I knew instantly what had happened. I'm lying there, moaning and groaning. You know you're going to be out for a long time. You're going to have to have surgery and it's going to be a long old road back. And he goes "Stop your squealing – you deserved it." I couldn't believe he said that. I just could not believe it.'

That night Gary underwent surgery to repair the medial ligament in his shattered right knee. The anaesthetic meant he did not fully regain consciousness until early the following afternoon. 'I was pretty groggy. At some stage a nurse came in and said I'd had a visitor and that he'd left me some magazines. It was Vinnie Jones. So he did come and see me, but the magazines were these boxing mags, kick-boxing, fighting and all that business. I thought "At least he's made the effort", but then he started saying that I'd refused to see him which was rubbish. I'd been under anaesthetic, and anyway, do you really want to see someone within 24 hours of that happening? The tackle had been hammered on TV and in the papers by then, but he kept popping up over the next few days doing stuff at schools and charity events. I'm lying in hospital and I've got "Stop your squealing – you deserved it" going through my head. I wanted to look at suing but [Spurs manager] Terry Venables didn't encourage it and the PFA [Professional Footballers' Association] didn't want it to happen because they represented both parties. It wasn't the end of my career. I

did get back playing again, but I didn't perform that well and was nothing like what I had been. I went down to Portsmouth and just slowly faded away really.'

Gary admits it took him the best part of 10 years to come to terms with not being a footballer anymore, citing the camaraderie and banter as the things he missed the most. He has considered club management (Gary is a UEFA 'A' qualified coach) and once applied for the vacant Albion position after Steve Coppell's defection to Reading in 2003. 'I didn't get an interview but Dick Knight did write me a very nice letter back,' Gary told me at the time, adding 'Of course it was the right decision, but unless you throw your hat in the ring you're not going to get anywhere.'

Since then his own football business, The Ball School, has continued to flourish in and around Tunbridge Wells. Aimed at children from a pre-school age right up to 18, according to Gary it is 'all about giving children and young players the best possible opportunities.' For some youngsters it is a way of having fun and developing their football skills. For others it is a bit more serious than that, several pupils having been referred on for trials with professional clubs. In 2007 his desire to find a permanent home for The Ball School led to him becoming the owner of Tunbridge Wells Football Club. 'It makes perfect sense really. The Ball School's aim is to develop talented young players who might just go on to become an asset to Tunbridge Wells Football Club and beyond. What we're doing is creating a Centre of Excellence together with driving the club forward. I live in Tunbridge Wells. I have done for five years. I've also dedicated my life to football. This is a way of continuing to do both.'

Gary has no elaborate five or 10-year plans for the club involving breaking into the Football League followed by Premiership domination. He simply wants it to grow within its means, becoming a sporting centre for the local community. 'I don't honestly know whether this area could support another Football League club. You've got the London clubs up the road and Gillingham and Brighton not far away, so I don't think it could. But my getting involved with them isn't really about that. It's about benefitting the town and getting young players playing to the best of their ability.'

Who knows? Maybe one day a protégé from The Ball School will find himself sitting down to dinner with the players of an ambitious football club on the verge of breaking into the Premier League, just like a very wet behind the ears Grease on

the eve of Albion's game at Newcastle in May 1979. 'As the head apprentice I went up for the final match of that season as the kit boy,' says Gary, squirming with embarrassment at the story he is about to tell. 'I roomed with Peter Sayer. I didn't have any real experience of staying in hotels or anything. We sat down to our first evening meal up there, and I'm looking at this menu thinking "What's this all about?" Peter Sayer says to the waiter "I'll have whitebait to start with." So I said, "Yeah, I'll have whitebait." Then Peter says "I'll have a fillet steak, medium rare", so I go "Yeah, I'll have a fillet steak medium rare as well." I just copied him because I was sitting with all the boys but felt so insecure. Sure enough, the starters arrive and it's "Who ordered white bait?" Peter Sayer says "You have this one, I'll have the next one out." So there's this little plate of fish and I'm thinking "Do you take their heads off? Do you eat the eyes? Are there bones?" Peter says "Tuck in" and I'm going "No, I'll wait until yours turns up." His turns up. He squeezes lemon over it. So do I. He grinds some black pepper in. So do I. He stabs his fork in and whooshes it into his mouth. So do I. So I learned how to eat white bait. I just winged it. I did that a lot back then, but I managed to survive!'

Chapter Three
Hello Mum!

Let's face it – left-back isn't exactly the sexiest position on any football field. Ninety-nine percent of number-threes will probably tell you that themselves. They rarely get the opportunity to shoot let alone score, hardly ever cross the halfway line unless it's to take a throw in and frequently pay for the reluctance of their particular team's left-winger to track back and help defend. Yet there are exceptions. Stuart Pearce springs to mind, as does that shaven-headed Brazilian who used to take free-kicks from ridiculous distances. They are two of the few who dared to attack. Gary Williams was another, and as a result he scored some absolute beauties. That's why Sussex school playgrounds were full of kids imitating Gary during the lunchtimes of the late 70s and early 80s, even with Peter Ward around.

'I was very lucky in that I played right at the beginning of the era of overlapping full-backs,' says Gary during our meeting at Caffé Nero in Hove, still this Lancastrian's home town despite having last played for the Albion in 1981. 'It was beginning to creep in when I first came on the scene, and I had an advantage as I'd started my career as a left-winger. I knew all about coming forward. I wanted

to come forward. My problem was that I just wasn't making it at Preston North End in that position. I'd been flying but then had a cartilage operation and the "jinkiness" wasn't quite there anymore. I'm sure they were thinking of letting me go. I was only 18 at the time and could see the writing on the wall as I wasn't making the breakthrough.

'Anyway, to cut a long story short someone got injured at left-back in one of the reserve-team games. I went and spoke to the guy who held the position in the first team and he gave me a bit of advice about tucking in, covering and all sorts of things. Sure enough I got the left-back spot in the reserves. Everything was about overlapping, and I was encouraged to do it. I was pretty nippy in those days and I could get up and back easily. I wouldn't say my defensive qualities were fantastic, but I got stuck in with the tackles and because I used to be a winger I knew which way to shepherd them to make it difficult to cut inside.'

It was Bobby Charlton who gave Gary Peter Williams his break in the Preston first team, playing him at left-back for the final half-a-dozen games of the 1974–75 season. Yet, when 'God', as Gary still calls him, resigned that summer, the future for this one-time sewing machine engineer once again looked uncertain. Fortunately, new manager Harry Catterick backed Charlton's judgement and decided to go with Gary for the 1975–76 season. The following campaign saw him win the Player of the Season award for his outstanding performances in a defence that included some bloke called Mark Lawrenson, who, word had it, was apparently being watched by Brighton, a club Gary had already developed something of a soft spot for.

'We were in the same League as Brighton, which would have been the old Third Division, with us hoping to get promotion and Brighton very definitely looking good for it. Most players in that Division played in front of around 6,000 people each week, and when the fixtures came out we always looked for Brighton away because they were getting 30,000. To run out in Division Three at the Goldstone in front of a full house was amazing. You knew you were in for a hard time but the atmosphere was just infectious.

'Alan Mullery had had his eye on Mark for a while, but I found out later that every time they went to watch him I played really well, so word began to get out that he fancied the left-back as well. I heard about that in the papers and, being Brighton, I was really pleased about it. At the end of the season Mark signed and my name wasn't even mentioned. That

seemed to be that. Then two or three weeks later I got this phone call from someone saying they were Alan Mullery. And I went "Yeah yeah, come on, who is it really?" and he said "No, it *is* Alan Mullery. I want you to come down and have a chat because we want to sign you. Jump on a train first thing tomorrow, get yourself to the ground and we'll go from there." I was dead naïve and wasn't on fortunes or anything, so I said "Well, are you going to pay for the train trip?" He laughs his head off at that and goes "Yes, we'll pay for it, just get your arse on the train and come down here!"

Like so many other Northerners to have played for the Albion, Gary knew absolutely zilch about Brighton or the surrounding area before signing for the club, other than that it was on the south coast and had a half-decent football team. Yet, within an hour or two of stepping off the train 'I knew I was never going to say no.' He was given a room at the Metropole Hotel on the seafront complete with a balcony. It was summer time. Looking out over the beach and the English Channel, it struck him how much the place was like Blackpool. And hailing from Lancashire, that was just fine by him. He signed immediately.

Then the hard work began. Albion had already started their pre-season training and, as Gary quickly found out, the pace was ferocious. Several new faces had arrived at the club, competing for places with men who had just won promotion from the Third Division. On several occasions the XI versus XI practice matches had to be halted after the competitive juices threatened to spill over. One such game saw Gary, so out of condition he had thrown up during his first training session, come off worse in a 50–50 tackle with the tough-tackling midfielder Steve Piper. His left ankle didn't break but was sufficiently beaten up for him to miss the opening few games of the season. Welcome to Sussex.

'We got off to a good start but I didn't really feel part of the team until I made my debut. The lads hadn't a clue what I could do, and, although I was around in the treatment room, it's hard to be part of the set-up when you're injured. When I did make my debut I just wanted to do well, which I did – I think we won 2–0 – and I thought "Great, I'll take it from there." But I got dropped three or four games later after a bit of a shocker at Charlton. It was a famous game. The train was running late and we had to get changed on board because the driver had gone the wrong way up the track and had to reverse. We arrived so late we pretty much ran straight out of the train onto the pitch. We got done 4–3 if I remember right, and three goals came down my left-hand side. I don't know what "Sully" (Peter O'Sullivan, Albion's left-winger) was doing that night, but he didn't give me the best of protection. It was two on

one the whole time. Mullers pulled me in afterwards, had a few words, dropped me but I got back in and was a regular pretty much from that day on.'

Well before the end of Gary's first season at the Goldstone it had become clear that the fight for the three available promotion places to what is now the Premier League (the Play-offs were still nine years away) would be between four clubs that had broken away from the rest of the pack. They were Bolton, Southampton, Tottenham and the Albion. Not that you would have known it from some of the media coverage doing the rounds at the time. 'We were having a great season, but we weren't getting a mention. Every time you read the paper or watched *Grandstand* or a football programme it would be 'And now for what's going on in the Second Division, these two teams – Spurs and Saints – are running away with it with Bolton', but they weren't. All the time we were about four points behind, that's all. Whenever they were winning we were doing exactly the same. We knew with 10 games to go we could still do it. Spurs came down and we walloped them 3–1. There was a pitch invasion and all sorts of things going on in the crowd, but it was a fantastic game and we were right on their tails. All we needed was for someone to slip up on that last day.'

Hindsight is a wonderful thing, but that was never going to happen. Not with

Southampton and Tottenham facing each other at The Dell as Albion took on Blackpool at the Goldstone. Bolton had already been crowned Second Division Champions and a draw between Saints and Spurs would be enough to send both clubs up behind them. Brighton, on the other hand, had to win and hope someone lost. In the event, Mullery's men won 2–1, but – surprise, surprise – things ended all square along the coast in Hampshire, opposing managers Lawrie McMenemy and Keith Burkinshaw having set the tone before kick-off by walking onto the pitch arm in arm. Despite having finished on 56 points (the three points for a win system had yet to be introduced), enough for Nottingham Forest to win the League 12 months previously, Albion had lost out on goal difference.

As far as I'm aware, Mullery's squad to a man still maintain what happened in Southampton that day to have been, in goalkeeper Eric Steele's words, a 'stitch up'. At the time their moods were hardly soothed by yet more sycophantic coverage of the promotion race in the press by journalists reared on Tottenham's 'Glory Glory Days' of the early 60s. 'It would have been a tragedy had they been pipped at the post having been one of the front-runners throughout the season', wrote Geoffrey Green in *The Times* of Spurs. 'No, it wouldn't' says Gary. 'We took three points

off them that season, or what would be four today. We were a match for anything they had to offer, yet we felt like we had been relegated. We were in tears. You're going to be, aren't you, having come so close after a long season and done virtually everything right. Heartbreaking. Then Mullers made his speech up in the grandstand to all the fans saying we'd definitely go up the next season. Him saying that was a real pick up. It helped give us the confidence to regroup and show everyone that we hadn't been one-season wonders.'

Which was just as well, as the race for promotion the following year proved to be as tight as it had been during the 1977–78 campaign. After an inconsistent start, Albion found their stride with a run of four consecutive wins around Christmas, setting the tone for 1979. The final fortnight of the season saw Albion, Crystal Palace, Stoke, Sunderland and West Ham all in the hunt for the three promotion places. Yet a crass piece of organisation by the Football League also meant that two of those clubs, Crystal Palace and West Ham, would finish their League programmes four days after the other three. This farcical situation only exacerbated the nerves, not just around the Goldstone but the whole of Sussex. 'It was nip and tuck all the way,' remembers Gary, an ever present in the team that season. 'With 10 games left we still had to go to places like Bristol Rovers and

Cardiff, neither of whom were in the promotion frame but who were both playing really well. I think it was Bristol where we won 2–1 in a night game in the rain and it was just sheer determination to get through. But at the back of your mind you're thinking "Not again, please God don't let it happen again."'

The pressure levels reached such an extent that Alan Mullery made the decision to take his squad up to the north east of England a full five days before Albion's final game of the season against Newcastle at St James' Park. Sunderland magnanimously threw open the doors of their training ground and the players got to relax over a round or three of golf, venturing out from their hotel on the Wednesday night to take in Newcastle versus Bristol Rovers. Despite having nothing to play for, the Geordies put on a devastating display to beat the west-country side 5–1. It was the best possible result, and Mullery knew it. If any of his players had expected Newcastle to simply roll over and die on the Saturday, thus handing Albion one of the sought after promotion places coveted by their deadly rivals Sunderland, they were very much mistaken.

There's no doubt that the opening 45 minutes of the Newcastle game saw that particular Albion side at their very best. In front of a full house, including 10,000 travelling fans hell bent on having a good time, goals by Brian Horton, Peter Ward and Gerry Ryan gave Mullery's men a 3–0

lead at the break. All of which made what happened inside the away dressing room at half-time all the more extraordinary. Nobody knows exactly how the verbal sparring started. Brian Horton once told me he thought Mullery had been the catalyst, firing up the players to such an extent with his rhetoric that they began falling out with each other. Eric Steele, booked supposedly for time wasting after 30 minutes, remembers Mullery freaking out over the possibility of him being yellow carded a second time and getting sent off, at which point Horton told him not to panic because 'Paul Clark can go in goal.'

So what does Gary recall of probably the strangest, most volatile half-time in Albion's history? 'If you ask everyone who was there you'll get a different story from each player. It was crazy. I seem to remember an offside decision starting it all. They got through and somebody hadn't stepped up. It might even have been me. Someone had a pop at somebody else, and it all went from there. Instead of everybody shutting up and taking it on board we were so hyped up and tightly strung we were just snapping. I don't think anybody grabbed hold of anyone but there was a hell of a lot of screaming going on.

'What you've got to remember is that the last two years of our lives were riding on that next 45 minutes, and even though we were 3–0 up no one was ready to get out the cigars. None of us had played in what is now the Premiership. It meant so much to us to get there, to play at places like Old Trafford and Anfield. At the end we talked about what had happened at half-time and were laughing our heads off, but at the time we meant it.'

Exactly what Newcastle's players – three goals down and with their minds on the beaches of Florida and Spain – must have thought of the rumpus next door is anyone's guess.

Newcastle did get a goal back but it didn't matter. Brighton won 3–1 to secure promotion to the top flight for the first and so far only time. Four days later Crystal Palace were confirmed as Division One Champions after their 2–1 victory over Burnley, Albion's players hearing they had missed out on the title while at 30,000 feet over the Atlantic on their way to a well-earned three-week break in the United States. As if to illustrate exactly how tight things were that season, Sunderland, top of the table with two games left to play, missed out altogether.

And so three months later Brighton made their debut in the old First Division. It would prove to be a memorable season, not least of all for Gary, who, for the second campaign running, would appear in every game. To begin with, the dream of playing in amphitheatres such as Old Trafford threatened to become a nightmare. It was Gary, after all, who was involved in that spot of fisticuffs with

teammate Eric Steele during an away game against Manchester United on 6 October 1979, the one that led to Steele being shown the door by Mullery and Graham Moseley becoming Albion's regular 'keeper.

'Everyone had looked forward to this game, no doubt about it,' says Gary. 'Everyone wanted to play at Old Trafford. There had been that extra bit of zest in training with everyone wanting to get picked. You look up at the scoreboard when you come out and there it is – 52,641 – the biggest crowd I'd ever played in front of, and the lads were up for it big time. But it didn't quite go according to plan.

'I think we were 1–0 down when it happened and we ended up losing 2–0. Before I go any further with this story I'd like to say that I get on really well with Eric. We always played tennis against each other and were good buddies. But there was this mix-up. A ball got played through and I thought I heard a shout to leave it, so I left it. Ashley Grimes goes past me, hits a great shot and Eric makes a fantastic save. Like most goalkeepers, he gets to his feet and gives me the point with two fingers, then throws another finger up in the air to say "You should have booted it into the crowd." As far as I was concerned, I got a shout off him to leave it. And from then it's probably my fault because the old red mist came down. I felt he was blaming me for something that wasn't my fault. So I actually ran at him and we're squaring up to each other and holding one another's shirts. There was no punching. We were just grappling. It happened right in front of the Stretford End, and I think we slightly came to our senses when we could hear the whole ground laughing their heads off. They were winning the game and we were at each other's throats.

'In a way I feel pretty guilty about it because I don't know if it had any baring on Eric leaving. Mullers asked me after the game "What's your version?" and then Eric had his say. Maybe he didn't shout but that's the way I saw it. We shook hands afterwards. Things like that can and sometimes do happen in the heat of the moment. As a group of lads we were so passionate about that football club and about what went on out there for 90 minutes. It was that kind of thing that took that team from the Third Division to what is now the Premiership. What we were lacking maybe in skill we made up for in heart. We never knew we were beaten.'

Unfortunately for Gary's conscience there's no escaping the fact that Eric's transfer to Watford less than a fortnight later was largely down to what happened at Old Trafford. As Steele himself admits in Chapter One, he should have stayed and fought for his place instead of jumping at the chance to leave. He had, after all, just signed a three-year contract at the Goldstone. 'It's the one thing that if I could have my time again, I'd do differently,' admits Eric.

Six weeks after that ill-fated trip to Old Trafford, Albion won 1–0 away against the reigning European Cup holders Nottingham Forest, thanks to a Gerry Ryan goal. It was the kick-start their season so desperately needed. From 17 November until the end of the campaign only seven League games were lost, the club finishing comfortably clear of relegation in 16th place. Yet it was the return fixture against Brian Clough's all-conquering Forest side on 29 March 1980 that was to become the defining moment of Gary's Albion career for many supporters.

The move that led to my all-time favourite Goldstone goal began with the young substitute Gary Stevens winning a tackle deep inside the Brighton half, launching a five-pass move that culminated with Peter Ward laying the ball back in Gary's direction around 30 yards out on the left. 'I was thinking of maybe moving it on again when Brian Horton shouted "Hit the ****ing thing!" And I thought "Alright, I will." When you hit the ball that sweetly you don't even really feel a thing. By the time I looked up it was heading for the top corner. I don't care what you say – no one aims for the top corner. When you take a shot you're aiming for the goal with your head down and you bang it as hard as you can, which is what I did. In it went and everyone descended on me. It came right in the last few minutes and meant we'd done the double over the European Champions. To

Gary Williams, scorer of 'that goal' against Nottingham Forest.

this day I remember running back and "Nobby" [Brian Horton] saying "There's the camera – shout to your mum and tell her what you've done." So I went "Hello mum."

Gary's wonder goal, dismissed typically by Clough as a 'fluke, an absolute fluke', was replayed on *Match of the Day* that night, those being the days when the show carried no more than two featured games instead of action from every top-flight match around the country. Chosen as one of the Goals of the Month, it went on to make the BBC's Goal of the Season competition where it lost out to a sublime Terry McDermott volley for Liverpool at Spurs. To this day, Gary describes it as his 15 minutes of fame. 'I still get stopped in the street and asked about it, which I'm thankful for. It's better than being remembered for something like a miss, which is why I always feel so sorry for Gordon [Smith] after what happened in the Cup Final.'

While that Nottingham Forest goal remains Gary's most memorable strike for the club, it is by general consensus far from his most important. That came 13 months later in the penultimate game of the 1980–81 season as Albion fought desperately against relegation to the Second Division after just two years in the top flight. An abject display at Middlesbrough on 11 April meant Alan Mullery's side pretty much had to win their remaining four matches to stand any

chance of avoiding the drop. Back to back victories over Crystal Palace and Leicester during Easter meant Brighton faced Sunderland at Roker Park on 25 April with their season still very much alive. In the dying seconds Gordon Smith played a one-two with Gerry Ryan on the right, the Scotsman advancing before chipping a cross towards the far post into Gary's path, and the full-back smashing a left-foot volley past Sunderland goalkeeper Barry Siddall to snatch a precious 2–1 win.

'The game had just been drifting with them kicking it towards the touchlines, happy with a point because it meant they would be mathematically safe from going down. It was our last attack of the game. Gordon knocks a good ball into the penalty area and I've just taken a gamble and gone up from the halfway line. I say so myself but it was a really good volley. It fell to me around 10 yards out and you could hear the net ripple because the crowd went silent. We were running around celebrating and you could hear us shouting and hollering, which isn't normal because there were 20-odd thousand people there. We had a few fans over in the corner at the far end going mad, but Sunderland's were thinking "God, we've got to go to Anfield next week." They thought they'd had it.'

In the end Sunderland stayed up, as did the Albion following a 2–0 win at home against Leeds on the last day of the season. Unlike Steve McQueen, Brighton had managed to pull off the Great Escape. However, Mullery's resignation during the summer of 1981 would ultimately signal the end of Gary's career at the Goldstone. His replacement, Mike Bailey, favoured a more defensive style of play than the frequently cavalier approach adopted by Mullery. That September the new manager went out and bought Arsenal left-back Sammy Nelson, himself surplus to requirements at Highbury following the arrival of Kenny Sansom.

'It came completely out of the blue,' admits Gary. 'I started off in Mike Bailey's team. I knew I had to prove myself all over again, but I thought I was playing the best football of my time at the Goldstone. Then one day I pick up *The Argus* and we have signed Sammy Nelson. I stormed in to see him [Bailey] and I say "So you don't think I'm playing well then?" And he says, "No, don't worry, we need extra players. He's a squad player who can play anywhere." And I'm thinking "Bollocks!" But he didn't play him straight away. He couldn't drop me because I wasn't doing anything wrong.'

That didn't stop matters coming to a head immediately after a home game against Manchester City on 3 October, Gary scoring again in a comfortable 4–1 win. 'It was another one of those goals where I'd gone on a run on the blindside with nobody picking me up. The ball got crossed to me, I brought it down and put it in the back of the net. Afterwards, he

[Bailey] came over to me in the dressing room and instead of patting me on the back he says "What are you doing?" I told him I'd gone on a run and what have you and he looked at me, shook his head and just went "What were you doing up there?" And I knew at that second that on the strength of scoring a goal I was going to lose my place. I think it had been 2–1 or 3–1 when I scored, but it was clear he wanted a solid back four the whole time, the one-nils in other words.'

Gary played his final Albion game the following month, after which Sammy Nelson took over the left-back berth. He played in the reserves until being rescued the following July by, of all teams, Crystal Palace in an exchange deal that saw Neil Smillie move from Surrey to Sussex. 'In the space of six months it had all changed. When we finished the 1980–81 season I honestly thought we had a really good side with the likes of Brian Horton and "Lawro" [Mark Lawrenson]. We were dominating teams towards the end of the season, particularly at home, and I thought we were going to go on from there. But then Mullers went, and Brian, then Lawro. All of that was an absolute bombshell. Don't get me wrong, some good players came in, like Jimmy [Case] for instance, but the manager had a different outlook on the game, different ideas. I always preferred the Mullery way – attack to him was the best form of defence.'

Ironically, for a man who had built up a reputation at the Goldstone for being Mr Consistency, playing in 146 consecutive games at one point, Gary's career at Selhurst Park lasted just 10 matches before injury forced his retirement from the professional game. He went on to represent Sussex while playing County League football with Whitehawk and used the proceeds from a 1984 testimonial to launch his own television and radio business in Brighton's George Street.

The ending may have been a sour one, yet Gary has staunchly refused to let the memory of those final months colour his view of the club. 'It was a different philosophy after Mike arrived, but I always look back on those three or four years beforehand as the glory years, going from the Third Division right up to the top. We had some excellent players and a team spirit that was just fantastic. I'd speak to many of the other lads after they left and we'd all look back on it and say "When you went to that other club, did you ever feel the same kind of thing as we had down here?" And to a man they'd say "No." What we had was pretty special. Other teams after games often go their separate ways but we used to go out for a meal. Some people couldn't make it every now and again, but there would always be at least eight couples because the wives all got on together.

'There were an awful lot of northerners in that team – myself, Lawro, Wardy, Brian Horton, Ken Tiler from Sheffield, even Sully from North Wales. Northern lads usually get on like a house on fire anyway, but lads are lads in football and we bonded straight away. The culture shock of moving south was compensated for by the fact that we were working-class lads who generally talked about the same stuff. You've got 15 or 20 ready mates on your doorstep, and unless you cock it up by being an arrogant so and so you'll always be alright. We were lucky. A lot of people move to a new area when they change their jobs and don't know anybody.'

Although most of those 15 to 20 ready mates now live outside Sussex, in Peter Ward's case as far away as Florida, Gary is one of the ones who remained. He continued to make regular visits to the Goldstone as a spectator, drawn by the atmosphere that had first attracted him to the club while he was still on Preston's books. It's fair to say that what happened to the old place in 1997 hit him harder than the vast majority of ex-Albion players, living as he did just a short walk from the centre circle.

'I was totally devastated. For one thing it was my club. That was where I played. There was always something special about it, the feel of it. It had been there 100 years. What made it all the more emotional for me was the way the fans tried really hard to do something about it. Some people said they were being unruly. No they

Gary Williams, Hove, 2006.

weren't – they were just trying to prevent it from being sold from under their noses. It was tragic, absolutely tragic, and the Football Association seemed to do nothing to help.'

Gary took his son Ben, then aged 14, to the last-ever fixture at the Goldstone against Doncaster Rovers in April 1997, a game Albion won 1–0 setting up a nailbiting showdown with Hereford on the final day of the season to determine which of the two sides would drop out of the Football League. After the final whistle had blown, the two of them joined thousands of others fans on the pitch, Gary taking a souvenir lump of turf from around the spot where he had let fly against Nottingham Forest 17 years beforehand.

'I stood there for around five or 10 minutes because I was never going to get the chance to do it again. I didn't realise it at the time, but a girl who used to write for *The Argus* had spotted me. She wrote, "I looked over to where Gary Williams scored that famous goal against Nottingham Forest, and I saw this slightly ageing, grey-haired man. I did a double take and yes, sure enough, it was Gary Williams." As I said, my 15 minutes of fame, but it's fantastic being remembered for something special like that.'

Chapter Four
Happy Days

Gary Williams, as he says, had his 15 minutes of fame. However, the showbiz bandwagon just keeps on rolling for one of 'Willo's' old defensive sidekicks from Preston. Albion set it in motion, Liverpool steered it into the fast lane and the British Broadcasting Corporation turned on the booster jets. Rarely a day goes by when Mark Lawrenson isn't doing some kind of football analysis via television, radio, newspapers or digital media. And why not? The man's effortless style, as lampooned by impressionist Alistair McGowan, may not be to everyone's tastes, but my God he knows his stuff.

First things first. There is a school of thought among a fair percentage of Brighton supporters that Mark is, for some reason, ashamed of his Albion connections. Why, for instance, doesn't he mention the club more on *Football Focus*, with a gleam of nostalgia in his eye at the memory of golden days on the Sussex Riviera? Couldn't he have used his media clout a tad more effectively in the ongoing fight for a new stadium? I for one have always been willing to give him the benefit of the doubt. If I name-checked Albion glowingly in every piece I produced for a national newspaper, for no

other reason than I happen to be a fan, then editors would stop using me. Mark is from Preston, hence his use of the word 'us' when referring to North End. He won over the world with Liverpool and owes his post-career job to what he achieved on Merseyside, not because he was promoted to the First Division with the Seagulls in 1979. For the record, there was no reluctance on his behalf when it came to this book. He wanted to be part of it.

So where does Brighton & Hove Albion lie in his football affections? 'It falls just behind Liverpool,' says Mark, as we talk in a make-up room deep within the bowels of the BBC's HQ at White City. 'Liverpool was just sensational in terms of what you won, which is, after all, what you show your kids and grandkids. I got another career out of playing for them. But the most fun I ever had was at Brighton, definitely. I've really got nothing but fantastic, fond memories of the place. I just hope people understand that Preston is a spiritual thing for me. I was born in a hospital 350 yards as the crow flies from Deepdale. My dad played for them. My stepdad was on the board there. It's where I made my debut in front of my schoolmates, so it's a very special place.'

So, hopefully, that helps clear that up then.

Mark Thomas Lawrenson came into the world on 2 June 1957 and grew up a North End fan, his heroes being the men of the 1970–71 promotion side which won a place in the old Second Division, guys such as goalkeeper Alan Kelly, midfield general Alan Spavin and centre-forward Bobby Ham. Peter Read, the club's official photographer, lived in the same village as the young Mark and used to pass any unused pictures on to him to decorate his bedroom walls. He did well at school, passing enough O levels to be accepted into the sixth form. It was in the middle of his A levels that Preston came knocking for his signature. He had already rejected one golden opportunity with Lancashire County Cricket Club, his talent with a bat and ball having been recognised with a place in the county's schoolboy side. This, however, was the call he had been waiting for.

'I'd had the chance of going on the ground staff at Old Trafford, but it was never really a goer with me. When the coach went "You've got to pick one or the other", it was probably the worst thing he could have said because it was always going to be football. There was just never any doubt. I'd done a deal with my mother that I would take my O levels. Then Bobby Charlton took over at Preston and it was like "You've got to come now or you will miss the boat."

Once that happened my mother's point of view was "Fine, go and do it." I was supposed to continue with my education but that sort of fell by the wayside.'

Mark made his debut for North End aged 17 during the 1974–75 season and went on to play 73 times for the club over the best part of the next three years. By the end of 1976 he was already the subject of transfer speculation, something that only increased the following April when Ireland selected him to face Poland in Dublin (Mark's grandfather on his mother's side was Irish). Despite the family connection, it was his first visit to the country. 'There's that famous story about Terry Mancini, who played for Ireland though he was born and brought up in London. The national anthem starts playing, "Amhran na bhFiann", Terry turns round and says "Christ, their anthem doesn't half go on a long time," and everyone else goes "Shut up you pillock, it's ours!" That basically applied to me. I'd never been there before. I can't even remember who I played alongside.'

Despite earning rave reviews for his performances in Division Three, not everyone was initially a Mark Lawrenson fan. 'Me and Steve Piper had been playing tennis over in Hove Park,' recalls former Albion captain Brian Horton. 'We were walking back to the Goldstone to get changed when Alan Mullery cornered us. He said "I'm about to sign the best centre-half in the Third Division. Can you guess who it is?" The two of us put our heads together and thought of a few decent centre-halves, but in the end I said "I can't think gaffer, no." He goes "Mark Lawrenson." I said "What! We battered Preston by five at our place!" And Alan replied "I'm telling you, he's the best in the League." We bought him and, of course, that's what he became, and then some.'

Brighton saw off interest from Liverpool to sign Mark in July 1977, having just won promotion from the Third Division. The defender was in Benidorm on Preston's end-of-season wind down when he received a telephone call from his stepfather Tom Gore, a North End director, saying Albion had made a bid. Mark said he would speak to the club on his return, but Tom was adamant that chairman Mike Bamber wanted to do the deal immediately, even if it meant him flying out to Spain.

'They were really insistent. I said "Look, I won't sign for anyone else", but that wasn't enough for "Miami Mike". He flew out with Dudley Sizen, who was one of the club's directors. They were due to arrive about midday but had loads of problems with the flights and ended up getting there at eight o'clock at night. I'd said to the lads "I can't drink, I've got to be completely sensible", but they arrived so late that I'd had a few. To cut a long story short, I signed a blank contract on the strength that Miami Mike had spoken

to my stepfather. The negotiations took place in a phone booth at their hotel. I was talking to my stepfather, the chairman was talking to my stepfather, and so on. At one stage the hotel manager came over to Dudley with a piece of paper to say the phone call was costing more than the overnight stay. Then the three of us went out to celebrate with beans on toast.'

There was, however, one brief moment when the celebrations looked as though they might have been premature. Tests had shown up abnormalities in Mark's blood, leading Albion's club doctor to conclude he was diabetic. His advice to Alan Mullery was not to sign him. Puzzled, the manager, together with the club's medical team, began probing the young Lancastrian for answers, at which point the truth became clear. While in Benidorm Mark had been drinking large quantities of Guinness laced with blackcurrant, enough to play havoc with his sugar levels ('You can imagine how many pints I'd had over the course of a day, let alone a week!') False alarm over, the deal finally went through.

Like Gary Williams, Mark's knowledge of Brighton as a place up until that point would not have covered the back of a postage stamp. And as for the Albion? Well he knew they got fantastic crowds and as an enthusiast of the game (even then), he appreciated the talents of various people with associations past and present to the

'In terms of fun and everything it was just the best' – Mark Lawrenson in the blue and white stripes.

club – Pat Saward, Brian Clough, Peter Taylor, Kit Napier and Fred Binney to name just a few. He moved into digs in Preston Park with the Doo family, plus their pet dog called, you've guessed it, Scooby. The welcome was a warm one, but having never lived away before homesickness was a problem. 'Those first few Saturdays I'd drive back to St Annes from Brighton. You imagine that, 270 odd miles with no M25. It seems crazy, but I didn't know any better, so I just did it. Then, at some point you suddenly realise "This is a great place. I like it here." And the trips home steadily become less frequent.'

It may have been 'a great place', but it was the faces around the club itself that made Mark feel more comfortable in his new surroundings. 'There was Nobby [Brian Horton], Wardy and Sully [Peter O'Sullivan], who was a really good player, but there were also a lot of really great characters like Chris Cattlin and Eric Steele. I loved it because the vast majority of all these players had been brought in from outside. There were only Steve Piper and Tony Towner who were remotely local. All of them had been brought in, lived in hotels, gone through all that kind of transitional stuff and because of that there was a real sense of camaraderie. Every time we went away if you didn't go back to the pub afterwards you were fined, which was great for team spirit. And nothing was ever too much trouble. The club honestly couldn't do enough. If you wanted to buy a house, they would be there to help you get sorted out. It was the classic case of a club on the up who had never been in the top League – and it was perfectly obvious that's what they were aiming for.'

For Mark the most disappointing thing about missing out on promotion to Division One during his first year at the club was the colossal gap between fourth-placed Albion and Blackburn, who finished fifth. Yet that did not prevent him feeling an immense sense of satisfaction over what the team had achieved. 'Yes, it ended in tears, but you can't deny that it was a really good season. If you'd said at the start that we were going to miss out on goal difference we would probably have accepted that. What did jar with me was the points difference between ourselves and Blackburn, which was plenty even back in the days of two points for a win (it was actually 11 points). Personally, that season was a big step for me and something to build on.'

And build on it he did. After a shaky start to the 1978–79 campaign, Albion knuckled down and began doing the business, with every man fulfilling the job asked of him by Mullery. Four or five, however, seemed able to go the extra mile, so often the difference between a good team and one that actually achieves things. Mark was one of them, his composure at the centre of defence shining out like a South Downs beacon on a clear night. His timing in the tackle and ability to read the game belied his relative youth, but what really caught the eye was his skill on the ball, which for a centre-back still earning his wages in English football's second tier was little short of remarkable.

'He was one of those players that when they had the ball you just couldn't get it off them,' says Malcolm Poskett, brought in by Mullery from Hartlepool in February 1978 to provide extra firepower up front. 'The difference was, of course, that Mark was a back and they're not supposed to be like that. He had these long legs that went on forever. He could creep up behind players and with one sliding tackle just whip the ball away from them. He would look like he was beaten but he was deceptive. He didn't look quick but he was.'

'The way he used to bring the ball out from the back had to be seen to be believed,' adds Brian Horton. 'I remember one game in particular. He came out with the ball and I went to drop back and fill in for him, which is what I used to do. He went on this mazy run where he just kept on going and going and scored a beauty. Jesus, if Sky TV had been around then they would have been showing it for months on end. It was the kind of thing (Franz) Beckenbauer would do, only it was happening at Brighton.'

Chances are the goal Brian recalls is the one Mark scored in an FA Cup third-round tie against Wolverhampton Wanderers at the Goldstone on 9 January 1979, to this day a popular choice among many supporters as the greatest ever scored by an Albion player. Mark remembers it slightly differently. 'I ran through and it parted like the Red Sea in front of me. I couldn't shoot for my life, but I ended up hitting it from outside the box and it must have skidded off the turf before going in the corner. When it left my foot I didn't think it was a goal. It seemed to pick up more pace when it hit the dirt. I think I scored better goals than that.'

Such as? 'I scored one at Bolton for Brighton which was on *Match of the Day*. I thought it would've been in the archives here but it's not. I beat two or three players, cut in and bent it round the goalkeeper but it got chalked off because of someone (standing offside) way out on the left-wing. There was another in a really tight home game against Sheffield United. I had my socks rolled down and it came from a corner. There's a fantastic picture somewhere – I've just hit it and it's going through a forest of players into the far corner. That would certainly have been one of my better goals. I had a similar one [to the Wolverhampton goal] against Manchester City, when we absolutely destroyed them once at the Goldstone. That would've been up there, but it hit the bar. That's in the archives. I know because I managed to find that one!'

Mark played in the first 39 League

games of what proved to be an historic promotion season, and probably would have made all 42 had he not come off second best in a challenge with Dave Staniforth at the Goldstone on 16 April 1979. Rising to head the ball, 'Lawro' went over the top of the Bristol Rovers centre-forward and came down hard on his right arm. 'You could hear the snap and there it was pointing to New York. Mike Yaxley was the physio then. They'd just invented these inflatable things to help deal with broken bones. He'd been blowing this thing up and I just said "Yackers, it's gone down", and the bloody thing had collapsed. I was saying "Just blow the f***ing thing up and get me out of here", because you can imagine the pain. So I went off on a stretcher and he chucked some morphine into me, then we went to the hospital where the specialist reset my arm with me completely conscious. I remember the arm being on some kind of plinth and he put an injection in, got hold of it and started putting it back in place. I couldn't feel a thing. I was watching him do it thinking "If I can't feel this, it must be okay." Then he took an x-ray, had a look at it and said "That's absolutely fine." And I haven't had any problems with it since.'

Crowned Player of the Season before Albion's final home game of the campaign against Blackburn, Mark travelled to Newcastle for the crunch promotion match with his arm wrapped in a sling. He watched events unfurl sitting next to Mike Bamber in the directors' box at St James' Park before making his way towards the tunnel as the final whistle approached. It was then that a local policeman, oblivious to Mark's identity, tried to escort him back onto the terraces thinking he was a punter. Thankfully, Mike Yaxley appeared in the nick of time to vouch for him, enabling Albion's star centre-back to join his teammates celebrating on the pitch.

'That was also the best train journey of my life on the way back,' says Mark, echoing the thoughts of just about everyone who rode on the 12-coach booze-soaked diesel-hauled special which lumbered back from north-east England complete with playing staff, directors and a few lucky supporters on board. 'It was just sensational. It probably took 12 hours but it went like that [clicks fingers]. I used to love the train rides anyway to away games but that one was something else. Some of the carriages were left over from the old *Brighton Belle*. They had buzzers in them for you to call the steward. There was an old boy who worked on it who would tell us all these stories about the Queen. He'd done the London to Brighton line for years and knew everyone and everything who used it. It was little things like that that made playing for the club so special and memorable.'

Mark's arm had healed well before the start of the 1979–80 season, allowing him to take his place in the first-ever Albion team to play in the top flight. But after just seven games he damaged ankle ligaments in a 2–1 defeat at Tottenham resulting in a two-week spell on the sidelines (the very same injury which allowed Gary Stevens to break into the starting XI). When he returned to the side it was in midfield rather than defence, as Mullery looked to change things around following a dreadful start to the season, employing new recruit Peter Suddaby alongside Steve Foster in Mark's old position. Lawro made the transformation look effortless, and it is no coincidence that his return went hand in hand with Albion's steady climb away from the relegation zone.

On 22 March 1980 Albion went to Liverpool, then undisputedly the best side in Europe, and narrowly lost 1–0 to a rare Alan Hansen goal. It was a measure of how far the club had come, the closeness of the contest illustrated by Gary Stevens going desperately close to an equaliser in the fourth minute of added time. The following day's newspapers were full of praise for the way Mark and Steve Foster had marked Kenny Dalglish and David Johnson respectively out of the game. 'People in Liverpool will tell you that they (Liverpool) signed me on the back of that day because of how I played against Kenny,' says Mark. 'Brighton had a director at the time called Tom Appleby. He came up to me afterwards and went

"You playing against him was better than watching the game", which is an unusual thing for a director to say.'

He may have done a decent job on him that day, but Mark still rates Dalglish as the best player of his generation. 'We spent the first half of that season in the dressing room looking at the names on the opposition team sheet thinking "Oh Christ!" That's probably why it took us so long to get started. I wasn't looking forward to playing against Joe Jordan, that I do know. Trevor Francis was another one that stood out. But Dalglish was the ultimate. Anyone who's ever played with him will tell you the same thing. He couldn't run, he couldn't head it and he had a big arse, but he was an absolute genius. Every 10 or 15 years there's a guy that plays football who stands alone, and that was Kenny.'

It would be over a year before Liverpool signed Mark from Brighton, but it was clear even then that the Merseyside club had him in their sights. Lawro insists he remained blissfully unaware of this but admits games against the Reds always had a certain aura for him. This was largely because whenever the two sides met, Mark knew he was going up against the very best in Dalglish. 'I remember playing them at home once when we were 2–0 up kicking uphill, and they pulled it back to two each. I was captain that day because there was something wrong with Brian [Horton].

Without Brian that would have been a decent result for us. I played in midfield and didn't touch the ball in the second half because we never saw it.'

That particular match came at the Goldstone on 21 February 1981, during Albion's second season in the top flight and Mark's last at the club. It would ultimately prove to be a vital point as Mullery's side fought successfully against relegation, winning their last four games with Gary Williams scoring that vital goal in the final minute of the penultimate fixture at Sunderland. 'A match that was so dire it wasn't true,' recalls Mark. 'What did help us over those last few games was all the players that got sent off against us. We played Leicester and they had a big centre-forward who was a good player but nuts – Alan Young, that was his name – and he got his marching orders. I think "Fozzie" (Steve Foster) had wound him up and he'd bitten. Then, against Leeds, one of their defenders, Neil Firm, also got sent off. What I'll always remember about that run in was a game at the Goldstone just beforehand where we got beat. We were sat in the bath and we're all like "Oh Christ!" because big Al [Mullery] had gone mad at us. "Smudger" [Gordon Smith] said "We need a snooker", which was really funny at the time but everyone suppressed their laughter in case Al heard. "We need a snooker" – and we got one, didn't we!'

Albion might have got out of jail, but behind the scenes all was far from sweetness and light around the Goldstone. The previously harmonious relationship between Mullery and Bamber had gone sour. The two had always been larger than life characters who shared an important mutual understanding – Bamber let his manager handle team affairs, and Mullery left boardroom matters to his chairman. The catalyst for this sea change had been the death in October 1980 of Harry Bloom, the club's vice-chairman. Harry died of a heart attack on the team coach in Stoke as it waited to transport the playing staff and directors from the town's railway station to a hotel. The club's medical team had attempted to revive him to no avail.

'Harry (Bloom) was about five foot five and always wore a suit,' says Mullery. 'He was like a father to me. Every morning when I arrived for work at the Goldstone he'd always be outside waiting for me. We'd have a cup of coffee together and then around 9am the chairman would arrive and we'd all talk about football. Harry once told me that as long as Brighton were in the old First Division he'd die a happy man. Within around three months of him saying that he'd died on the team coach up at Stoke. When he died the buffer between Mike and me had gone. For the last six months I was there, there was no buffer.'

Mark still clearly remembers that fateful day in Stoke. 'We were having lunch on the train going up from Euston – I'll never forget this. There was this bloke who worked in the restaurant car who we'd met a few times and sort of got to know. We nicknamed him "Mr Shadrack" after a character in a TV series about a funeral parlour that was on at the time, because he looked like him. He was good fun. The two of us were chatting away and he suddenly said "Who's that fella over there in your party?" And it was Harry. He said "He doesn't look very well." To me he didn't look any different than normal. When we got to the station at Stoke we had a really long walk from the platform to the coach, and I remember him [Harry] getting on board coughing and wheezing. He got into the very first seat and by then he really didn't look well. And he just went like that. They had him in the passage way and George Aitken [Albion's trainer] was pumping his heart, beating it, trying to get it started.'

Without their 'buffer', the relationship between manager and chairman rapidly went downhill, fuelled by what appeared to be a losing battle against relegation. Mullery resented the way Bamber kept going behind his back regarding players' contracts. Money – or rather the lack of it – became an issue as chairman asked manager to make cuts in his backroom staff, ones Mullery, to his credit, resisted. However, with debts mounting both men saw eye to eye on one thing. If cash had to be found then selling the club's star asset

seemed the easiest option. And that's where Mark came into the equation.

Bamber, God rest his soul, is no longer with us and so cannot comment on what happened next. Mullery's version of events goes along the following lines: once the club had reluctantly decided to sell Mark, Mullery phoned Ron Atkinson – poised to become the new Manchester United manager – and gave him the opportunity of making Mark his first signing. Atkinson provisionally agreed to the asking price of £400,000 plus two players. The pair agreed to finalise things at a football dinner they were both due to attend in London later that week. The morning after the dinner, Mullery told Bamber what he had agreed with Atkinson, only to hear that the chairman had already done a deal with Liverpool for £900,000, all the money being paid in one attractive lump sum. An argument ensued which resulted in Mullery resigning.

'I've heard so many different things but it was obvious I was going,' says Mark. 'I was getting phone calls from everywhere basically saying "They need the money, you're going to go." Liverpool, Manchester United and Arsenal had all been in touch so I knew I was off. When Al (Mullery) went Mike Bailey took over and then almost straight away Brian Horton left as well. We went away on a pre-season trip to Holland, and I got sent off in a friendly. Afterwards Mike Bailey came in to see me promising all these things, and I just said "I'm not being funny, but I think it's time for me to go." Mullers had gone, Brian had gone and there was just this synergy saying "This could be the time." To be fair to Mike, he did me a favour by letting me go, and he managed to change it round because players like Tony Grealish and Don Shanks came in. In fact, "Skanksy" came with us to Holland. I remember him telling me at one point "For f**** sake hurry up and go and I'll get a contract!"'

It is at this point where Mark's story differs slightly from the popular perception around Brighton of what happened. 'Some of the things I've heard don't particularly ring true. For instance, the night before I actually signed (for Liverpool) I'd been given permission to speak to Arsenal. As far as I was concerned I could've said "Yes" or "No" to Arsenal, but I turned Terry [Neill, Arsenal's manager] down. He was trying to sell me the marble halls and playing with [David] O'Leary, but he actually offered me less money than I was on at Brighton. I went "Terry, I'm not a mercenary at all, but you're offering me less money to come and play for your team. That doesn't quite work." The next morning he called me saying "We've been having a think about it. We're going to offer you more money." And straight away something inside me said "Why didn't you offer me that yesterday?" I told him I was speaking to Liverpool at lunchtime

that day in a hotel at Heathrow. Terry said he would be in the hotel next door if things fell through because Arsenal were going on a pre-season tour of Greece. But it didn't and I signed.

'When I was speaking to Liverpool I was getting all sorts of messages along the lines of "Don't sign for Liverpool until you've spoken to Ron." And Ron was going "I'll give you more money, I'll get you a better deal", which he probably would've done. But once I'd spoken to Liverpool that was it. So I don't know about the politics with Al and Bamber because as far as I was concerned, if I'd told Terry Neill "I'm signing for you" then that would have been that. I'd have gone there. I suppose the Liverpool deal – £900,000 plus VAT in one lump sum in the bank – was probably more attractive to Miami Mike because of the way the club [Brighton] was at the time.'

Four weeks later Mark and Terry Neill came face to face with each other in a corridor at Anfield, Arsenal having drawn Liverpool away in one of the opening fixtures of the 1981–82 season. 'He said to me "Do you think you've made the right choice?" I replied "What do you think?" And he went "Yeah, okay."

Mark's situation was not too different to that of most Brighton fans at the time – everyone knew he was going to leave, it was just a question of when and to where. The man had served the club admirably for four years and was ready for a bigger stage, so there were no hard feelings. His value had multiplied by nine times, resulting in a nice little cheque to bank in Albion's vaults. What did make his departure during the summer of 1981 hard to take was that it formed part of a steady exodus away from the Goldstone. Besides Mullery and Brian Horton, the long-serving Peter O'Sullivan together with future England international right-back John Gregory had also left for pastures new. Exactly how Albion survived this exodus is a subject for other chapters in this book. At least supporters had the consolation of exacting some revenge over Mark the following season as Brighton won 1–0 at Anfield, having fought back from 3–1 down to snatch a point at the Goldstone five months previously. Not that either result prevented the Reds being crowned League Champions in May 1982.

'That was probably my biggest highlight because I always said I was going there to win things,' says Mark. 'It completely justified my decision to leave Brighton. The first three years I was there we won the League Cup three times, the League three times and then the European Cup in the third of those three years. The first time we won the League we had to beat Tottenham at home on the last day of the season. I was playing in midfield again – I played all over for them that year. Glenn Hoddle was my opposite number and he scored an unbelievable

goal from outside the box, which meant it was brown trousers time for us. Then I scored with a header from a corner and hooked the ball on for Kenny [Dalglish] to make it 2–1. After two years surviving and fighting everybody off at Brighton you're suddenly top of the pile, and as good as Brighton had been that was an amazing experience. But even then there was a business-like way to it. Nobody got carried away with anything. We had great players and massive crowds, but with it came this expectation that you had to win things.'

As Mark says, his third year at Anfield brought with it a European Cup-winners' medal, generally regarded as the Holy Grail for any player at club level. Liverpool made it to the Olympic Stadium in Rome thanks largely to some outstanding performances away from home against the likes of Bilbao, Benfica and Dynamo Bucharest. In the Final, fate decreed that they would face Roma inside the Italian side's home ground. The game itself finished all-square at 1–1 and was eminently forgettable. The real fireworks took place during the subsequent penalty shoot-out as Liverpool goalkeeper Bruce Grobbelaar distracted Roma's players with his 'wobbly knees' routine. It paid off, as Joe Fagan's side triumphed by four kicks to Roma's two.

'Our away performances that year were just unbelievable. We went to Benfica when Sven [Goran Eriksson] was manager there and absolutely buried them. The semi-final was against Dynamo Bucharest, where we won 1–0 at home and Graeme Souness allegedly broke one of their fella's jaws. We went back to the Eastern Block and there was a crowd of 75,000, of which 74,999 were Soviet guards. It was a very daunting prospect as they had identified Graeme and just tried to break his legs. In fact they tried to boot us all off the pitch but we won 3–1. In the dressing room after a game, the Liverpool way was always to play things down, so we got in and were quite sombre. Then Bobby Robson, who was England manager at the time, burst in and went "That's the best performance from an away team that I've ever seen!" Joe [Fagan] was probably going to say something like "We didn't play well but we're in the Final", but even he had to join in a bit then.

‘That team was full of strong characters and we needed them in Rome. That was when Graeme Souness took us round the ground while a kids match was going on and the place was absolutely full at four in the afternoon apart from our end. He went "Come on, let's walk round and wind them up," which worked. There was a narrow corridor at the Olympic Stadium going from the dressing room down to the pitch. We were standing in it before the game and somebody, I think it might have been Dave Hodgson, started

singing *I Don't Know What it is but I Love it* by Chris Rea, who was getting to be a big deal at the time. Their manager, a Swedish guy called Nils Liedholm, said afterwards "Picture me. We're at home, a fantastic advantage, the Italian press think we've already won it, I've got my players and I'm talking to them about the game and this singing starts. It gets louder and louder. And as it gets louder and we realise who it is the colour drains from the faces of my players." He knew they were in trouble. We only knew the chorus but we kept singing it. Nobody thought "This could be a really good idea." It was just a complete fluke.

‘Everyone forgets that Brucie never saved one [of Roma's penalties]. When Alan Kennedy left the centre circle to take what proved to be the winner we were all arguing about who was going to go sixth, seventh, eighth and so on, because we were sure he wasn't going to score. We'd practised penalties on the Monday against the apprentices and lost. I remember [Alan] Hansen and me standing there and I'm saying "You're 10th, I'm 11th" and him going "No, I'm 11th and you're 10th." I'd taken a penalty before but that night no way did I want one.'

Kennedy scored and Liverpool won the European Cup to add to the League Championship and the League Cup, then known as the Milk Cup. The only trophy they failed to collect during the 1983–84 season was the FA Cup – and that was because they lost 2–0 to the Albion at the Goldstone in the fourth round. Nice.

Mark's success with Liverpool meant he was always one of the first names on the Irish team sheet, adding to the 14 caps he won while at Brighton. Jack Charlton had yet to take over as the Republic's manager and the concept of Eire making it through to the Finals of a major tournament seemed about as remote as pigs flying. Inevitably, the 'if only he was English' line came up at regular intervals in the media and among followers of the England team. 'I think he would definitely have made it into the [England] side while he was still at Brighton,' says Malcolm Poskett. 'He was good enough, no doubt about it. But on his performances at Liverpool he'd have been an England regular. It was strange because he was about as northern as they come, yet he'd made his choice (to play for Ireland) and that was that. He probably didn't think when he was 19 or 20 that playing for England would be a possibility.'

Amid all the silverware and international call ups there is one memory Mark would rather not have, that of the Heysel Stadium tragedy of 29 May 1985 when 39 people were killed following a surge by Liverpool supporters before the European Cup Final against Juventus. What happened that night in a dilapidated arena in north-west Brussels remains one of

football's darkest moments, an act of hooliganism leading to a crush among the Italian supporters which resulted in a wall collapsing.

Mark, together with the rest of the Liverpool team, knew there had been trouble on the terraces. Some of the players had ventured outside to see with their own eyes what was going on, and their reports back to the dressing room made depressing hearing. 'We were totally numb then, even though we didn't know the scale of it all at that point. The idea of people dying at a football match just doesn't add up. What did surprise us was when the police chief came in and said we would have to play. That seemed like a ridiculous idea given the circumstances, but he said if we didn't play there would be more trouble so it kind of made sense.' Does he think it was the right thing to do now? 'No, I don't, but as I said, I don't think we really knew the scale of it until afterwards.'

Liverpool continued as the dominant force in domestic football post-Heysel, their European reign halted by the five-year UEFA ban on English clubs that resulted from the tragedy. In March 1987 Mark snapped an Achilles tendon, which, by his own admission, he never really recovered from. The tendon was in the same leg as the ankle ligaments he had damaged while playing for Brighton at Tottenham way back in September 1979. He returned to the side but found the

Mark Lawrenson's BBC publicity shot.

injury hampered his ability to run properly. The old ligament wound was also now affecting his blood supply, to the extent that Mark was having to sit on the team coach with his leg in the air before games to allow fluid to drain from the affected areas.

Determined to extend the playing career of one of their key players, Liverpool sent Mark to a specialist in the Welsh border town of Oswestry. 'He basically taught people to walk again after serious car accidents and was a great guy. We did a series of tests over the course of a day involving hopping, skipping, jumping, the whole thing. The next day he came in and said "How do you want it?" I asked him what he meant.

He said "Do you want it in black and white?" I said yes and he went "You should finish. If it goes again it will be difficult to repair, you're already 25 percent down on what you can do with your Achilles", and so on. I already knew in my mind that it was over but that was what I needed to hear.'

And so, at the age of just 30, Mark retired. He carried on playing non-League football, ran a pub in Oxford and had brief stints managing both Oxford and Peterborough United. He even become player-coach of the Tampa Bay Rowdies in Florida and was responsible for bringing a certain Peter Ward to the club from Vancouver Whitecaps. By 1996 he had become defensive coach at Newcastle United. It was what you might call a varied CV, yet 10 years after hanging up his boots Mark still felt like a ship without a port career wise. It was around then that he began receiving the odd offer to do TV work.

'I literally stumbled into it. I think Alan [Hansen] was the same. You think because of who you are and where you played that the phone is going to ring every minute of every day, and it doesn't. When Sky asked me to do a bit of freelancing I thought "Why not?" Then HTV in Bristol got me in to analyse City and Rovers which was good fun, and it just went from there.' So how does he rate himself as a pundit? 'I try to be honest. I've upset one or two people because of it

and fallen out with a couple of managers, though never for long, but it's the only way to be. You can't con people because people know. They know players, they know teams, they know performances. They know what's right and they know what's wrong.'

As for the Alistair McGowan impression? 'My only argument with him is "murment". I don't know where he got that from, because that's what he says all the time – "murment". I say "moment". But it helps. I know him well. That's happy days, that is.'

Mark Lawrenson might not be the most popular player ever to play for Brighton, but in all my years supporting the club it is hard to think of a better one. He came to Sussex a decent Third Division player. He left a good First Division one. And he went on to become world class. Hats off to him. The boy done well and has continued to do so in his TV career. Next time you hear someone accusing Lawro of being anti-Albion, remember the following lines, which he delivered towards the end of our meeting.

'Brighton was just great. I'm sure everyone you've spoken to who went there has said the same thing. In terms of fun and everything it was just the best, apart from big Al occasionally going mental at us after games. It was a great time to be there with a great set of players and fantastic supporters. So many wonderful memories, both on the playing side and the social, like when Al sent us on that trip to Jersey with 'Craggsy' [Ken Craggs, assistant manager] and 'Mose' put his hand through the window. Someone else threw up in reception. No training, no nothing. We just went on the lash! Craggsy was going "What are we going to tell Al? What are we going to say happened?" And, of course, Mullers completely lost his head – but it was great for team spirit. My four years there, plus the Republic [of Ireland], got me to Liverpool. It seems a bit harsh to say it was a stepping stone, yet it was. But what a stepping stone!'

Chapter Five
'Nuts as a Bloke, But a Nice Kind of Nuts'

Stop me if the following scenario sounds familiar. You are at a house party in, say, London. At some point during the evening you fall into conversation with a group of people about football. Someone asks which team you support, and you reply Brighton. Almost immediately the questioner raises his or her arms and starts drawing imaginary lines across their forehead, uttering something like 'That bloke. Oh, what's his name? With the headband.'

His heyday at the club may have been during the early 80s, but there is no denying that for an awful lot of football followers Steve Foster, aka 'that bloke with the headband', remains the public face of Brighton & Hove Albion Football Club. They might not always remember his name, yet the image still remains. What is more, the average Joe still associates Steve with the Seagulls, despite the fact he went on to play for Aston Villa, Luton Town (whom he led to victory in the 1988 League Cup Final) and Oxford United. That, ironically, probably has as much to do with one game in which he did not appear for the Albion rather than the 332 he did. But more about that later.

'He was the best centre-half I ever played with, without a doubt,' says Brian Horton, from whom Steve ended up inheriting the club captaincy in 1981. 'He was also a great lad. Our team spirit was fantastic and Fozzie played a huge part in that because he was a big, strong, jovial character, a better footballer than a lot of people gave him credit for. The thing people always remember him for is that headband. Some thought it was a gimmick but it wasn't – it was because of his scar tissue.'

'Yeah, scar tissue that Michael Robinson helped start off,' says Steve with a smirk as we chat over a pint or two in the bar at the Courtlands Hotel in Hove. 'We used to do a free-kick routine where I would go in, he would go in, then he would turn around to come back out and block my marker. We played Wolves in a League match. He went in. As he started to come out I went in, only he forgot to block Andy Gray, so I smashed heads with Andy and split my head open. There was blood everywhere. I wanted to carry on playing, so the only thing to do was put a bandage on it with some tape wrapped around. Nowadays, if you get blood on your shirt you have to come off, but back then you didn't.

'About four weeks later we played Norwich and exactly the same thing happened. Robbo forgot to block off Justin Fashanu, who smashed the other side of my forehead. With all the scar tissue after that it was impossible for me to play 90 minutes when I'd probably be heading the ball 50 times, or trying to. It would always puff up. You couldn't just wear a sticky pad because when you sweat it falls off, so for years I had sticky tape to hold the pad on. And that's how it started.'

Stephen Brian Foster was born in Portsmouth in September 1957. As a schoolboy he was on the books at Southampton, a club that at the time boasted a fearsome youth team, including the likes of Steve Williams and Nick Holmes. Nine ended up being offered apprenticeships. Steve, then a centre-forward, was not one of them. 'Please do me a favour – go out and prove me wrong,' Southampton's manager Lawrie McMenemy told the dejected 16-year-old. The following week he was invited to play in a youth team game for Portsmouth against, of all sides, Southampton. He scored twice but there was a problem. Portsmouth had already selected their 10 apprentices from the youth ranks for that year. Fortunately for Steve – and I suppose the Albion – one youngster from Wales grew homesick and decided on a return to the Principality. He took the spare place, earning £5 per week for the privilege.

Steve played 10 games as a forward during the 1976–77 season and failed to score in any of them. It was then that Portsmouth manager Ian St John, once of Liverpool but probably more famous to anyone under 50 as one half of ITV's Saint and Greavsie partnership, had an idea. The club had an injury crisis among its centre-backs. Maybe his misfiring striker could plug a gap in defence? Twenty-five minutes into game number one in his new position, Steve scored an own-goal. He made amends the following week by notching the winner in an FA Cup tie against Aldershot, and from that day on was a regular in Portsmouth's first team.

'When you look back, it was pure luck. Sure, you need skill and heart and everything to succeed as a kid, but a lot of it is being in the right place at the right time. Unfortunately, that doesn't always happen to a lot of youngsters. You can be the best centre-forward at your age level, only for new people to take over at the club who want you to fail. They want you to fail because if you succeed it makes the old youth team manager look good. It's sad. If they were man enough they would want to turn those kids into better players. But they don't. It happens at senior level as well. Mind you, I suppose it happens in all walks of life as well as sport.'

'Luck' is a word that Steve Foster uses a lot. I would have put his success as a player down to a combination of skill, determination and sheer brute force, but

'Nuts as a bloke, but a nice kind of nuts' – Steve Foster.

in his opinion luck played a greater part than any one of those attributes. 'I ended up playing for England. Why? Because Alvin Martin and Dave Watson were injured. If they had been fit, I wouldn't have gone to the World Cup. That was luck. Escaping bad injuries is luck. Coming to Brighton was luck. Everything you do is luck.'

Steve was on holiday in July 1979 when he received a phone call saying Alan Mullery wanted to buy him. Several people had warned the Albion boss not to sign Pompey's number five because he was, in short, a nutcase. But Mullery decided to take a gamble. Brighton had just been promoted to Division One as it was then known for the first time, and he believed Steve's wild qualities, if channelled in the right direction, could be just what the club needed to survive in the top flight.

The early signs were not good. Steve was fined during his second week at the club for a breach of discipline and then suspended a fortnight later for breaking a Friday-night curfew in Manchester, the same one which landed Graham Moseley in hot water. Then that word 'luck' intervened again. Regular centre-back Andy Rollings picked up an injury, forcing Mullery to lift the suspension ahead of a League Cup tie against Cambridge at the Goldstone. Albion won 2–0 and the renegade defender kept his place for the rest of the season.

'Sometimes you have to believe in yourself. I thought I should have been playing anyway. At one point I'd said to Mullery "I'll piss off back to Portsmouth, at least I'll get a game there. I'm not staying here to not play games." But after he stopped the suspension and brought me back I was in the team from then on. It was unlucky for Andy and lucky for me. You have to take those opportunities.'

And so, by the age of 21 Steve had managed to achieve the incredible feat of playing in all four divisions of the Football League. The opening months of the 1979–80 season proved to be something of a baptism of fire both for the young centre-back and his teammates, none of whom had played regularly at that level before. Fortunately, they proved to be fast learners. 'The abiding memory of this game in which Forest had 80 percent of the possession will be John Robertson's crosses being headed clear by Brighton's vastly-improved, 21-year-old centre-half Steve Foster', wrote the *Daily Mail's* Jim Hooley of Albion's infamous 1–0 win at the City Ground on 17 November. Come April 1980, and with the club's place in Division One virtually assured for another season, Steve was selected for England's Under-21 side against East Germany alongside Peter Ward. He was booked but played well, having been introduced as a substitute. The following month he was chosen as Player of the Season by supporters, Mark Lawrenson and Ward finishing in second and third place respectively. His prize was a television – not just any television mind you, but a 'colour' one.

Steve puts his vast improvement as a player during that first season in Division One down to a simple philosophy he learned while still at Portsmouth. 'I always say to kids, not just my kids but also other kids who are playing the game, that you've got to have the balls to go and make another mistake. The moment you make a mistake, roll your sleeves up and go and make another one. I know it sounds silly but it's the right thing to do. As a footballer you can hide, not receive the ball, not tackle, just keep out of the game. But that doesn't work and you get found out, so what you have to do is go and make another mistake. After a period you learn to cut the mistakes out. You still make them, only not as frequently.'

Something else Steve acquired from Portsmouth that would stand him in good stead against the best strikers in the land was the importance of balance. 'Frank Burrows was my last manager at Portsmouth and one of the two biggest influences on my career. He used to take me out every afternoon just smashing balls at me to improve my heading and control, showing me how your strength is in your legs, not your arms. If you stand with your feet together, I could push you over with my finger. If I stand with my legs apart, you physically can't move me even if you run at me. It's all about balance. Frank taught me that and it's something I always try to teach kids who play at centre-half.'

The second biggest influence on Steve's career was Brian Horton, who as Albion's captain would also play a key role in the club's transformation from relegation certainties to First Division thoroughbreds during the 1979–80 campaign. Brian's tendency to berate his teammates throughout games had a huge effect on the young centre-back, who, as the months passed, seemed almost to morph into an Austin Powers-style 'Mini Horton'. 'He shouted and screamed for 90 minutes to help us get results and to keep everyone on their toes,' says Steve. 'If he made a mistake 10 other people would shout and scream at him, and he would take it. When I was captain at Brighton and my other clubs, that's how I tried to be.'

Although Brighton struggled throughout much of the 1980–81 season, only saving their Division One skins by winning those crucial last four games, Steve's reputation as a top-class centre-back continued to grow. Whether he was up against the skill and grace of a Kevin Keegan or the brawn of a Joe Jordan, Albion's number five usually had what it took to cancel them out. 'My hardest opponent without doubt was Peter Withe. He never stopped working, taking you here, taking you there, going short, going long, aggravating. I ended up on the same side as him at Aston Villa, and I was far happier to play with him than against him, I can tell you. After that it had to be Mick Harford. He was hard. I only played against him once and that was enough. We got beaten 1–0 at Birmingham. He scored a header at the far post and split my head open in two places.'

If there was one minor criticism of Fozzie it was his lack of goals since moving to the Goldstone. Prior to the final game of the 1980–81 season against Leeds, Steve had scored just once in 79 League starts, a paltry return for someone who promised so much in attack from set pieces. He would, however, make up for it that day, hitting Brighton's opener and creating the second for Andy Ritchie in a 2–0 win, ensuring First Division football for another year.

Steve's willingness to put his neck on the line for the cause earned him hero status among the fans, together with the complete respect of the Albion dressing room. When Brian Horton was sold to Luton during the summer of 1981, there was really only one candidate to replace him as captain. Even before 'Nobby's' departure, the players had increasingly been turning to Steve for guidance, as much about off-the-field matters as on it. 'He was a fantastic person, great fun and a terrific centre-half,' says Gordon Smith. 'He was also our captain, our manager,

our chairman, our social director, the lot. Even if the club hadn't appointed him captain, Fozzie would still have been our leader.'

Gerry Ryan concurs. 'Fozzie was a huge player with a huge personality, a real leader and deceptively quick for a big man. When he played against the best, like Ian Rush and Kenny Dalglish, he was the best. People talk about players giving 100 percent, but Fozzie gave 150 percent in everything that he did, and I mean off the field as well. He was, without a doubt, a real character and somebody we all looked up to – nuts as a bloke, but a nice kind of nuts.'

The man who handed the captaincy to Steve was Mike Bailey, Alan Mullery's successor as manager. Bailey had his critics – the soon-to-be-sold Gary Williams among them – yet it is hard not to look at Albion's League results throughout the lion's share of the 1981–82 season without a sense of pride. Early wins against the likes of Middlesbrough, Wolves, Manchester City and Spurs, together with a string of respectable draws, meant that with a third of the season gone Albion were perched comfortably inside the top half of the First Division, somewhere that had been unknown territory under Mullery.

On Tuesday 8 December Bailey's side travelled along the south coast to face high-flying Southampton, who included the likes of Kevin Keegan and Peter

Shilton in their number. That night produced quite possibly the best example of a textbook performance that I have ever witnessed from an Albion XI. Everyone did their jobs and then some. A 2–0 win courtesy of second-half goals by Andy Ritchie and Steve Gatting saw the club rise to sixth place, the highest in its history. There was still a long way to go, but a UEFA Cup spot was beginning to look like a distinct possibility.

However, not everyone was happy with the way things were. Mullery was always going to be a hard act to follow because of what he had achieved during his five years with the Seagulls. Bailey was getting results having jettisoned the gung-ho style of his predecessor. The problem was that many fans longed for a return to the more attacking, less defensive approach. A European place was honing into view, yet, incredibly, attendances at the Goldstone were falling for the first time in years.

For what it is worth, my opinion at the time was that Steve was far happier with Albion's tighter tactics. His main job description was, after all, to stop goals being conceded. It is not an opinion that has changed having spoken to him. 'We sacked Mike Bailey because we weren't playing attractive football, allegedly,' he says sardonically. 'Things were changing. Brighton had never been so high. They do say crowds were down but, if you remember, the ground was also going

through changes and had one or two difficulties. The massive crowds of a few years earlier just couldn't fit in anymore.

'When things are going well, everyone wants to be there,' he says, changing tact slightly. 'When you're not doing well people will turn their collars up, put a hat on, sneak in and keep quiet. We were doing well, but we weren't seen as a flamboyant side. I was never happy with the press, as in the *Evening Argus*, during that year or the next when we got to the FA Cup Final because they were creating this boring talk. Some of the stuff they used to write really annoyed me, and not just about the way we played. I remember one match against Manchester City. They used to do a Man of the Match for us, and a Man of the Match for whoever we were playing. Their Man of the Match according to *The Argus* was Steve MacKenzie. Steve MacKenzie never even played!'

An impressive 1–0 triumph over Liverpool at Anfield on 6 March 1982 meant that with 14 games remaining Albion lay eighth, having won 11, drawn 11 and lost six of their 28 matches so far. In the process they had bagged 33 League goals compared with 22 from fifth-place Arsenal, not bad for a side deemed by large sections of its own support to be dull (none of the three sides in the relegation zone had managed to reach 20). Unfortunately, with the finishing post in sight the wheels began to fall off

Brighton's UEFA Cup bid. Defeat to already-doomed Leeds on the final day of the season saw the Seagulls consigned to 13th place. It remains the club's highest finish in the League pyramid, but for everyone associated with the Albion it felt like an anti-climax.

The season had ended in disappointment, but at least Steve had one massive consolation to look forward to. Ever since that Under-21 appearance against East Germany in April 1980 there had been talk of him breaking into England's full international side. On 23 February 1982 the talk became reality when Fozzie took to Wembley's turf to partner Dave Watson at centre-back against Northern Ireland. England scored through Bryan Robson after just 44 seconds and went on to win 4–0. Three months later Liverpool's Phil Thompson was selected alongside Brighton's skipper against Holland as manager Ron Greenwood looked to whittle out the probables from the possibles ahead of that summer's World Cup Finals. Once again England kept a clean sheet, winning 2–0 thanks to a brace of goals within five second-half minutes from Tony Woodcock and Graham Rix. Steve had done enough to make it onto the plane for Spain. He was now an official member of Ron's 22.

Besides Thompson and the ageing Watson, Steve's main rivals for the England centre-back spots at the time were West Ham's Alvin Martin and Terry Butcher of Ipswich. However, Watson and Martin had picked up injuries. Butcher and Thompson were always Greenwood's first-choice partnership, leaving Steve as first reserve should anything go wrong in Spain.

England got off to a flyer in their first appearance at the World Cup Finals since 1970, defeating France 3–1 in Bilbao on 16 June with Bryan Robson scoring the opener after just 27 seconds. Four days later the same XI, featuring Butcher and Thompson as centre-halves, saw off Czechoslovakia 2–0. However, the manager faced a dilemma ahead of the third and final group game versus Kuwait. Butcher had already picked up a yellow card during the tournament – a booking against Kuwait would make him unavailable for the following match in the second phase of the competition. The solution was obvious – replace Butcher with Steve for one game.

And so on 25 June Fozzie did Albion fans everywhere proud by lining up in Bilbao against the minnows from Kuwait, a side England were expected to beat comfortably. It did not turn out that way. The Kuwaiti side battled hard and showed a surprising amount of skill, the only goal of the game coming after 27 minutes when Trevor Francis capped a 30-yard run by slipping the ball past the oncoming 'keeper. Steve had done everything asked of him, but a West

Germany side boasting the lethal Karl-Heinz Rummenigge looming in the first game of the second phase immediately made way once again for Butcher.

A dull 0–0 draw against the Germans in Madrid meant England had to beat Spain by two goals on 5 July in order to make the semi-finals. They failed in their objective despite Greenwood throwing on Keegan and Trevor Brooking as substitutes for the last half-hour, both players going desperately close to goals during a frantic climax. Despite remaining unbeaten in their five games, England were out of the competition. Keegan would controversially never again be selected for England duty under Greenwood's successor Bobby Robson. And neither, somewhat surprisingly, would Steve.

Quite why Robson chose to ignore Fozzie from the moment he took charge of the national team, only the former Ipswich and Newcastle boss will know. Many of us expected Steve to become a regular in the England set-up, especially with Phil Thompson coming towards the end of his career. Yet somehow three caps and no goals conceded just was not enough. His face didn't fit, whereas those of Graham Roberts, Terry Fenwick, Russell Osman and Alvin Martin – all of who went on to partner Butcher over the next few years – clearly did.

'But there's no regrets,' says Steve. 'It just never happened. I wasn't first choice anyway. I was probably fourth or fifth, so it was just an honour to be at a World Cup. And it really was a great experience. Me, Glenn Hoddle, Kenny Sanson and Graham Rix were the younger ones in a squad that included players like Keegan, Brooking, Ray Wilkins and Joe Corrigan. You can't help but enjoy yourself and learn when you're around players like that. Sharing a room with Glenn Hoddle for six weeks, a man who could tune a television with his left foot, was just amazing.

'After that Northern Ireland game, my first cap, I got a telegram from Lawrie McMenemy, a lovely fellow and someone I still see at luncheons. It said "Well done, you proved me wrong." That was class, nothing but class.'

It is, of course, just possible that Albion's horrible form throughout much of the 1982–83 season had something to do with Steve's omission from the England set-up under Bobby Robson. Away from home the goals against tally was little short of abysmal, 27 being conceded in the first eight fixtures alone. With attendances continuing to dip at the Goldstone, Mike Bailey's dismissal in December 1982 was somewhat inevitable. His replacement, Jimmy Melia, would guide the club to an FA Cup Final at Wembley for the first time in its history, yet in Steve's eyes he was completely the wrong man for the job of keeping Albion in Division One.

'When Jimmy took over it was more of a circus than a football club. We didn't train properly and everyone got involved in the FA Cup run. We weren't concentrating. We were caught up in it, and in that respect the fact we were relegated at the end of the season was as much the fault of the senior players as the coaching staff. We shouldn't have allowed it to happen. A year or two later I was at the bottom with Luton when we went on a great run in the Cup. We played Everton at Villa Park in the semis and got beat. It was the best thing that happened to us because we went and won our last two or three League games and stayed up. Getting to the FA Cup Final is lovely, but staying in the League is the most important thing.'

On 30 April 1983 – having qualified for the FA Cup Final by defeating Sheffield Wednesday at Highbury in the semis a fortnight earlier – Brighton travelled to Notts County for a League game, their battle against relegation to the old Second Division fast appearing to be a futile one. In the first half Steve picked up what many regarded as an unfortunate booking which took him over 31 disciplinary points, triggering an automatic two-match suspension. Everyone connected with the club knew immediately what this meant – Albion's captain would miss the FA Cup Final. Throughout the remainder of the game Steve did his level best to get referee

Norman Wilson to send him off, something one or two fans I know have never quite forgiven him for considering the club's precarious League position. In mitigation, all I can say in Steve's defence is that if I had been in his boots, I would have done exactly the same.

'I think I committed 22 fouls in the second half and the referee just refused to send me off. If I had got sent off, I'd have missed just one game, which I think would have been at Norwich, so I'd have made the FA Cup Final. At one stage their 'keeper kicked the ball and I jumped up, caught it, showed it to the referee and he said "I'm not booking you." He just wouldn't bend.'

Albion already knew Manchester United would be their opponents at Wembley on 21 May. The common consensus, not just among supporters but within the club, was that without Fozzie victory would be a very tall order indeed. With relegation to Division Two by now confirmed, Brighton set about finding ways of having Steve reinstated for the Final. First up was an appeal against his suspension, rejected immediately by the Football Association. On Thursday 12 May Albion went to the High Court in London, where Mr Justice Vinelott granted the talismanic captain leave to serve proceedings on the FA against his suspension, claiming it had been against FA rules. With Steve's counsel Daniel Serota stating the 'matter was of considerable urgency', Justice Vinelott set a date for the full hearing of Monday 16 May.

It was a hearing that would end in disappointment for the Albion. After listening to four and a half hours' worth of evidence, Justice Vinelott refused to grant the club an injunction that would have prevented the FA from implementing Steve's two-match suspension. Fozzie's representative on the day, Peter Sheridan QC, had claimed the player stood to lose a £5000 match fee plus a potential £10,000 win bonus, not to mention the experience of a lifetime. However, Leonard Hoffman on behalf of the FA said Steve knew exactly how many penalty points he had accumulated and should have behaved accordingly. He added that Manchester United had accepted a similar suspension ruling their midfielder Remi Moses out of the Final, plus Albion had already beaten two sides during their Cup run – Manchester City and Norwich – who were also missing suspended players.

'I am not unsympathetic and insensitive to his position, but it must also be borne in mind that interference at this stage would be unjust to all the other players suspended this season,' said Justice Vinelott afterwards, his decision making both the BBC and ITV news bulletins that evening. 'The Cup would also be affected because to interfere now would be to destroy the basis on which the competition has been compounded.' Ted Croker, the FA's General Secretary at the time, added 'I'm pleased for sport in general and football in particular that the case has gone the way it has because it is vital that the rules of sport should be upheld.' Steve, mindful that Albion's lawyers could still appeal against the decision and speaking through the hefty beard he had been cultivating throughout the Cup run, told the waiting media scrum 'Until the lawyers make their decisions I can't say whether I'm confident of playing in the Final. I certainly didn't enjoy it today. It was like having all your teeth pulled out slowly.'

The following day the club announced it had given up on its attempts to have Steve made available for the Final, adding that Tony Grealish would replace him as captain at Wembley. So what in hindsight is Fozzie's opinion of all the legal shenanigans that proceeded the big day? 'It was Mike Bamber who wanted me to go to court. He wanted me to play and I just went along with it. Obviously they couldn't change it otherwise everyone who gets suspended would go to court. I had no problem with the decision. It was more upsetting for my sister and parents that I missed the Final because I was big and ugly enough to take it on the chin. Looking back it's all part of life. It was my own fault that I was in that position, nobody else's. I shouldn't have played.'

In a twisted way, Albion's 2–2 draw

against Manchester United at Wembley meant those trips to the High Court had all been wasted time, the result leaving Steve free to play in the replay the following Thursday. Whether he would have been chosen to start had right-back Chris Ramsey not been almost decapitated by Norman Whiteside on the Saturday is another matter altogether. Fozzie's own verdict is this: 'If Chris Ramsey hadn't got injured the same XI would have played. I would not have played. How could I have taken anyone's place? I wouldn't have done it. Jimmy might have asked me but whether I'd have gone along with it or not I don't know, because it's all about the team. And we had a fantastic team spirit.' Other players I've spoken to from that squad are, however, slightly less magnanimous in their opinions. 'Fozzie was an immense figure who had played a huge part in us getting to Wembley,' says Gerry Ryan, Albion's substitute for both the first game and the replay. 'If he was available for selection, then you selected him.'

I ask Steve what he remembers of the replay, in particular the United fans goading him with chants of 'Stevie Foster, what a difference you have made' as their side cruised to a comfortable 4–0 victory. 'Even my mum was singing it!' he laughs. 'I had a great time in the Final, but I don't tend to recall that much about big games because they get too intense. We started off playing better than we did in the first

game, then a couple of goals went in and that was it. When you've got someone like Brighton playing Manchester United, in a one-off game they [Brighton] have got a great chance. When you play them twice, three times, four times, you've got less and less chance. They were more nervous than us in the first game, and they were definitely more nervous in the second because they were under pressure and we weren't. But sometimes nerves are good. They can help you concentrate.

'If you asked every single player what the highlight of that Cup run was, I bet they'd all say the semi-final. The Final was nice but knowing you'd actually got there was incredible, not just for us but the whole town.' While we're on the subject, I'll mention Steve's acrobatic overhead kick from close to his own goalline during the closing stages against Sheffield Wednesday, which helped deny the Yorkshire side a certain equaliser. 'I only had to do it because Mose [Graham Moseley] had dropped it! But he saved me a couple of times as well. That's what you do. I mean Mose played fantastically. How he got to two of their shots I don't know.'

Following Albion's relegation from the top flight and public humiliation at the hands of Manchester United, it was generally assumed that Steve, like Gary Stevens and Michael Robinson, would be snapped up by some big fish. So it came as something of a surprise to find him still on the club's payroll as the 1983–84 season kicked off in the unglamorous surroundings of Oldham. However, even with the likes of Fozzie and Jimmy Case on board, Albion still struggled to shake off the poor League form that had dogged the club more or less since that 1–0 win at Liverpool back in March 1982.

In October 1983 Jimmy Melia resigned. His replacement, the former Albion defender Chris Cattlin, had been working at the club as a coach since the summer and selecting the first team, something that had caused friction with Melia. The appointment did not exactly strike a chord with supporters, who questioned what Cattlin – a man with no previous managerial experience who since retiring as a player had been running a shop selling 'Brighton Rock' – could bring to the table. It also went down like a lead balloon with Steve, who, it is fair to say, had not exactly been Cattlin's biggest fan as a player. 'I felt it wasn't one of the best moves the club had made. He came in and wanted everyone out. For four years he had been running his rock shop never having watched a game and suddenly he's got his heart on his sleeve. He was definitely the wrong man. I told him the truth and what I thought of him.'

The manager may have been at loggerheads with one of the club's most-prized assets, but that did not prevent Steve from remaining a key figure in Albion's dressing room, one that had been steadily filling with new faces since

Cattlin's arrival. 'His leadership was just fantastic,' remembers Danny Wilson, a future club captain in his own right. 'He was very much like a guy called Nigel Pearson who I played with at Sheffield Wednesday later in my career. Both of them were leaders on and off the park. Those types of players are few and far between now. The game is less physical and they've tended to disappear, which to me is a big shame.'

Ultimately, not even Steve's standing among his peers could prevent the inevitable from happening. Something simply had to give between him and Cattlin. It was just a question of when. In January 1984 Albion embarked on another FA Cup run, disposing of Swansea City and (for the second consecutive season) Liverpool in the third and fourth rounds respectively. The day after the Liverpool game Fozzie and Cattlin held what were described in the press as 'clear the air' talks at the Goldstone. 'I am a volatile character and so is Foster, so we are bound to have our problems and no doubt will clash again,' the Albion manager told the media, before adding 'But Foster remains club captain.'

A more accurate quote would probably have been 'But Foster remains club captain until we get knocked out of the FA Cup, after which he'll be on his bike.' On 18 February Albion lost 3–1 to Watford at Vicarage Road in the fifth round. Within days he had been sold to

Aston Villa and another link with the club's residency in the top flight had been severed. No doubt about it – the mini Cup run helped Cattlin win over the hearts and minds of supporters, the club finishing a respectable ninth that year before missing out on promotion in May 1985 by just three points. But not having Fozzie at the back, cajoling all around him in his inimitable style, didn't half take some getting used to.

If 1983 represented international rejection for Steve, then 1984 turned out to be its equivalent at club level. Within months of leaving Brighton to aid Aston Villa's push for a European place, he found himself out of favour following the arrival of a new manager by the name of Graham Turner – the very same Graham Turner who, 13 years later, would be unable to prevent Hereford slipping into the Conference at Albion's expense. 'My face didn't fit so straight away I was out.' To, as it happened, Luton, where just like at the Goldstone he became a hero, playing in 163 First Division games and captaining the Hatters to League Cup glory following a dramatic 3–2 win over Arsenal at Wembley. He was made player-assistant manager at Kenilworth Road and looked a shoe-in to one day become boss in his own right. Until July 1989 that is, when a familiar face came calling.

'Brian Horton asked me if I wanted to come and join him at Oxford where he was the manager. I've already said what a big influence he was on my career, so I said yes.' During the next two years Steve turned out over 100 times for United, including three times against the Albion, before an injury forced him onto the sidelines in November 1991. And that, at the age of 35, appeared to be that. 'I didn't really know what to do. The Luton job was up and they asked me to apply for that but I refused. I'd been assistant manager there for a year and it was too much work to do what with the travelling and playing. So I phoned up Barry Lloyd and said "Is it alright if I train with you because I don't know where I'm going to go or what I'm going to do?" And I ended up staying four years.'

Barry Lloyd, for the uninitiated, had at that time been Albion's manager for well over five years. If Steve really wanted a living, breathing example of why becoming a football manager can be a bad, bad thing, he need have looked no further than Lloyd's own experiences as boss at the Goldstone. Regarded by many today as the right man for the job at the wrong time, the former Fulham player had been vilified by supporters since taking over as manager from Alan Mullery in January 1987. Even promotion from the old Third Division in 1988 and an appearance in the Division Two Play-off Final at Wembley in 1991 hadn't been enough to sway some of Lloyd's detractors, many of whom still cruelly refer to him as 'Barry Who?'

What was not fully appreciated by Albion supporters were the constraints Lloyd was working under. The club was venting money and had been for years. Just five months after Steve had originally been sold to Aston Villa, Albion had pulled out of a deal to sign the highly-rated Newcastle United centre-back Jeff Clarke because of the £20,000 asking tag. Lloyd had papered over the cracks thanks to his canny knack of picking up players on the transfer market for next to nothing. However, come the summer of 1992 the financial crisis had reached 'Everything Must Go' proportions. In Fozzie, Lloyd spotted an opportunity to put a smile back on the club's face.

'Brighton were really on a bad downward spiral at the time,' says Lloyd. 'Everyone was leaving because all kinds of bills needed to be paid. The fans needed to see the club progress somehow. When he [Steve] rang me up to ask if he could come training I had absolutely no problem with that whatsoever, because in my mind I was going to assess his level of fitness. I knew all about him as a player, what an influence he'd been and what he meant to the club. Now I wanted to know whether he could still do a job for us. If he could, it would be a fantastic opportunity for both parties.'

Steve proved without any shadow of a doubt during pre-season that he was far from ready for retirement and Lloyd, unable to believe his luck, popped the question regarding whether or not he fancied playing a couple of League games. 'It's quite funny actually,' says Steve. 'I said "Barry, you can't just ask me to play and not pay me. How about giving me what I was getting in 1982 on my old contract?" Which was something like £1,400 a week. They'd have probably been better off accepting that!'

Money issues ironed out, Fozzie went straight into the team for the first match of the 1992–93 season away at Leyton Orient. With Nicky Bissett beside him plus Gary Chivers and Ian Chapman in the full-back positions, the defence leaked three goals but became a steadier unit once the Irish Under-21 international Paul McCarthy came in for the injured Bissett. Add the likes of promising goalkeeper Mark Beeney, Welsh forward Kurt Nogan and ageless winger Clive Walker to the cocktail and somehow Albion, despite all their money worries, had a team that could compete. A narrow 2–1 aggregate defeat to Manchester United in the Coca-Cola Cup was followed up by three wins in the FA Cup including a third-round victory over Portsmouth, Lloyd's motley crew exiting the competition at the next hurdle only after an agonisingly tight 1–0 reverse at Old Trafford. Steve even managed to develop something of a striker's touch at one point, scoring three goals within the space of four games.

Fozzie during his second spell as an Albion player.

'He was always someone I had looked up to,' says Mark Beeney of Steve. 'He'd played in Cup Finals and for England and there was I, just this whipper snapper. You took notice of him. He was coming towards the end of his career but was still reliable as anything. He still had it. In many ways he was the John Terry of his day, always talking and never afraid to put his head where it hurts.' Beeney, it should be said, is better qualified than most to make the John Terry comparison, having worked as a coach at Chelsea for several years.

'Fozzie might not have been so mobile then but his positional sense was absolutely brilliant, as was his ability in the air,' adds Clive Walker, before making one slight criticism. 'We had quite a few experienced players in the side at the time who tended to organise themselves. Sometimes he would try and organise us like a bunch of kids. He'd done it throughout his career. I mean this in the nicest possible way, but sometimes you just wanted to say "For goodness sake, GIVE US A BREAK!" I know he did it partly to keep his own concentration, and anyway he was great to have in the dressing room, so most of the time we put up with it.'

Despite Albion's relative success on the pitch, the money worries were continuing to pile up. In April 1993 Beeney was sold to Leeds United for £350,000 to stave off a winding-up petition brought by the Inland Revenue, allowing a court case scheduled for the following day to be dismissed. The former Maidstone 'keeper had been in excellent form all season but was still pipped to the post in the fans' Player of the Season competition by Fozzie some 13 years after he had first received the accolade. Once again Lloyd asked his star centre-back if he fancied sticking around for a few games the following season. Steve went one or two better than that, appearing in 36 matches. Come the end of the 1993–94 campaign he was just four months shy of his 37th birthday. And still the end was far from nigh.

Unfortunately, the same couldn't be said for Barry Lloyd. Caught between a rock and the hardest of places in his combined role as team manager and managing director of the club, he left by 'mutual consent' in December 1993 after a series of demonstrations against him by supporters. His replacement was the former Arsenal and Ireland midfielder Liam Brady, one of the most gifted footballers of his time who was tempted into taking the Albion job by his fond memories of the Goldstone Ground during the late 70s and early 80s. In hindsight the euphoria which welcomed Brady's appointment helped deflect attention away from what was really going on behind the scenes at the club, which, as some of you may recall, proved to be shady beyond belief.

Just weeks before Lloyd's departure, the Albion had been taken over by Bill Archer, managing director of the Focus DIY chain, who was working in tandem with a director of the club called Greg Stanley. Archer immediately installed the former Liberal Democrat Member of Parliament for Eastbourne David Bellotti as chief executive. In July 1995 it was announced Brighton had sold its ground supposedly to pay off mounting debts and would, from the beginning of the 1996–97 season, be playing its home games 40 miles along the south coast at Fratton Park, Portsmouth. One supporter, a chartered accountant by the name of Paul Samrah, was so alarmed by the developments that he made a trip to the Land Registry's office in London accompanied by local journalist Paul Bracchi. There they discovered that the club had sold the land occupied by the Goldstone to a property company called Chartwell, developer of retail parks, superstores, shopping malls and such like. The land was worth £7 million. The club's debts were said to be around £4 million.

The two Pauls considered who would benefit from such a sale. Scouring the small print, it became evident that Bill Archer had gained control of the club for just £56.25, the equivalent of 5,625 shares bought for one penny each. He had then reorganised the structure of the club by creating a holding company called Foray 585. To their horror, they also discovered that a single paragraph in the club's memorandum and Articles of Association had been changed – one that would now allow Archer and the other shareholders in Foray 585 to benefit from the sale of the ground. Archer later claimed that this had been 'an oversight,' but the damage had been done. The long running and frequently bitter fight to save Brighton & Hove Albion Football Club had begun.

Never one to shy away from a confrontation, Fozzie became one of the new board's biggest and most vocal critics. The future of a club he loved was in jeopardy, and there was no way he was going to stand aside and do nothing. 'It was robbery. You had people fighting to change the use of the Goldstone Ground, and they got it. No one at the council thought to say "You can have planning permission when you've got another site to go to, and when the money comes it goes to build the club." They fought to get the change of use, got it, and took the money.

'You could see it coming, or at least I could. It was like trying to flag down a runaway train. I used to tell people like Liam what was about to happen. He was fantastic. We had a great relationship. I'd say to him "This is really happening" and he'd be like "No, it can't be." But it was. They [the board] would come in and say "We swear to God we're not doing this" but it was all lies, lies, lies, lies.'

Steve, together with thousands of others, was of course proved right. In 1997 Brighton played their final match at the Goldstone before relocating not to Portsmouth but Gillingham, where the club staged its home games until 1999. Archer and Bellotti disappeared into the ether to be replaced by a new board led by long-time supporter and former advertising guru Dick Knight. Fozzie finally decided to call it quits during the 1995–96 season, having played 131 games during his second spell at the club, giving him an overall total of 332 appearances. 'Funnily enough, during that second period I played probably some of my best football. I had to because of the position the club was in. There was no money so you had to pull out all the stops. Liam was promised this and that and had to cut wages, but we still had some great games. We drew with Manchester United, beat Portsmouth, won at Leicester with Stuart Munday scoring from 40 yards. I had a great time when I came back and the thing was a lot of the supporters who had been kids when I'd first played were now adults. They were always good to me and I appreciated that.'

Since retiring Steve has concentrated on running his insurance business for footballers. He is still as passionate and outspoken about all things to do with the sport (and in particular the Albion) as he ever was, something that has, on occasion, led him into conflict with the board led by Dick Knight. When interviewed for this book Steve told me he was banned from attending Brighton games, the result of him introducing a wealthy friend to the board who was keen on buying the club (an approach that Steve says Knight rejected as it involved him stepping down as chairman). The club categorically denies that a ban exists. Whatever the truth, you cannot say the man doesn't care. If anything, he cares a little too much.

He still lives in Hove. In fact, Steve has lived in Hove since 1979 when he signed from Portsmouth. 'It's like a village really. Everyone knows each other, from antique dealers to estate agents to landlords. You always know someone who knows someone, and I think that's because I've always lived here. When I went to Aston Villa I used to commute and come back on weekends after games. When I went to Luton I did the same. When I went to Oxford I did the same. Why would you want to leave? It's a fantastic place. If anything it's got even better over the years. It's just sad that during the same period of time the club has been allowed to go downhill so much. That annoys me. It annoys me a lot.'

And in that sentiment Steve Foster is far from alone.

Chapter Six
Nobby

In 2006, while interviewing Alan Mullery on the subject of his recently-published autobiography, I asked the former Albion manager exactly how influential Brian Horton had been both as a captain and player. 'He was the manager on the field,' replied the ex-Spurs and England midfield star. 'He was just a natural born leader and without a doubt the best captain I ever had. We couldn't have achieved what we did without him because everybody followed his example. And he was a fantastic player. The only time we ever really faltered as a team was when he was missing, which says everything.'

And who am I to argue with Alan Mullery?

When it comes to deciding who will be the captain of my dream team there's really only one candidate. And that is saying something when you have got Steve Foster in your side. Between the years 1976 and 1981, Brian 'Nobby' Horton was the epitome of everything good about Brighton & Hove Albion Football Club, the dictionary definition of that overused football term '110 percent'. With those trademark bulging eyes, every vein in his body standing out the size of an Alaskan pipeline, he was just like Popeye. Except Brian didn't need spinach to pump himself up.

'Brian was our total leader, an inspiration to all of us,' says Gary Williams. 'He was far more than just a player. On the pitch we were always a better team with him around. Even if he was having a bad game, which was rare, he would keep us all going and focused with his clenched fist and stuff. I really cannot overemphasise his importance to that side.'

If there was one chink in Brian's armour, it was this. During the early part of April 1980 he made a promotional visit to Warnham Comrades Club near Horsham along with Peter O'Sullivan and Gerry Ryan. At one point during the evening Brian was introduced to an 11-year-old defender described by the manager of the local boys' football team as 'Our tank,' a nickname that had been bestowed at the time on Albion midfielder Paul Clark. 'Well we'd better sign you up then,' said Brian to the lad in question, who just happened to be me. For the record, I was never signed up. Didn't even get a trial. Not that I'm bitter. The fact Nobby had spoken to me was reward enough.

Considering what he went on to achieve, it is amazing to think that Brian was almost lost to the game forever as a teenager. Born in February 1949 in Hednesford, just 13 miles from where Peter Ward would enter the world six years later, Brian made a name for himself playing for Staffordshire Boys before leaving school at 15. There was talk of him going to Aston Villa, Birmingham City and West Bromwich Albion, but all decided to pass owing to his height, or rather lack of it.

'I was small, very very small,' says Brian during our meeting at the extremely swanky Mottram Hall Hotel near Wilmslow, the same spot where Albion chairman Dick Knight successfully persuaded Brian to take over the managerial reigns at the club following the sacking of Steve Gritt in 1998. 'I was

only around 5ft 1in or something. I ended up going to Walsall where I spent two years, but I was still very small. During my second year there I broke into the reserves and thought I was on my way. Then they let me go on a free transfer. I was devastated, absolutely devastated. It came as a total shock.

'But then again some things happen for the best. I went back to my hometown team, Hednesford, who were in what was then called the West Midland League, and supported myself by getting work in the building trade with a mate. I'd spend Monday to Friday on the site, train Tuesday and Thursday, and play on Saturday. We had some very good players and were winning things like the

Brian Horton, Cheshire, 2007.

Staffordshire Senior Cup. It was hard work, but I think it was the best thing that ever happened to me, because working on the buildings I all of a sudden grew and got stronger. I was fit as anything, probably fitter than many League players. And I was better off, earning double what my mates were on at Walsall.'

Brian may have been performing admirably for Hednesford Town, but it was not until he was 21 that a professional club finally came along to rescue him from non-League obscurity. Gordon Lee, then manager of Port Vale, who would later take over at Everton, hailed from Hednesford and had heard about the builder–cum–footballer anchoring Town's midfield. He went to watch him in action in a game at Brierley Hill and liked what he saw. Afterwards Lee struck a deal with Hednesford's secretary. Port Vale had no money, so instead they would bring their first team to Hednesford for a pre-season friendly, with Town keeping 100 percent of the gate receipts.

Over the next six years Brian played 236 times for Vale and scored 33 goals in the process, all of them coming in the old Third Division. His all-action never-say-die attitude made him a big hit with fans of the Potteries club. When it became public knowledge during the early part of 1976 that Vale were prepared to sell their captain the news went down like a lead balloon, especially considering the cut-price fee Brian was available at. Both

Hereford and Plymouth had offered £25,000 but two other clubs were prepared to go higher. They were Crystal Palace and Brighton.

'We played Crystal Palace at Selhurst Park on the Tuesday night before the transfer deadline. It was a year when we were having a really good season. We were right up there along with a few clubs including Brighton, Palace and Millwall. Right before the game I got a shout saying "Don't do anything stupid because Palace are coming in for you in the summer." We'd beaten them in the home match earlier that season and I'd scored two goals. We drew 1–1 that night in front of a massive crowd, and I got a penalty. As we came off the pitch our manager Roy Sproson, who by then had taken over from Gordon, said "We've done the deal. You're leaving." Only it wasn't Palace I was going to, it was Brighton. The deal had been done while the game was taking place.'

Having showered and changed, all bar one of Vale's team boarded the team coach for the return journey north. The exception was Brian, who stepped into a stretched limousine sent by Albion chairman Mike Bamber, which took him to – you've guessed it – the Metropole Hotel in Brighton. There waiting for him was Peter Taylor, then Albion's manager, who had initially come to the Goldstone along with his long-term partner in crime Brian Clough in November 1973, taking over the reigns himself following 'Old Big Head's' defection to Leeds in July 1974. 'I met him for about 10 minutes in a suite at the Metropole. He said "Would you like a drink?" I said "Okay, I'll have a beer." He made me an offer – a very good offer compared to the money I was on at Port Vale. I said "I'll come providing this and that" and he said "No, no, that's the offer. Take it or leave it. There's a ticket back to Port Vale if you want to go back. It's up to you. We're playing Shrewsbury Town at home tomorrow night. Why don't you speak to your wife, get her down here, come and watch it and we'll discuss it further on Thursday morning?" They ended up losing to Shrewsbury and on the Thursday morning I went in and he didn't increase the offer one penny. He said "It's a good offer. Some are on more, some are on less. You'll be captain. Do well for me and I'll look after you." And I signed that Thursday morning.'

As with the Preston duo of Gary Williams and Mark Lawrenson, one big attraction of signing for Brighton at that time was the healthy attendances at the Goldstone. 'I'd always enjoyed playing there because of the big crowds. Port Vale were getting three, four, five thousand maximum and Brighton were on 18,000 at the very least, probably the biggest in our division. And the pitch was always lovely. I knew nothing about the town at all. I only knew it to drive in, stay Friday night, play a game and drive out of.

Funnily enough, we played Port Vale at home a couple of games after I'd joined, and beat them one-none.'

Despite knowing zip about Brighton, Brian and his family quickly settled into the area with the club's new captain doing enough to earn the respect of the Goldstone public during what remained of the 1975–76 season. Then, just a month before the start of the following campaign, came the bombshell: Peter Taylor resigned as manager, a week later joining forces once again with Clough at Nottingham Forest. Worse still as far as Brian was concerned was the identity of his successor – Alan Mullery, one of the most combative and effective midfielders of recent years. 'We had heard that he might come in as player-manager, so straight away I thought "I've come down here, not even moved house, and I'm going to be gone again." We started that pre-season and won away at Brentford, then beat Coventry and Wolves at home. Then we started the season for real, and I don't know how many games we went before we lost. And he just never played. We had a good side. He must have thought "Well, I'm enjoying this, I'm going to sit out of it."

'You know sometimes in football you either click or you don't click with people, and we clicked. We both had similar personalities and attitudes towards the game. I just got on great with him. And it went from there.'

Brian 'Nobby' Horton, the best captain Alan Mullery – and arguably the Albion – have ever had.

Having missed out on promotion to the Second Division during the 1975–76 season by three points, Albion went all-out to make up for the disappointment under the guidance of their new manager. 'The team picked itself most of the time that year – Peter Grummit, Gerry Fell, Steve Piper, "Sully", "Wardy", Ian Mellor. We were belting teams at home. Training used to be very relaxed because we were winning games. The gaffer would come into the team meeting on Friday with a cigar and the team sheet and say "Well if you can't beat that lot!" And he'd screw it up, throw it away and say "See you tomorrow." He gave us so much confidence. But he did ask a lot of his players, in that he was very much like Alex Ferguson or Graeme Souness, he always wanted more. He wasn't the best coach in the world – he'd probably say that himself. What he had was the ability to motivate and pick players rather than the tactical side.'

Albion were promoted that season scoring 83 League goals in the process, Mullery building on the foundations laid by Peter Taylor to guide the team to second place behind champions Mansfield with Crystal Palace finishing third. Peter Ward took the lion's share of the headlines with 36 goals in all competitions, but it still wasn't enough for him to capture the Player of the Season award. That honour went to Brian, a measure of the high esteem he was now held in by the club's supporters.

The icing on the cake came with an emphatic 7–0 win over Walsall at the Goldstone, Ward scoring four and Mellor three. For the first time since returning to the professional game, Brian managed to get one over on the club that had dumped him on football's scrap heap as a teenager.

It is fair to say that success on the pitch around this period was not all down to Mullery and the players. Since moving into management in 1984 Brian has worked with many boards, some good, some not so good. Down the years he has come to realise that the Albion board of the 70s and early 80s, led by ambitious chairman Mike Bamber, was by far the best of the lot. 'You'd never come across a better board than that. They used to travel on the coach or train and mix with us, which just doesn't tend to happen. Mike Bamber used to call me Capitano – "Anything you want Capitano?" I can remember one time saying to him that I wouldn't mind a Christmas do for all the players and the wives. "Good idea" he says. "Get down to the Metropole, see the general manager and make it for all the staff, all the directors, all the wives." Instead of being a little Christmas bash it became a massive party. I think some supporters even came. And that was what it was like. "I could do with a golf day chairman." "Well, you arrange it and we'll pay for it."'

Although Mullery would later criticise his chairman for trying to interfere with transfers and players' wages, at least Bamber made money available for his manager to strengthen Albion's squad when the need arose. Take the summer of 1977 for instance. Having just achieved one promotion, the aim now wasn't to consolidate in Division Two but to get into the First Division as soon as possible. In came Gary Williams and Mark Lawrenson to beef up a defence bolstered by the signing of goalkeeper Eric Steele towards the end of the previous season. Soon Paul Clark, able to play in midfield or defence, would arrive from Southend. Quietly optimistic would be a good way of describing the mood around the club on the eve of the 1977–78 season.

One evening shortly before the opening game, most of the Albion squad together with a select band of press men convened in a pub in Kemptown that had recently been bought by Eric Steele's uncle. Also present was Eva Petulengro, a well-known local clairvoyant. Petulengro told Brian that Brighton would miss out on promotion by the slimmest of margins. However, she added that the season afterwards would see the club realise its dream of bringing top-flight football to Sussex for the first time. Not being the most superstitious of people, Brian remembered her predictions but paid little attention to them.

Nine months later the first instalment of Petulengro's prophecy came horribly true on the day when Albion entertained

Blackpool, with Southampton and Tottenham going head to head along the south coast at The Dell. Like Gary Williams, Brian had become fed up with the media's love-in with Spurs, who had to secure at least a point against the Saints that day to pip Brighton to promotion. 'We were getting 30,000-odd people for our home games and yet they were saying it wasn't a football town. Absolute rubbish. We were as good if not better than Spurs that year, but we just weren't getting the credit we deserved.'

Towards the end of the Blackpool game Albion won a penalty that, if converted, would (barring a very late equaliser) give them the victory they required to keep the pressure on Southampton and Spurs. The players had no idea what the scoreline was at The Dell, the presumption being that things were still level. 'I always wanted the penalties and so did Wardy, so if he missed I'd take them, and if I missed he'd take them,' says Brian. 'That's how we did it. We got the penalty that day and I looked at him, and he went "No" and shook his head. I'd had to go off earlier because someone had done me, and I needed stitches in my right foot. It was killing me. Anyway, thank Christ I scored, then we heard the crowd roar again and thought we'd done it.'

But Albion had not and Brian, together with the majority of the team, was soon in tears in the dressing room, cursing events at The Dell. 'I think if they had played until now they wouldn't have scored. I was thinking "It might never happen again. What if that was our chance?" You try not to think about it but it's on your mind – "Can we ever do it again?" It takes a good side to bounce back from something like that. Fortunately, that's what we had.'

And so it came to pass that the second instalment of Eva Petulengro's prediction came true, following that 3–1 win at Newcastle on the final day of the 1978–79 season. For the record, Brian's recollection of the row that broke out at half-time inside the away dressing room at St James' Park goes like this: 'We had a succession of corners and I took a gamble on one from the edge of the box. Gary Williams took an outswinger, and I bulleted a header straight in. We were three up! The gaffer used to go mad and shout sometimes, so as we came off at the break I was saying to the lads "If he starts, just shut up and let him spout off", because if anybody went back at him he'd go off even more. Anyway, somebody said something, he went off, and I'm like "****ing hell gaffer, calm down! We're 3–0 up!" I think maybe it had something to do with a misplaced pass by Gary Williams.'

For Brian, not to mention Alan Mullery and many of the players, the journey back home to Sussex that night proved to be as memorable as the game

itself. In those days the club would charter a train to virtually every away game, with the team and fans travelling on board in separate coaches (for particularly important matches sometimes two, three or more trains would make the trip). This became known as the 'Seagulls Special', although the players had another name for it. 'We used to call it the 'Paralytic Express', because of the atmosphere on board when we won,' says Brian. 'We'd have wine, brandy and a three or four-course meal coming back. Mullery would throw me a cigar – that was the only praise he'd give sometimes. If I got a cigar I knew I'd done okay. If we lost it would be totally different. There would be no smiling or drinking. He wouldn't even speak to us. But that journey back from Newcastle was incredible, just one big party on wheels rolling for mile after mile with all the players, directors and fans mixing. By the time we got back to Brighton I don't think anyone could stand up.'

Brian is far from alone in believing that those two promotions within the space of three years were as much a result of the camaraderie among the players as any amount of training, tactics or hard work on match days. 'The team spirit was excellent, absolutely faultless. We went out together, played golf together, ate and drank together. I think it helps when you all live in the same place like we did then. We had success after success after success, unbelievable times not just on the pitch but off it as well. When I came back to Brighton as manager it was different. I had people living in London, Southampton, all over. As a result something of that spirit was missing.'

However, team spirit was only going to get the Albion so far in the First Division. As the club struggled to find its feet in the top tier during the early months of the 1979–80 season, so several players discovered their Goldstone days were numbered. Paul Clark, Teddy Maybank, Malcolm Poskett, Andy Rollings, Peter Sayer and Eric Steele were all either dropped or sold, with Ken Tiler departing for Rotherham before a ball had even been kicked. Having just turned 30 it had crossed Brian's mind during the summer whether he would become surplus to requirements. As it turned out, he need not have worried. The League might have changed but Brian's effectiveness was as constant as ever. Liam Brady may have had the style and Glenn Hoddle the vast repertoire of passes, but neither possessed Brian's leadership qualities or work ethic.

'That's what it was all about for me, playing against those top-class players week in week out. And I relished it. Every game you were up against a Bryan Robson, or a Jimmy Case, or a Graeme Souness, or a Glenn Hoddle, or a Liam Brady. Liam was different class. His vision was amazing. Hoddle was a fantastic footballer. Souness had everything. He

was hard, he could pass and he could score. I would say those three were the best while I was at Brighton, but Bryan Robson was the best I ever played against, when he was at Manchester United and I was at Luton. He was all of them put together, the top of the tree.'

Brian played in every Albion game during the 1979–80 campaign as the club overcame those early-season jitters to finish a respectable 16th – not great but not bad, having won two, drawn three and lost nine of their opening 14 matches and conceding 29 goals. In the process he earned the respect of his midfield peers in the First Division and many a top manager. There were enquiries regarding his availability, including one from Bobby Robson at high-flying Ipswich. All were dismissed with a curt 'Thanks, but no thanks.' Brian had signed a three-year deal during the summer of 1979, and he intended to honour it. Anyway, why would he want to leave Sussex?

It is so often the case that a club promoted to what is now the Premier League excels beyond all expectations during its first season in the top flight, only to be relegated come the second, that initial burst of enthusiasm making way for the harsh realities of having to compete week in week out with the big boys. It happened to Bradford City in the late 90s, Swansea City in the 80s and (no laughing at the back) the Crystal Palace side promoted with Brighton in 1979 and subsequently dubbed 'Team of the 80s'. For the vast majority of the 1980–81 season it looked like something similar would happen to the Albion. There were highlights including outstanding wins against Aston Villa and Ipswich at the Goldstone, the clubs that would finish first and second in the League respectively, but there were also some dire lows such as the two Middlesbrough games. Boro lost all bar three of their away fixtures that season yet still managed to win at the Goldstone. After the return match on 11 April 1981, a lacklustre 1–0 defeat seemingly dooming Albion to relegation, Mullery was so angry that he threatened to run any member of the team over if he saw them crossing the street.

Just days prior to the game on Teesside, Brian had once again found himself sitting opposite Eva Petulengro along with journalist John Vinnicombe, who for many years covered the Albion on behalf of *The Argus*. 'We met at a hotel owned by Harry Bloom, one of the club's directors and a lovely fella. There would have been about five or six games of the season left to go. She said "I don't like these vibes – you're going to be relegated." It wasn't a hard call to make as we were in the bottom three anyway. Then she said "By the end of July both you and Alan Mullery will have left the club." I turned to John and said "Mate, you can't print that!" Then I called the gaffer and told

him what Eva had said. "Print it!" he said, and I'm pretty sure *The Argus* did.'

Petulengro's relegation prediction turned out to be false, a run of four consecutive wins at the tail end of the season sending Norwich down along with Leicester and Crystal Palace. 'That Middlesbrough away game was the turning point. We were shocking, absolutely dreadful. I don't think Mullers said too much after the game, but on the Monday morning we all got told there was a meeting in the boardroom at the Goldstone. Mike Bamber was there. When we had meetings like that, Mullery would always start with me because I was the captain. He said "What do you think?" And I'd probably got "Well…" out of my mouth before he went "*You* don't make a tackle anymore, *you* don't compete anymore." It was no good arguing with him when he was like that. He hammered me. Then he turned to Steve Foster. "Come on, you're the England whizz-kid with the headband on, what do you think?" And before Fozzie could get a word out it was "*You* don't head the ball anymore, *you* don't compete."

'Next up was Mark Lawrenson. "Come on Mark, you're the superstar." And Mark said "Do you ever think we're just not good enough gaffer?" And if Mullers could have hit the roof then he would have done. He went berserk. I think I was the only player in the room at the time he hadn't signed, and he was going "You bastards, you're letting me and the club down." Then he turned to Gary Stevens, who was only 17 or 18 at the time. "What do you think?" he says. And Gary goes "Maybe we could try a bit harder." And Mullers says "You're spot on." It was then he said he'd run any of us over in his car if he saw us crossing the street, and Mike Bamber – who was the nicest man you could ever wish to meet – stood up and said "So will I." At that point they both walked out, and we all turned and slaughtered Gary Stevens for being a goody-goody!'

Two months later, having fallen out with Mike Bamber over the sale of Mark Lawrenson to Liverpool, Mullery resigned. Straight away the now ex-manager went round to tell his captain what had happened. 'He knocked on my door and when I answered it the first thing he said was "I've resigned." I said "Gaffer, come in, don't be daft." He said it was all about Mark, and that he and Mike had had an argument. Sometimes that happens in football. He said there was no going back. That's the kind of man he was. It was crazy really because had we got relegated you could maybe understand it, but we hadn't – we'd survived.'

Mullery also told Brian that 'they' wanted him to leave the club as well. Just a few weeks previously Nobby had heard a whisper that Luton were lining up an exchange deal to take him to Kenilworth Road, with Tony Grealish coming in the opposite direction. Brian asked Bamber about this and was told that an approach had been received – and rejected – from Luton boss David Pleat. However, Mullery's decision to walk meant the goalposts had now been moved. To Brian's amazement and anger, his successor, Mike Bailey, immediately made it clear that the long-serving captain's future was far from secure at the Goldstone.

'Mike came in and obviously wanted to do the deal with Luton. Initially I thought I'd get on with him and stay. I had a year to go on my contract, had just bought a new house, and I didn't want to leave. But he said "I'll take the captaincy off you. You'll have to prove yourself to me." And I said "I don't have to prove myself to anyone at this football club or in this town. But if that's the way you feel I'll speak to the chairman and think about going." Mike [Bamber] didn't want me to go. The problem was he had just appointed a new manager and had to be seen to be backing him. He offered me a financial package for the year left on my contract, and I went to speak to David Pleat. He told me all about his plans and said I'd be captain. So I weighed it up and thought "Well if Mike doesn't want me, then I'll go." Luton had a good team then and it made sense. But I remember thinking "whoever puts that number-four shirt on now will have to do some winning over".

'The really sad thing about it, and I'll never forgive him [Mike Bailey] for this, was that we beat Leeds 2–0 on the last Saturday to stay up and that was my last game. I never got the chance to say cheerio to the fans and thank them for everything that they'd done and meant to me. That hurt.'

On 29 August 1981 Brian made his debut for Luton at Kenilworth Road against a Charlton Athletic side now managed by, you've guessed it, Alan Mullery. Town won 3–0 on the first step to what would be a promotion season. The following campaign saw the Hatters batter Albion 5–0 at home and 4–2 at the Goldstone, Brian playing a starring role in both games. Come the end of the season Brighton were relegated after four years at the highest level, while Luton stayed up with a final-day victory at Manchester City, Pleat performing a memorable celebratory jig across the Maine Road pitch before jumping into Brian's arms. Damn right it was hard to take.

Seven days later Brian, together with his then wife Denise, went to Wembley to cheer on the Albion against Manchester United in the 1983 FA Cup Final. Beforehand they met up with former Seagull Peter Suddaby, a veteran of the club's first season in the top flight, who was accompanied by the singer Maureen Nolan, his partner and one of the famous Nolan Sisters. 'We went to a massive pub

on the outskirts of Wembley which was full of Brighton and United fans. Maureen was stunning and the whole pub came to a hush because she had walked in. I'd like to think a bit of it was for me as well, but I know it was Maureen who caught everyone's attention!' So did he have mixed feelings about watching Albion at Wembley, having served the club so well in the not-so-distant past? 'No way. I never look back. I'd had a promotion with Luton in the meantime and was happy there, but of course I desperately wanted Brighton to win. And they were so close in that first game.'

In 1984, at the age of 35, Brian took the logical step of moving into management by becoming player-boss at Hull City, guiding them to promotion from the old Third Division at the first attempt. Over the next 14 years he went on to manage at Oxford United (following Mark Lawrenson's dismissal), Manchester City and Huddersfield Town. With Albion's fortunes taking a dive both on and off the field during the early to mid-90s, many supporters hoped Nobby would one day return to occupy the hot seat at his spiritual home, yet somehow the time was never right.

Not until February 1998, that is. The previous May had seen Albion survive by the skin of their teeth in the Football League, a nerve-wracking 1–1 draw against fellow strugglers Hereford United at Edgar Street on the final day of the season consigning the home side to the Conference instead of the visitors. The man credited with achieving the impossible was former Charlton player Steve Gritt, whose initial introduction as manager to the Goldstone public in December 1996 had been greeted with a chorus of boos. Marooned at the bottom of the table and having seemingly reached a point of no return, Brighton somehow managed to avoid relegation by winning 10 and drawing two of their remaining dozen home games.

During the summer of 1997 the Goldstone Ground was consigned to history, the circumstances behind its demise being documented elsewhere in this book. Unfortunately, Albion's excellent home form went with it, the team being unable to replicate their winning ways at Gillingham's Priestfield Stadium – Albion's temporary home from August 1997 to May 1999. Come the start of 1998 Brighton were once again struggling to avoid demotion to the Conference with only Doncaster Rovers – another club dogged by a board with dubious intentions – beneath them in what by now had become Nationwide Division Three. That February Albion's new chairman Dick Knight decided a change was necessary.

'I was out of work having lost my job at Huddersfield,' recalls Brian. 'Dick rang to ask if I'd be interested in taking over. I can't remember if Steve had been sacked

or was in the process of going, but I said "If Steve goes then I'll speak to you". Sure enough they sacked Steve, and Dick was up on business in Manchester so we agreed to meet here at Mottram Hall. There were about 12 games left to go and we were second bottom. Dick said would I come for the rest of the season? So I went in, we stayed up and he asked if I wanted to stay. We did a deal for a year with me commuting from where I live up near Manchester.

'I'd followed events at the club from a distance over the years and didn't like it. I mean, to lose the Goldstone – blimmin' heck! The memories I've got of that place you couldn't buy. To see them where they were after everything that had happened in my time at the club was almost unbearable. I'd left them in the top flight and here they were, struggling to keep themselves in the League. Crazy, just crazy.'

Despite the huge commuting distance, Brian enjoyed being back in Sussex working for a club he loved. 'The training ground was okay because that's where my office was. You had lovely people around the club and the town. We were getting the playing side sorted out. I think I gave 14 free transfers and got 14 new players in, including Gary Hart, and we started off well.' Yet there was one tremendous down side to it all – having to play those home games in Gillingham, a round trip of 140 miles by road from Brighton via four motorways. To make matters worse, nobody really had any idea about when the club might be moving back to Brighton. Possible dates were mentioned, but nothing firm.

'I really couldn't comprehend the Gillingham business,' says Brian. 'Eventually it became clear that we'd be playing at Withdean, but the date kept getting put back and back and back. I was like "When will it happen Dick?" Forget about me. It wasn't good for the club being at Gillingham, for the players and the fans having to make that trip every week or two. It was torture. And the fans were amazing. There aren't many clubs in this country who would be taking four or five thousand over that distance to home games.'

On the field, Brian appeared to be getting results as the team set their sights on a Play-off spot during the first half of the 1998–99 season. But off it he was struggling. A typical weekend for Brian when Brighton were at Priestfield went something like this: travel with the team to the match, play the match, travel back to Brighton, drive home to Cheshire that night, return to Sussex on the Sunday ready for training on the Monday. Somewhere in the midst of this transient existence he had to juggle the needs of his players, the club, the media, his family…and so on. Sooner or later a ball or two was going to get dropped.

The board at Port Vale were only too

aware that Brian had bitten off more than he could chew. He still had connections at his former club, lived only 30 miles from the ground and was on good terms with the chairman. In January 1999 the Staffordshire outfit approached Brian to become their manager. To Albion's horror he accepted the offer, citing Vale's greater potential as a key factor behind his decision. It was a stark reminder of just how far Brighton had fallen since those halcyon days of the 70s and early 80s.

Brian attracted plenty of flak from Albion supporters for defecting after less than a year in the job. At a time when fan solidarity was the order of the day, the sight of one of the club's legends turning his back on the cause did not go down particularly well. He had, after all, been aware of the club's precarious position when he joined. In hindsight it is easy to feel a chunk of sympathy for Brian. Since 1999 the constraints of Withdean have proved too much for Micky Adams, Peter Taylor and Steve Coppell, all of whom departed for more glamorous surroundings. When Brian left, Albion did not even have Withdean.

'It is without doubt the hardest decision I've ever had to make in football,' admits Brian. 'Port Vale was a stable club. It had its own stadium. At Brighton we were aiming for the Play-offs, but there seemed no end in sight to Gillingham. Maybe I should have stayed and gone for promotion, then left for Port Vale in the summer, because Brighton fell away from the promotion race after I went, didn't they? I still got a good reception from 99 percent of the people when I went back with Port Vale, which says everything about Brighton's fans. But what happened gave me a few sleepless nights, I can tell you. It was sad.

'I don't have many regrets in football, even leaving Brighton as a player. I look back now and think it all worked out because I got to meet David Pleat who was like a mentor to me. I still speak to him every week. David was calm and a tactician, whereas Alan [Mullery] was more of a motivating manager, brilliant at spotting players. But I learned so much off the both of them. When David went to Tottenham he could and should have

been one of the contenders for the England job. That's how high I rated him as a coach. And he'd have gone for it as well.'

Since leaving Brighton Brian has joined the select group of managers with over 1,000 games under their belts, although when we met he was seeking employment having recently been fired by Macclesfield Town ('I knew I should've taken that job at Carlisle in the summer when I was offered it!') But Brian's not in my Albion dream team for his managerial record. Nobby is in because of his outstanding efforts both as a captain and player for Brighton & Hove Albion between March 1976 and May 1981, an era that was, in his own words, 'incredible, just incredible'.

Chapter Seven
Jimmy's Gonna Getcha!

Brian Horton had left the building, his departure to Luton Town begging one big question: how do you replace the irreplaceable? The answer, Albion fans were about to discover, was by bringing in someone with more medals than Douglas Bader.

Lord knows the supporters needed a tonic during the late summer of 1981. Alan Mullery had gone. Nobby had gone. John Gregory had gone. Peter O'Sullivan had gone. Mark Lawrenson was in the process of leaving. Give or take the odd cashflow problem, the ship seemed in pretty good shape having lived to sail another day in the old First Division, yet the sailors seemed intent on abandoning her. All of which made the news that broke one day in August all the more remarkable. Jimmy Case was coming.

It is easy to forget so many years later the seismic effect his arrival had on the club and its supporters. Forget about those dark days during the tail end of 1996 as Jimmy, then Albion's manager, struggled to deal with the chaos that reigned around the Goldstone. In 1981 the man was dynamite and him coming to Sussex had the same effect on my 12-year-old senses as a million-pound lottery ticket has on a teenage mum surviving on income support. I, everyone, was blown away. We had not heard the rumours from Merseyside that he had become difficult to handle off the pitch, but we just knew that Jimmy had won medals, lots of them, playing in a midfield that many still regard as one of the finest ever seen in Europe (Case, Graeme Souness, Ray Kennedy and Terry McDermott). He had also developed a reputation as a hard man, perhaps the hardest of them all. You just didn't mess with Case. Those who did quickly came to regret it.

James Robert Case was born in Liverpool in May 1954. Despite the bombsite reminders of World War Two it was a good time to be in the city. Work was plentiful and the place seemed to be on the cusp of something that would manifest itself in The Beatles and the Mersey Beat sound of the early 60s. His dad, who worked on the railways, had played rugby and boxed while in the forces, but it was football that caught Jimmy's eye. Whenever the opportunity arose, he would play it – at Toxteth High School, at the local Boys' Club, for Saturday teams, you name it.

'I just missed out on the Beatle thing,' he says, as we sit down to a pint (mine) and a Coke (his) in the bar at the

'Oh Jimmy Jimmy, Jimmy Jimmy Jimmy Jimmy Jimmy Case!'

Southampton Hilton. 'My brother and my sister, who are six and seven years older than me, were right in the mix of it, but I was just a little bit too young to go out and do the pubs and whatever. You're still in amongst it in a way. My sister was always bringing mates round to play records so I was getting interested in what was going on along with my football. Every lad wanted to be a footballer for Liverpool or Everton. We'd go out to the parks, throw our coats down as goalposts and play. I'd always watched Liverpool as a kid. I was never an Evertonian. But every kid was either one or the other.'

In common with the vast majority of working-class households (particularly at that time), the important thing to do post-school was to get a trade behind you. On leaving Toxteth High School in 1970 Jimmy went for two interviews – one with Dunlop, the other at a firm called Evans Medical in Speke. He got the latter and started out on a four-year apprenticeship as an electrician. By then he was already excelling at football, playing at a semi-professional level for South Liverpool. A couple of clubs had taken a look at him including Burnley, who passed on his services after a trial lasting five days. Legend has it that Albion also expressed an interest after Mike Bamber watched him play for South Liverpool. 'Possibly, I don't really know. I've heard something mentioned about that,' is all Jimmy can recall the best part of four decades later.

Two years into his apprenticeship Liverpool Football Club came calling. It was dilemma time. 'A young player can sign, say, for a club on a two-year contract but what happens if they don't make it? The money is better now, but if I didn't make it, and I had no apprenticeship to fall back on, I would have had nothing.' The answer was for Liverpool to take over his semi-professional contract and Jimmy to have two jobs, one as a footballer and the other as an apprentice electrician. 'I had two mornings a week off work to do full-time training with the team, then I would have to go back to work. I had college on the Wednesday, training two nights a week with the kids to keep my fitness levels up and playing in the reserves on a Tuesday night or on a Saturday. For two years that's what it was. I knew it was going to be hard work, but you just do it. When you're young stuff like that doesn't phase you. You have the energy.'

During the latter part of 1974 Jimmy completed his apprenticeship. However, by that time it was clear he had what it took to make it as a professional footballer with Liverpool, the club Bill Shankly had guided from the Second Division to Championship glory over the course of an astonishing 15-year managerial reign. When 'Shanks' resigned in July that year his right-hand man Bob Paisley stepped into the void and led the Reds to even greater heights. They won the European Cup in 1977, 1978 and 1981. Only 16 goals were conceded and 15 players used on their way to the 1978–79 League title. Jimmy was a vital cog in the team throughout this period, a favourite with the fans who loved him because he was one of them – an inner-city lad who supported the club. The Italian press voted him Young European Footballer of the Year. The only thing missing was international honours. In fact, Jimmy never won a single full cap throughout his whole career, although he was chosen once to play for an England Under-23 side.

Make no mistake about it – the Liverpool side of that era worked hard. They could also play hard. Their success at home meant the players got to know Europe and its cities better than your average travel agent. More often than not, Jimmy would sample the local nightlife in the company of fellow midfielder and close friend Ray Kennedy, the two men always making a point of hunting down the best restaurants in the area around the team's hotel. Pranks were also pulled. Goalkeeper Ray Clemence and right-back Phil Neal once returned to their room after dinner to discover the beds had been turned upside down. This baffled them as the keys had not left their pockets all evening. Later the pair discovered that Jimmy and Ray had scaled a wall, climbed in through an open window and done the deed before exiting the same way they had come in.

Occasionally, however, things did spill over. During one post-match dinner in

Tbilisi, Georgia (then part of Russia), Ray punched Jimmy full in the face after the latter had insulted a group of British sports writers accompanying the Liverpool party. In April 1980 both players made the national headlines for a court appearance on charges of affray resulting from a fight that had erupted at the Bryn Howell Hotel near Llangollen during what was meant to be a few days' rest and relaxation for the Liverpool squad. Having returned guilty pleas they were each fined £150 plus costs.

Whether such incidents played any part in bringing both Ray and Jimmy's Anfield careers to a close the following year, only Bob Paisley together with the other members of Liverpool's famous 'boot room' knew. Jimmy did not talk about Tbilisi or Llangollen during our meeting, so out of respect for the man I decided to mention neither. What is for certain is that the arrival of little Sammy Lee on the scene during the 1980–81 season certainly hastened Jimmy's departure after eight years at the club, during which he made 236 appearances and scored 45 goals.

'Sammy was getting to the stage where he could play in the first team and was going for my position,' says Jimmy. 'Me and Sammy get on great, always have done. It was just one of those things. I got the feeling he was going to get the nod without anybody actually saying so. He'd played in the [1981] European Cup Final in Paris and I'd been substitute, coming on for Kenny Dalglish towards the end of the game. Just prior to that we'd been abroad somewhere and Bob Paisley had mentioned in passing that John Toshack had been on the phone and wanted a word with me. A lot of players had gone out of Liverpool around that time to Swansea, which is where "Tosh" was managing. Out of politeness I said "He can call me if he wants", because you don't just turn people away, you speak to them. So Tosh was trying to persuade me to go down there. Then before the beginning of the following season we were on a tour of Switzerland and Bob said Brighton had been asking about me. Once you get told twice that clubs are asking about you, you begin to get the picture. If they wanted to keep me, they wouldn't have told me.'

Unlike so many transfers, Jimmy's switch to Brighton came about remarkably quickly. 'All the decisions I've made in footballing terms have been quick ones, and I've never regretted any one of them. When I think it's right, I'll do it.' So why did he think this move was right? 'I didn't really want to go to a big city club again. I fancied something totally different. I didn't want London or anywhere like that. I spoke to Mike Bailey and his coaching staff when I got off the plane from Switzerland in a hotel in London and arranged to go down and see them. And that was it. By later that afternoon I'd signed.

'It was around that time that Mark [Lawrenson] was going the other way and that deal had to be done. Not that there was any pressure. If he didn't want to go, he didn't want to go. But I think there might have been a certain queue of players that were available in the wake of Mark going to Liverpool, and they [Brighton] plumped for me.'

With the exception of the FA Cup, Jimmy won just about every honour available at club level with Liverpool, including four League Championships, three European Cups and a UEFA Cup. But they had come at a price. The pressure to succeed – both from within Anfield and among supporters – was immense, something Mark Lawrenson would discover during his seven-year spell on Merseyside. Not winning at least one honour per season was unthinkable. It is a cliché, but few places on this planet eat, sleep and drink football like Liverpool, and for those members of the squad living in or around the city centre there was simply no escaping this goldfish-bowl existence. By 1981 the pressure had begun to get to Jimmy.

'Ray Clemence put it well when we were sitting in a café outside our hotel in Paris the morning after we'd won the European Cup. He said "Ah, but it wasn't as good as the first time, was it?" We'd had eight solid years of winning trophies and you do tend to get to the stage where you compare things. That's what happens when you're playing at a club where the demands for week in, week out performances are huge and the professionalism is that great. I'm not saying Brighton was any less professional, it's just that things were done differently. It was enjoyable at Brighton. We played some good football and had some good times. You have a life outside football that you are able to enjoy. That didn't always happen in Liverpool. Even now I go back up there and it's hectic.'

In what way? 'I'd go shopping with my wife in a precinct and the next thing you know there's 15 to 20 people watching you buy a piece of meat at the butchers. I wouldn't mind but you're only after a pound of sausages. And it's still like it. Even now I go back and you can get cornered for three-quarters of the evening by people who want to chat about the game, which is hard when you're supposed to be with other people. It's a full on situation, whereas Brighton was a little easier. You still get recognised – "All the best for Saturday" – but there's nothing wrong with that. It's not like an obsession.'

Jimmy was 27 when he joined Brighton and had never lived outside Liverpool before, let alone north-west England. Nevertheless, he immediately felt welcome on the south coast, and it was not long before he 'got a feel for the place'. Jimmy had always respected Mike Bailey as a player and now the two men found themselves starting afresh in new surroundings. Jimmy Melia, another Scouser, was part of Albion's backroom at the time, working as the club's chief scout, and immediately helped the club's new £350,000 signing settle in with his Mersey brand of humour. He made his debut in a 1–1 draw at West Ham on 29 August 1981 and opened his scoring account a week later in a 2–0 home win over Middlesbrough. That October he was on target with a bullet header against Liverpool at the Goldstone as Albion fought back from 3–1 down to claim a point. The supporters immediately took a shine to him as did the players, who revelled in having an 'enforcer' in their midst – one who could also play a bit.

'Jimmy was a friendly character and definitely old school,' says Gordon Smith. 'If someone did a bad tackle on either him or anyone else on our side he never remonstrated. You just watched him clock whoever had done it, because you knew at some point he would get his revenge. Everyone always talks about Graeme Souness being the hard man, especially up in Scotland. I always say "Yeah, except for when he was playing against Jimmy." For a guy who was quite quiet, he was the proverbial hard man.'

'When he came to Brighton everyone was amazed,' adds Gerry Ryan of Jimmy. 'He was an enforcer in the old type of way. He would protect us. If anyone got hit bad then he would seek retribution.

But he was also a great footballer. Every game Jimmy played, he played to a high standard. He also gave the team an aura. When you saw his name on the team sheet it stood out. It meant something.'

One man who played against Jimmy twice during the 1981–82 season was Graham Pearce, the left-back whose appearances for Barnet versus the Albion in the third round of the FA Cup earned him a transfer to the Goldstone during the summer of 1982. 'We all knew about his reputation, everyone in the game did,' he says. 'But in those two FA Cup games I found him to be hard but fair, no more than that. Having said that, I wouldn't have wanted to get on the wrong side of him. He was a good footballer, but he didn't half carry an air of menace with him on the pitch.'

That air of menace initially extended to some of Albion's squad, not to mention opponents. In his first few weeks at the club several of Jimmy's new teammates commented privately on how quiet he was while in action, almost unnervingly so. 'We all wondered why he never said anything on the pitch,' adds Gerry Ryan. 'He rarely said a word. Sometimes you'd say something to him and he just wouldn't reply. None of us realised at the time that he was deaf in one ear!' Which is something we will return to later.

Jimmy's all-action and sometimes close-to-the-bone style of play quickly gave rise to a popular chant among Brighton's supporters. When an opposition player nobbled one of Albion's XI, fans would almost immediately start singing 'Jimmy's Gonna Getcha' over and over again in the full knowledge that Jimmy was, well, 'gonna' get the culprit at some point during the next five to 10 minutes. A second Case favourite on the terraces was a song that usually did the rounds when the team was announced before kick-off or when Albion won a free-kick outside the penalty box, giving Jimmy licence to have a pop with one of his long-range speciality shots. 'Oh Jimmy Jimmy, Jimmy Jimmy Jimmy Jimmy Jimmy Case!' was a simple yet well-loved ditty, which gave opposing goalkeepers a fair idea of what was about to come.

There is a saying in life that everything is relative. Albion ended the 1981–82 season in 13th place, still the club's highest-ever finish. By contrast, Jimmy had never been so low, the runner-up spot in the League having been deemed unacceptable at Liverpool. In the knock-out competitions Brighton struggled to get past non-League Barnet in the FA Cup before losing at home to Third Division Oxford United in the next round. Their performances in the League Cup were not much better, an aggregate 2–1 win against lowly Huddersfield Town being followed by a humiliating 4–1 away defeat to Second Division Barnsley. After year upon year of silverware, Jimmy had entered the real world.

'In those days there was more of a competitive edge right the way down through the First Division. It wasn't unusual for a team at the bottom to beat a team at the top, like it is now. These were the times when Nottingham Forest came up from the Second Division and won the title in their first year. It just wouldn't happen now. Because of that, 13th place would have been good for Brighton. We really weren't a bad side at the time.'

Did he find the 1981–82 campaign a comedown from his days at Liverpool? 'It was something different from what I'd been used to and where I'd been playing, but I would enjoy my football almost anywhere really. I work hard at it. By that I mean I work hard for others and at my game. I don't stop trying. So yeah, it was different, but no less enjoyable for me.'

If 13th place represented a reality check for Jimmy, it was nothing compared with what would happen the following year. Brighton's dire away form (their opening three League games on the road resulted in 14 goals being conceded and none scored) meant they were always relying on good home performances to stay out of trouble. On 27 November 1982 Notts County became the first team to win at the Goldstone that season. Albion would win only four of their remaining 26 League fixtures (three at

home, one away) and finished bottom of the table, having collected 40 points from 42 games. Mike Bailey had made way for Jimmy Melia as manager, Albion's chief scout being offered the job on the strength of the club's outstanding form in the FA Cup – of which Jimmy played a major part.

In the third round Brighton drew 1–1 at home against Second Division Newcastle United, winning the replay on Tyneside 1–0 thanks to a Peter Ward goal and a couple of debatable decisions in Albion's favour by referee Trelford Mills. 'The first goal I disallowed came when the ball went to Imre Varadi: he handled, I blew, but he went on and put the ball in the net,' Mills told me many years later. 'The second was just a couple of minutes later. There was a free-kick that went to the back post. Jeff Clarke [United defender] went up to meet it and put an arm across the neck of a player. I blew but the ball went across to Kevin Keegan, who headed it into the net. He ran off towards the halfway line doing his Mick Channon impression, not realising I'd disallowed it.'

Jimmy then proceeded to net goals in the following four rounds as Albion progressed to the 1983 FA Cup Final and a date with Manchester United.

Fourth Round – Manchester City (Home), Saturday 29 January

Two goals by Michael Robinson against his old club together with a strike apiece by Jimmy and Neil Smillie gave

Brighton an emphatic win against a poor City side. 'I can't remember too much about the goal, but I'm pretty sure it took a deflection off someone before going over the goalkeeper,' says Jimmy. 'The biggest thing for me about that game was the fact that we were through to play Liverpool in the next round.'

Fifth Round – Liverpool (Away), Sunday 20 February

Albion's first appearance in the fifth round for 23 years. Gerry Ryan put the visitors ahead only for Craig Johnstone to equalise. Nineteen seconds after the restart Jimmy let fly with a shot that took a slight deflection off Ronnie Whelan to beat Liverpool goalkeeper Bruce Grobbelaar. 'Apart from the goal the thing I really remember about that particular game is me and Tony Grealish playing against Graeme Souness and Kenny Dalglish, their midfield pair. I took Souness and Tony took Dalglish. They used to do this thing where they would move around each other and cross over to mess you up. You could end up with two of your players on one side and one of their guys coming through the gap from nowhere. So what we did was, whenever they crossed, Tony and me would rub shoulders and go back out again. We never changed sides. We never got messed up. That's what always used to excite me about playing, not so much the physical side as competing through thinking. They had some class players, and I was thinking

"How can I stop this happening?" If you're not thinking right, you get done.' It was Liverpool's first home defeat in any Cup competition since 1974, a run of 63 matches.

Sixth Round – Norwich City (Home), Saturday 12 March

Albion's first appearance in the quarter-finals ever. The game was settled by one goal in the second half, Jimmy out-muscling City centre-back Dave Watson in front of the North Stand before slamming the ball past goalkeeper Chris Woods. Norwich appealed to referee Alan Robinson that Watson had been fouled, but the effort stood. 'I go to Norwich quite a bit, and they've never forgiven me for that. It's the old-fashioned shoulder to shoulder, fighting for space to get onto the ball. You've just got to be stronger. I finished it and wheeled round – you're always looking to see if it's okay. I knew I hadn't fouled him. I grew up leaning into players from a young age because I was smaller than most other players. If you give a little nudge at the right time and he's off balance or not expecting it, you can knock over the biggest players. He shouldn't have got caught.'

Semi-final – Sheffield Wednesday (Highbury), Saturday 16 April

Wednesday manager Jack Charlton had spent a fair proportion of the week leading up to the game showing his side how to defend against Jimmy's free-kicks from outside the box. Fat lot of good it did. 'I wasn't going to take it because it was a fair distance out, but Tony Grealish bent down and just nudged it to his right. I hit it and it took off like a golf shot. I didn't even feel the weight of the ball on my foot, it was so sweet. It just rose and kept rising just under the bar, hit the net, hit the floor, then hit the roof of the net again. A shot has got to be travelling pretty hard and fast to do that. The important thing about it was it got us off the mark against them. The first goal in a semi-final is always a terrific boost.' Ante Mirocevic equalised in the second half, but Michael Robinson capped a historic day for Brighton with the winning goal.

Although Gordon Smith had won medals north of the border with Glasgow Rangers, Jimmy was the only player in Albion's squad who had appeared regularly in the latter stages of major Cup competitions in England (and Europe). His experience proved invaluable as the club crept ever nearer to the Final itself. 'It's like you're looking at the draw thinking "We can do this!" We had a little bit of luck here and there, which is something you need, and you start to believe you can get a bit further. The belief was there, especially when you draw a team that's not fancied like Sheffield Wednesday. Once you start counting down how many are left in the competition, you know you're getting close.'

To this day Jimmy is not sure exactly how many times he had played at Wembley prior to the 1983 FA Cup Final. One thing he does know is that getting there with Brighton meant as much to him as any previous appearance with Liverpool. 'It [Wembley] had become like my second home. The supporters used to call it the second Anfield. But to get there with someone else was a big deal for me – a real big deal. It was a new thing for the club, a new thing for the players around me, and you get wrapped up in that. The closer it got the more the town was buzzing. It's infectious.'

Jimmy remembers the squad being upbeat and relaxed on the morning of Saturday 21 May, even as they took to the skies over London to become the first side to arrive at Wembley for an FA Cup Final in a helicopter. Nobody needed to tell him his job that day – 'a little bit of intimidation on my part on certain players in their side to make them think they can't dwell on the ball or they are gonna get a challenge.' Certain player number one proved to be Manchester United midfielder Ray Wilkins, who felt the full force of a Jimmy special during the opening exchanges. A few minutes later United captain Bryan Robson caught Case in a revenge tackle, followed shortly afterwards by Case going in hard on Robson. 'That was the nature of the game in those days. If somebody caught you, or gave you a good kicking on the side of the leg, as long as they connected with the ball as well it was okay. You went through leaving a little bit of damage to the player as well, making it sore for them without intending any breakages. Then get up and get on with it. Say, for instance, I got caught by Bryan Robson. I would blame myself. I would've said "Well, I shouldn't have got caught there, that's my fault. I gave him the opportunity to catch me, and he did." The idea was not to get caught in the first place.'

Jimmy's midfield battle with Robson remains one of the enduring memories of Brighton's first match against Manchester United, together with Gordon Smith's miss, Norman Whiteside's dreadful tackle on Chris Ramsey and, of course, the goals. Unfortunately for Albion fans, the replay was a night to forget. It might have been so different had Jimmy's deflected long-range effort in the first half arched over Gary Bailey into the net. Instead, the United goalkeeper made a superb save, and the Red Devils went on to record an emphatic victory.

Why the very same side that made it to the FA Cup Final performed so miserably in the League that season remains something of a mystery to Jimmy. Reading between the lines, he may just agree with Steve Foster that Jimmy Melia was the wrong man to be appointed manager at such a critical time – although I should stress he did not actually say that himself. 'The team was looking after itself

basically. I'm not saying it picked itself but there were some strong characters to deal with. We'd suggest stuff to Jimmy and half the time he would go along with it. We had the players to do well – Gerry Ryan, Gordon Smith, Michael Robinson, Gary Stevens, Tony Grealish, Fozzie – so I can't tell you why we dipped so much. It's not like we didn't try in the League, but when the Cup came along you could see the lads were right up for that. That's what carried us along, not our League form. Maybe that was the problem.'

No player has a divine right to play at the highest level. However, watching Jimmy line up in the Second Division against Oldham at Boundary Park on the opening day of the 1983–84 season was like listening to a favourite record being played at the wrong speed. It just seemed wrong. Not that Jim appeared to care. He just carried on doing what he was good at, scaring the living daylights out of second tier midfielders and scoring long-range efforts like the 25-yarder he fired into Blackburn's net on 24 September 1983. The following week he scored a hat-trick in the 7–0 home drubbing of Charlton. Afterwards he cornered striker Terry Connor in the tunnel at the Goldstone. Not out of any malice – he simply needed Terry to remind him what the final score had been.

At a time of big transitions, Jimmy was a vital constant in the side as Albion recovered from a poor start to finish a respectable ninth under Melia's successor Chris Cattlin. Now fast approaching his 30th birthday, there were no signs, at least as far as the fans and his teammates were concerned, that age was catching up with him. He seemed as dynamic as ever and an inspiration to those around him, many of whom were newcomers to the club in the wake of relegation and defeat in the FA Cup Final. 'He was an icon, and to play alongside him then was just the most fantastic experience a player at my level could want,' says Danny Wilson, who partnered Case in Albion's midfield having joined the club initially on loan from Nottingham Forest in November 1983. 'I learned so much from him, not just about football. He never back-chatted to referees – it wasn't his style. So I didn't. He just went about himself and you learned from his example.'

The 1983–84 campaign had ended with Jimmy as club captain and the supporters' choice for Player of the Season. As Cattlin began to stamp his authority on the squad he had inherited from Melia, there were high hopes Albion could finish in the top three the following May to return to the First Division after an absence of just two years. With the likes of Frank Worthington, Danny Wilson, Steve Penney and Eric Young on board, not to mention Jimmy, the team certainly seemed strong enough to mount a decent promotion push. Come March 1985 and with the finish line in sight,

Brighton were still well placed to bag one of the three coveted places. And then something strange happened. With 11 games left to go, Chris Cattlin went and sold Jimmy to Southampton for – wait for it – a miserly £30,000.

After a rocky start Cattlin had developed a strong bond with the supporters during his first 17 months at the club. His reputation as a disciplinarian initially led many fans (including myself) to assume that Jimmy had transgressed some kind of rule. Why else would you sell one of your best players for such a pittance when you are striving for promotion? However, the truth was far starker – Cattlin simply did not fancy him anymore and believed his playing days were drawing to a close.

'When Brighton went down from the First Division I think I had another year of my contract left,' says Jimmy. 'A lot of players were leaving, but I was more than willing to stay and try and get them back up again. I never instigated anything about moving to Southampton. I've heard stories, but I can tell you I didn't. Chris Cattlin came up to me and said Lawrie [McMenemy] had been on the phone with a view to moving down there, which would have been back into the First Division. What had happened was that Chris had basically said to the board "Lawrie has been in for Jimmy, and I think his legs have gone." I think it was a Tuesday. He [Chris] said to go over and speak to them. They were very persuasive. Steve Williams had just left and Lawrie McMenemy said "I want somebody to come in and not be overawed by the dressing room, someone who will sit in the middle of the park and get us ticking." I think I left for £25,000 or £30,000, and I went on to play six seasons for Southampton in the First Division. It wasn't about the money. I've never gone anywhere for money. Whenever Lawrie gets asked about me at functions, he always says I was his best signing because I cost so little and played for so long, always on a yearly contract.'

Back at the Goldstone several members of Albion's squad were unimpressed with Jimmy's departure to say the least. 'Why didn't we go up that season? Because we sold Jimmy Case to Southampton,' says Gary O'Reilly, then one of Brighton's regular centre-backs. 'It just seemed like a crazy thing to do. We were doing okay. Jimmy was doing okay. And the timing was awful, with something like 10 or so games to go. No doubt about it, we missed him.'

Albion ended up missing out on promotion by three points. Only once since then have they ever come close to returning to the First Division (or what is now the Premier League), Barry Lloyd's side losing in the Play-off Final to Notts County at Wembley in 1991.

For Jimmy the move to Southampton turned out to be a dream one. He went on

to play over 200 times for the Saints and regularly captained sides boasting such talented individuals as Alan Shearer, Matthew Le Tissier, Andy Townsend, Peter Shilton, Joe Jordan and Danny Wallace. The Hampshire club failed to win anything during Jimmy's spell on its payroll, but they were entertaining to watch and difficult to beat.

'I was still more than capable of playing at that level when I was 38,' says Jimmy. 'I put my work in, but I was mainly a holding man, getting stuck in and passing the ball to good young players around me like Glenn Cockerill, Andy Townsend and Barry Horne. They helped me prolong my career. Really we had all the ingredients. You had [Alan] Shearer through the middle. You could knock it by the side of him, and he would power through. You could give is to "Tiss" [Le Tissier], who could do anything with it. You could hit it from the halfway line into the corner where the flag is and Rodney [Wallace] would get it before their centre-back. So I had an array of balls I could play.'

Roy Evans, a member of Liverpool's 'boot room' who would later go on to manage the club, once admitted to Jimmy that the Reds let him go too soon. History had repeated itself, only now Albion were the ones losing out.

Jimmy's Southampton career would be brought to an end by a managerial change during the summer of 1991. The new incumbent, Ian Branfoot, planned on adopting a more high-tempo game based around long balls rather than midfield artistry. Or, in Jimmy's words, 'He didn't think I would be able to keep up with the way they were gonna play.' Harry Redknapp immediately gave him the opportunity of making Bournemouth his third south-coast club, and Jimmy went on to become one of their outstanding performers during the 1991–92 season. However, a financial crisis that summer brought the curtain down on his spell at Dean Court. For the first time in his life, Jimmy found himself unemployed and waiting for the phone to ring.

When it finally did, the voice on the other end belonged to one of his former Albion teammates. Frank Worthington wanted to know if he fancied playing a few games for Halifax Town, where he was now coaching. Jimmy accepted the invitation and spent the first half of the 1992–93 season at The Shay before moving to Wrexham to join forces with the ex-Liverpool defender Joey Jones, then assistant manager at the Racecourse Ground. That, in turn, was followed by a couple of months playing for the British Wanneroo club in Australia, one game for Darlington and a month with Southern League Sittingbourne. Which takes us up to December 1993.

'Gerry Ryan called me and says "Do you fancy coming back and seeing Liam? We need a hand. He wants you to play in the middle of the park." I said "Yeah,

sure."' The Liam in question was, of course, Mr Brady, recently appointed Albion's new manager with Gerry Ryan working as his number two. Brady wanted Jimmy to perform the same role as he had at Southampton, acting as a holding player in midfield and bringing those around him into the action with his vast repertoire of passes. Despite his age (39) and a lack of recent League experience, Jimmy did exactly what was asked of him, helping Albion recover from a dismal start in what by then had become Division Two (the third tier of English football). Besides making 21 appearances he also managed the reserve team. 'He was the best signing I ever made,' Brady later admitted.

Jimmy remained part of the first team set-up during the opening weeks of the 1994–95 season as Albion looked to better their 14th-place finish last time around, despite the club's acute financial problems. One of his 11 appearances as a 40-year-old came in an outstanding 2–0 League Cup win away at Premier League Leicester City. It was, however, a game he failed to finish, not that age or low energy reserves had anything to do with him leaving the pitch early.

'I've got a growth on the bone inside my right ear which means I'm pretty deaf in that ear. It's a kind of hereditary thing. It's been there all my life but has got slightly worse with age. I was offered an operation in Brighton but there was a risk of total deafness so I didn't have it done. Anyway, we went to play Leicester in the League Cup at their ground. In the first half the ball went to go over my head and I had handled it and obviously got a booking. In the latter stages we were winning 2–0, meaning they had to score four goals within a minute or two to go through on aggregate. The referee then noticed that Jeff Minton had his chain on, so he sent him to the bench to take it off. While he was doing that we got a corner, but Jeff was our usual corner taker. I went over and Jeff was coming back on towards the middle of the pitch. The referee was standing close by and unbeknown to me he was saying "Come on, keep the game flowing", while I was saying to Jeff "Do you want to take it?" The referee was shouting at me, but I couldn't hear him because I'd taken my hearing aid out to stop it getting full of sweat. So he comes up, books me and sends me off. I was saying "I couldn't hear you mate!" Jimmy Greaves was upstairs at the time doing some commentary and he just went "That's absolutely ridiculous." Me, a seasoned campaigner, I know about the game. I know you keep it flowing – Crazy.'

They say you should never go back. Steve Foster proved during his second spell at the Goldstone that you can. On the other hand, Brian Horton's brief managerial stint at the end of the 1990s demonstrated it is not always the best of ideas. Jimmy's return to Sussex would fall

somewhere between the two. As a player he exceeded all expectations right up until the day of his retirement aged 41, following a horrific looking yet ultimately minor neck injury suffered during a reserve game. But as a manager he proved to be a disaster, though there were of course mitigating circumstances.

'I didn't even want it in a certain way,' Jimmy says now of his ill-fated 13-month reign, which corresponded with the club's spiral into apparent meltdown under the stewardship of chairman Bill Archer and chief executive David Bellotti. 'When Liam decided he'd had enough because of everything that was going on, me, him and Gerry [Ryan] sat down and talked. They reckoned they [Archer and Bellotti] might offer me the job. The possible takeover involving Dick Knight was already boiling up. There was always lots of talk going on about getting them out and Knight in, which is what eventually happened. I took the job because I liked the club and its supporters, but also on the understanding that if Dick Knight came in it wouldn't be a problem for me to revert back to running the reserve team, with Liam coming back through the front door to sit in the main seat. That wouldn't have been a problem for me at all. I thought it was just round the corner.'

As corners go, it proved to be an agonisingly gentle one. 'I stuck it out for a year. They threw a bit of money my way to make it look as though they were interested, but it's difficult to get players to come and play when fireworks are getting thrown into the directors' box, riot police are in the tunnel and everybody walks out of the ground when rockets go up. I don't blame the supporters, but when you're trying to manage it was impossible.'

With Jimmy as manager Albion were relegated into the fourth tier of English football in May 1996 for the first time in over 30 years. On 17 August the club won its opening game of the 1996–97 season. Within two months they had slipped to the foot of the table, the 92nd best (or worst, depending on your standpoint) team in the country. And that was the way it stayed until the penultimate game of the season, when a 1–0 victory over Doncaster Rovers in the last game ever to be played at the Goldstone saw the Seagulls rise one place to 91st. The following Saturday, 3 May 1997, a 1–1 draw against Hereford – the only club below Brighton in Nationwide League Division Three – was enough to preserve their Football League status.

By that time Jimmy was long gone, sacked the previous December when Albion were still nine points adrift at the bottom of the pile. Determined to do his duty, he had initially refused to quit but as defeat followed defeat his position became untenable, especially once the support of the fans had been lost. In an ideal world Jimmy would have arranged

for Messrs Archer and Bellotti to go swimming with the fishes off the Palace Pier, bullied councillors and planners into green lighting a new stadium, then led the club to successive promotions culminating in a 5–0 win over Liverpool at the New Goldstone on the opening day of the 1999–2000 season. Unfortunately, real life, as Albion supporters know only too well, just is not like that.

'If they had got the ground down there years ago the club would be flying by now because the support base, in my view, was, and is, phenomenal. They've always had a hard core but a lot more would've come out to follow them. Instead, they're playing home games in front of people sat in the rain in kagouls. It's unbelievable. I was speaking to Mike Bamber when I first joined them in 1981 about a new ground, and there had been talk about moving to Waterhall in 1974. And now we're in 2007. You tell me where it's all gone wrong.'

Today Jimmy lives near Southampton and works for the club's own radio station, providing commentary and analysis on home and away games. He also does the odd bit of work for BBC Radio Merseyside covering Liverpool matches. Should all else fail he still has his grounding as an electrician to fall back on. 'It was always said in most households when I was growing up that if you could get a trade behind you, then that was everything. You weren't setting yourself up for life but you had a licence to do

(picture courtesy of Southampton Football Club)

Jimmy Case, 2007

something that other people couldn't. You would probably always be in demand. As it turns out, now you can't get a plumber anywhere and electricians are scarce. I still sometimes jump in with a friend of mine in Norwich who used to work on the rigs. He's an electrician and he's snowed under with work so I give him a hand. There's new appliances and fittings but the basics don't change. You get the wiring wrong, you blow the fuse. It's not rocket science.'

Despite the sour ending to his managerial career at the Goldstone, Jimmy still has a massive soft spot for the Albion. It was, after all, where he proved

himself to be more than just a one-club wonder post-Liverpool. 'The top and bottom of it was I loved the place. I've still got good mates who live down there. Even to this day I get excited going to the Withdean because it means I'll see people like Derek Allan, the club secretary who's always been there. Even Dick Knight once said to me "You're always welcome here." That means a lot. It's just a shame the club hasn't been allowed to move on because the supporters deserve better, what with everything that happened with the directors and selling the ground. If anyone deserves some kind of success, it's them.'

Chapter Eight
Penney's From Heaven

His name was, I'm not ashamed to admit, one of the first on my wine-stained team sheet the night I decided to pick a dream Albion XI. And although a couple of players I've spoken to while in the process of writing this book have expressed some surprise at my choice, it's one I'm sticking to like a limpet. Steve Penney just had to be in.

'Why don't you have a 4–3–3 formation instead?' said one of the dissenters, who, funnily enough, just happened to have been a forward. 'How can you go for him over Neil Smillie?' remarked another. I thought about both options for all of, oh, five seconds. It is not that I don't rate Neil. Quite the opposite. A 4–3–3 formation would also have allowed me to accommodate one of the myriad of great Albion strikers from down the years in danger of not making the final cut. But I ask you, can you ever recall seeing Brighton fans wearing T-shirts in homage to Neil Smillie, Garry Nelson, Mike Small or even the fabulously impressive Michael Robinson? I rest my case.

'Can you tell my young girls about that because they don't believe me,' says Steve when I remind him of how some female supporters used to wear tops carrying slogans such as 'Penny's From Heaven' and 'Penny Lover', the latter borrowing from the title of a popular Lionel Richie song of the time. 'They just laugh and tell their father to stop making things up. It does seem kind of funny, though, looking back on it, almost unbelievable, so I can't blame them.'

I can only hazard a few guesses at why Steven Alexander Penney had the odd dissenter from among the ranks of ex-Albion pros. Maybe it was because the Northern Irishman arrived at a time when the club was in a state of flux, the heady days of the late 70s and early 80s making way for an era of stark home truths regarding expectations and finances. Perhaps it's down to some of the underachieving sides he played in while at the Goldstone (how people forget about the significant part he played during the 1987–88 promotion campaign). Then there were the injuries that made him something of a forgotten man towards the end of his Brighton career. If Steve had been a racehorse he would have been put down half-a-dozen times, maybe more.

In my eyes all of that pales into insignificance when I cast my mind back to his first two or three years at the club.

He didn't score many, but that wasn't his job. Manager Chris Cattlin bought him to create goals, and in that department Steve repaid his £25,000 transfer fee time and time again. He was, in short, a breath of fresh air, a flying winger whose close control and devastating pace left opponents and spectators alike lost for words. Former Albion hero Peter O'Sullivan describes Steve as 'a very good player, far more of a natural winger than I was.' That tribute to his ability says it all.

Steve was born on the 16th day of 1964 in Ballymena, the town he returned to after his playing days were over and where I travelled to meet him one crisp February day in 2007. His father was a teacher, and his mother a nurse. It was, he recalls, a relatively safe place to grow up considering what was going on in other parts of Northern Ireland at the time, though perhaps a little too austere. A local councillor once successfully banned a proposed concert by the Electric Light Orchestra because of fears it might encourage Satanism among local youths. Maybe he played *Mr Blue Sky* backwards and discovered something that has so far escaped the rest of us?

'Ballymena was one of the better places to be,' says Steve. 'We had the odd bombing. Someone once left a car where the main shopping centre now stands which exploded and killed several people, but most of the day to day stuff was down to bigotry rather than terrorism, you

know Catholics and Protestants not getting on too well. It wasn't like Belfast, Londonderry or round the borders. Unless your parents were RUC (Royal Ulster Constabulary) officers or army, in which case you had to be very careful, it didn't really affect you. It's like Israel now. You could go there and see nothing, but you constantly see suicide bombers on TV so you think it's happening everywhere all the time. We knew the areas to stay out of, the ones you didn't go to. In that way you were probably just at risk in, say, London.'

Thirteen months after Steve joined Brighton, the IRA bombed the Grand Hotel on the town's seafront during the 1984 Conservative Party Conference, killing five people in the process and hospitalising 34 others. 'The guys were telling me not to open my mouth for about a week afterwards what with my accent. It was strange, going all that way and something like that happening so close by. But thankfully times have changed. It's easier to bring up kids here now. It's a lovely place. Belfast has fantastic restaurants and shops. There are bad spots but everywhere has bad spots. I feel comfortable here. Your home is your home. I don't care where you come from, you feel more comfortable when you're at home. That's why I always wanted to come back.'

Steve grew up playing football, or soccer as he sometimes calls it, at primary school and in the Boys' Brigade. He passed his 11-plus exams and went to Grammar School, where he also excelled at rugby union in the scrum-half position. At 15 he had to make the choice between turning out for Ballymena Reserves or continuing with the rugby. Steve chose football. There hasn't been a moment since when he's regretted the decision, even though his rugby side went on to win the Northern Ireland Schools' Cup the following year without him.

His football idols were the mavericks of the game, players like Frank Worthington, Stan Bowles, Tony Currie and, it almost goes without saying baring in mind his birthplace, George Best. He didn't have a favourite team, realising from an early age that he preferred playing sport to following it. The first major football match he remembers going to as a spectator was a European Cup semi-final first-leg tie between Nottingham Forest and Ajax, Steve having been offered the chance of signing apprentice forms at the City Ground under Brian Clough. 'I was in the process of doing my schooling back home and had reached the O level stage. My father said to me "If you're good enough, you'll get over there eventually. There's hundreds of kids go to England and maybe one or two make it. Concentrate on your education first." I didn't particularly see it like that at the time, but I can see where he was coming from now.'

Back home he continued playing for Ballymena United, making enough of an impression in their first team to be noticed by Roy Coyle, manager of Linfield and the Alex Ferguson of Northern Irish club football. Coyle invited Steve to play in a tournament in Holland as a guest player. He scored in a 3–1 win over a Celtic side featuring Charlie Nicholas, Linfield losing in the Final to an Ally McCoist inspired Sunderland. One evening shortly after this he was sitting in the Ballymena team bath after a match when the club's goalkeeper Jim Platt, a former Northern Ireland international who had played for Middlesbrough, decided to give Steve's career the push it was so patently crying out for. 'He said to me "What are you working at doing?" I told him that I was just going to college and didn't really have any intentions. He said "Well I've played in England and I reckon you're talented enough." I told him if I got the chance I'd jump at it. Jim and Sammy Nelson (Albion's reserve-team coach at the time) were friends from their international days, and I think Jim obviously mentioned that to him. Liverpool were apparently interested, but a thousand kids go to Liverpool. Why go there and get disillusioned? Better to go somewhere you've got a chance.'

Which is where Brighton came in. Steve was invited over to train with the club for a week and play in a couple of

Steve Penney, one of the first names on the Albion dream XI team sheet.

reserve-team games. He was installed in a house close to the Goldstone (recently vacated by one Mr Jimmy Melia) along with another young hopeful, a brash Londoner by the name of Ian Wright. Steve performed well in his trial matches whereas Wright, then a left-winger, failed to shine. The Irishman was offered a contract and the Londoner returned dejected to the non-League scene. By the end of the decade Wright would be the darling of Arsenal's North Bank and an England international striker.

'Brighton had, of course, just been in the FA Cup Final. I knew all the players. Well, I knew their names and what they looked like. In those days you sat down with your family and watched the Cup Final. It was an occasion, not like now where every match is on TV and you can take it or leave it. I went over on something like the Tuesday, signed on the Friday and made my debut in the first team on Saturday. I didn't even have a chance to go home and get more gear. We played away at Barnsley, and after about five minutes I set up a goal. I beat the full-back, crossed it and big Alan Young – who could head a ball as hard as I could kick it – put it in. Then we get stuffed 3–1 and you realise you're in the big League now. This is serious. I'm at a different level.'

Steve's arrival in Sussex coincided with a period of huge transition at the club. The big-name players from Albion's days in the top flight were leaving, as was

Jimmy Melia who had been in charge for the run to the 1983 FA Cup Final. His successor, Chris Cattlin, still had a long way to go in winning over the fans (and some of the players), despite having been a member of Alan Mullery's squad between 1976 and 1980. The turmoil was reflected in the side's fluctuating fortunes throughout the first third of the 1983–84 season, which ranged from a 7–0 home win over Charlton to a 5–0 thrashing at the hands of Grimsby. The 3–1 reverse at Barnsley on 26 November was Albion's eighth from their opening 16 League games, not good for a club whose supporters had expected a concerted push for an immediate return to the old First Division.

'You could pick up that things had been going on. I'd missed most of it because I'd only just arrived from Ireland, but I wasn't interested in all the political stuff. I was interested in this fantastic opportunity I'd suddenly been given. I was straight in, playing first-team football, getting win bonuses. I'd gone from being at Ballymena maybe making £30 a week to making decent money. I was just glad to be training every day and playing with these guys, realising after a few weeks that I wasn't out of place.'

It's easy to forget that Steve was still a teenager when he made his Albion debut. For his age he handled the hurly-burly world of England's Second Division with remarkable maturity, something that allowed him to concentrate on doing the job in hand. That, as the Goldstone public soon realised, involved giving opposition defenders (especially left-backs) nightmares while looking to create goalscoring opportunities for the likes of Young, Terry Connor and Gerry Ryan. 'The physical side really didn't bother me. I'd played in the reserves at Ballymena at 15 and in the first team from 16 to 18. I was used to playing against men and not boys. The guys were a bit quicker and trained harder, but everything else was more or less the same. If anything, you were probably protected better by referees in England than you were in Northern Ireland.'

On Sunday 29 January 1984 the rest of the country woke up to what Albion fans already knew – that Steve Penney was a cast-iron, genuine talent. That was the day when Brighton took on and defeated Liverpool at the Goldstone in the FA Cup fourth round in front of a live TV audience of millions. The winger absolutely terrified the European Champions in waiting, particularly in the second half as Cattlin's side grew in confidence, launching wave after wave of attacks. Completely in the dark as to the identity of his tormentor, Liverpool left-back Alan Kennedy simply didn't know which way to turn. Two goals within the space of a minute did the job, Steve laying on the second for Connor with a through pass that made a mockery of the offside

trap. It remains one of the greatest results and performances in Albion's history.

'He was our weapon, an unknown one to start with,' says Danny Wilson, who had become Cattlin's second managerial signing the previous December a week after Steve's arrival. 'Teams just didn't know how to play against him. I know Alan Kennedy quite well because I played a bit with his brother. Steve took him apart that day, something Alan admits himself. He thought he was amazing.'

'We went to a little bar in town that night and the Liverpool players came with us,' adds Steve. 'I'd only been there six weeks and these guys were legends to me. We'd beaten them 2–0, and I thought they were going to be gutted and would just slink home, but they all came out. I thought that was good of them. They weren't bad losers, not that they lost much back then anyway. What helped us that day was [Graeme] Souness having to go off in the first half. He was an extremely creative player as well as being a hard man. They seemed to miss him, and we were able to come at them a bit more after he'd gone. Aye, I did well that day.'

Within the space of 90 minutes, Steve had gone from being a complete unknown in the English game (at least outside Sussex) to the talk of the managerial and scouting circuits. He had just turned 20 and had plenty of years ahead of him. Graham Taylor at Watford tabled a bid of £200,000. Bobby Ferguson at Ipswich did likewise. Yet Steve didn't want to move, and Albion, somewhat surprisingly given the amount of money on offer, weren't keen on selling. 'All I wanted to do at the time was play every week for Brighton. I hadn't come across the bad side of football then, with the injuries or the manager who doesn't fancy you and wants to bring someone else in. Everything was going right. It was only once I'd been in the game for a number of years that I started to realise I should have used the situation a bit more to my advantage. I always remember [Albion goalkeeper] Joe Corrigan saying "Son, you should be in there with a suitcase", but I was naïve in those days. Maybe I should've gone in and said "You sell me or you give me a really good contract." That's where Dean Saunders was very well led. His father was an ex-professional. My father wanted me to do well, but he wasn't over there. He didn't know the ins and outs of the game. If I had a son playing football now I'd make sure he made a lot more money out of the game than I did.'

Steve played in all of Albion's remaining games that season bar one, his absence from the FA Cup fifth-round tie at Watford proving crucial as the Hornets cruised to a comfortable victory. Although still prone to the occasional collapse (five goals conceded in the second half at Portsmouth having led 1–0 at the break, three goals down at Fulham with 40 minutes gone), Cattlin's side, in

the main, were playing good football and getting results, remaining unbeaten at the Goldstone from mid-December until the end of the season.

On Saturday 12 May, having already assured themselves of ninth spot, Penney and his teammates played the supporting role at St James' Park to the retiring Kevin Keegan. As the former Liverpool and England legend brought down the curtain on his remarkable career by climbing into a helicopter after the match and flying off into the Northumbrian skies, cheered to the rafters by 36,000 Geordies, Steve Penney couldn't help but reflect on his own remarkable rise over the past six months. Runner-up to Jimmy Case as Player of the Season, he had developed a reputation as the danger man in a side which 12 months earlier had appeared in an FA Cup Final. The fans loved him. What's more, his overall game was steadily improving. 'I'm not sure whether he had the heart to make those big tackles when he first came, but he soon learned and that made him a better player,' says former Albion left-back Graham Pearce. 'He made tackles that maybe Neil [Smillie] might not have made. I always thought of Steve as a bright young winger, very naturally talented, who had all the attributes you need in that position, especially pace.'

Just when Steve thought life could not get any better, it suddenly did. Frank Worthington, one of his boyhood idols, joined the club. It did not matter that the Yorkshireman was almost 36 and regarded as something of a journeyman. Just watching him in training was entertainment personified. On 25 August 1984 the two lined up alongside each other at Carlisle in Albion's opening game of the season. To cap a memorable day Steve scored in a 3–0 win, confirming what many of the bookies already knew – Chris Cattlin's new-look side would be among the favourites for promotion.

Steve scored again in Brighton's next away game, a 4–2 victory at Cardiff, before landing another from long range against promotion rivals Birmingham City at the Goldstone to make it six wins from the opening nine games. 'When I scored I normally scored good goals. They were never tap-ins because I was usually having to cut inside from a wide position. That one against Birmingham I remember because it bobbled just as I was about to hit it. It was one that could've gone a mile wide or flown straight in. Fortunately it flew right over their goalkeeper and into the net. Danny [Wilson] ran up to me straight away and said "Steve, you've got to take a bow after that!" I'm not sure if I scored a better one ever.'

However, Steve had to wait seven months for his fourth goal of the season, by which time Albion had slipped to the fringes of the promotion race. That Birmingham game signalled a dry run of results spanning seven League

matches, which produced no wins and just two goals. It would prove to be the difference between Brighton going up and staying down. Come the last match of the season against Sheffield United, Albion needed to win and hope that results elsewhere went in their favour. The only goal of the game came when a visiting defender diverted one of Steve's crosses into his own net. Wins for Manchester City, Portsmouth and Blackburn Rovers meant the Seagulls finished a disappointing sixth, yet spirits remained relatively buoyant among the players.

'We felt we weren't too far away from doing something. The season after that was when we really thought we could make a push. We just needed to add to that squad, get another couple of players in. That's when we bought Justin Fashanu, but he had a bad knee and it didn't really take off for him. Justin had said he was fit, but he clearly wasn't. I think Chris [Cattlin] felt pretty let down by that.'

If Fashanu was a flop, quite the opposite was true of Dean Saunders, another centre-forward brought in during the summer of 1985 on a free transfer from his home-town club of Swansea City. Although still only a raw version of the player that would go on to win silverware from Liverpool to Galatasaray, it was clear by Christmas that the 21-year-old rookie was something special. Dean and Steve quickly became close friends. 'They were great mates,' recalls Danny Wilson. 'If you ever wanted to know where the two of them were, it was a case of if you find one then you'll find the other. They used to play for this little snooker trophy every week, and it would get pretty competitive between the two of them, I can tell you.'

Brighton needed both Dean and Steve during the 1985–86 season. The previous campaign had seen the defence at its tightest, conceding just 34 goals in 42 games. Now it began to spring more than just the occasional leak. Supporters joked that Albion would have to score at least three because they were bound to concede two, but that did not prevent Cattlin's side from being in the shake-up for promotion as February made way for March.

An added bonus was the club's form in the FA Cup. Away wins over Newcastle United of the old First Division and Hull City set up a fifth-round tie at Peterborough United of the Fourth Division. The tie was played in sub-zero conditions on a frozen pitch covered by an inch or two of snow, cancelling out any technical advantage Brighton may have had over their opponents from two Leagues below. A giant killing seemed in the making when United went 1–0 and then 2–1 up during the final 20 minutes after Dean Saunders had equalised. With the clock running down, Steve, probably the one player to have made light of the conditions, slalomed his way in from the right and crossed low for Steve Jacobs to equalise. In the replay at the Goldstone Saunders scored the only goal of the game, having been set up by another one of Steve's crosses.

'That game at Peterborough will always stand out in my mind because there's no way it would've taken place today, the conditions were just too tricky,' says Steve. 'One of their goals was this tremendous fluke. A guy let fly along the ground, but the ball hit a lump of snow and took off into the roof of the net over Perry [Digweed], who just didn't have a chance. I think he had been making little piles of snow on which to take his goal-kicks and it came off one of those. But we fought back, won the replay and were through to the quarter-finals against Southampton.'

There was only one problem with that. Bad weather meant Southampton had not played for a fortnight and were fighting fit for the challenge ahead at the Goldstone. Albion, on the other hand, had been pushed hard by Peterborough in the replay five days earlier. 'We needed to be fresh for Southampton, but we were knackered and didn't recover in time,' says Terry Connor. 'They got an early goal and we couldn't come back. By the time we got going they'd got another and the game was over, and we were out of the Cup. It was a flat way of ending what had, up until then, been a memorable little run.'

Although Brighton won their following three League games, a complete loss of form from the end of March only compounded the gloom brought on by the Southampton defeat. A 2–0 reverse at Hull City on 2 May 1986 consigned managerless Albion to mid-table obscurity, Cattlin having paid the price for the crash days earlier with his job. 'Next season has to be our year' he had written in his final programme notes for the home match against Sunderland on 26 April. 'I badly want to be a First Division manager with First Division players here at Brighton.' He would never write another set of programme notes for any club at any level.

In 1982 Steve Foster had the consolation of a World Cup in Spain to look forward to following Albion's dismal end to the season. Four years later it would be Steve's turn to find comfort in the biggest sporting extravaganza on the planet. Northern Ireland had managed to qualify for Mexico '86, despite being drawn in an extremely tough qualification group. Needing at least a win and a draw from their last two games, they managed to pull off a surprise 1–0 win in Romania before holding England 0–0 at Wembley thanks, largely to an inspired performance from goalkeeper Pat Jennings. Having wrapped up a disappointing year at club level in the dilapidated surroundings of Boothferry Park, Steve – by now an established

member of manager Billy Bingham's side – packed his bags and prepared to face the altogether different proposition of a World Cup Finals group featuring Spain and mighty Brazil.

'It was a good time to be part of the Northern Ireland set-up. A couple of years ago we went God knows how long without winning a match, but it was different back then. We played big games against the likes of France, England and Romania and never lost, and were the last team to win the old Home International Championships. Billy Bingham had been a right winger and obviously appreciated what I could do, which was a source of great strength to me. He'd been part of the team that had played in the World Cup in Sweden in 1958, a lovely man who was very good at getting the best out of his players and encouraged me no end, something I'll always be grateful to him for.

'The big thing about playing in Mexico was going to be the altitude, so two weeks beforehand we went to Albuquerque in New Mexico because it was 7,000 feet above sea level. I'll always remember the first day we went out and Billy [Bingham] says "We'll just take a walk up the mountain here." So we walked up, walked down, got back in the coach and I'm thinking "This is quite nice. This isn't hard work." The next day he put a couple of bollards about 200 yards apart and had us doing three-quarter paced runs between the two of them. My nose was bleeding all over the place! After about a week or 10 days your blood gets used to it, but if we'd gone out there directly to play we would have collapsed.'

Northern Ireland's opening match of the tournament was in Guadalajara against Algeria, something of an unknown quantity on the international scene. After six minutes Steve was brought down on the edge of the opposition's penalty area, and Norman Whiteside stepped up to drill home the resulting free-kick. It was after this that things began to get nasty. 'The Algerians really weren't nice people. They would spit on you, stamp on you, anything to put you off your game – and I mean anything. It was the first time I'd come across that kind of thing. We went 1–0 up, but they equalised and that's the way it finished. We really should've won that game, but we got distracted, which is exactly what they wanted.'

Next up was Spain, one of the World Cup's perennial underachievers. Northern Ireland started badly, going 2–0 down within 20 minutes. Around the half-an-hour mark Sammy McIlroy played what is known in the game as a 'hospital pass' in Steve's direction. The lurking Emilio Butragueno, scorer of Spain's opener and renowned as one of the hardest players in Europe, sensed blood. 'They used to call him "The Vulture". He shot in from nowhere. If I didn't make an effort to get

the ball he was straight through on goal. So I stretched my leg to try and flick it away and he goes over the top of me. And that was it. I managed to limp on until half-time but missed the second half. My ankle was still up ahead of the following game, so that was my tournament over. I would love to be sitting here now telling you I played against Brazil. Instead, I can only tell you I sat and watched it.'

Northern Ireland lost 3–0 to the Brazilians and exited the competition having picked up just one point from three games. But for Steve it had been an experience to savour, even allowing for Butragueno's stud marks. 'The strange thing was that because of the way the group system was set up, we could've gone through as one of the best third-placed teams had we beaten Algeria. That was a bit of a sickener, as we would have played Mexico in the Aztec Stadium in front of 100,000 people. That would've been nice.'

Instead, the Irishman's next match was played out before a slightly smaller crowd of 13,723 for the visit of Portsmouth to the Goldstone on 23 August 1986. For Steve it was the mother of all reality checks. After seven weeks abroad he returned to discover the bubble of optimism from 12 months previously had well and truly burst. Alan Mullery's appointment as manager in place of Cattlin had been a good public relations move, but no amount of gloss could hide the fact that cuts were the order of the day. Players on relatively high salaries were being axed, Graham Moseley among them. Steve had been one of the lower paid members of the squad, something that probably saved his bacon. That, plus a glorious goal he had scored against Sunderland in the final home game the previous season.

'Alan was a very charismatic man, with his cigar and glasses. I came back from the World Cup. My contract was nearly up; I wasn't on as much as most of the other guys and I was doing the usual "All these other clubs are showing interest in me" stories. He said "Son, I want you to sign for me. I can't offer you much, but I really want you." It turned out he had been at the Sunderland game when I'd played a one-two with Dean Saunders and bent a shot into the top corner from outside the box. He'd had his hat pulled down and coat done up. He didn't want anyone to recognise him because he knew he was about to take over from Cattlin. He said "Son, when you scored that goal it was better than sex!" You couldn't help but warm to the guy, so I signed for him for three years. He charmed me. A good manager can do that. They can make you feel special in the simplest of ways.'

Despite a couple of good early home wins against Birmingham City and West Bromwich Albion, Brighton struggled throughout the 1986–87 season from the word go, as indeed did Steve. His left knee

had started to play up, sometimes becoming sore less than 30 minutes into a game. Unbeknown to him he was suffering from bursitis. Remember that word – we are going to come back to it.

For the time being Steve played through the pain barrier. At least he did until 7 March 1987, when a late tackle by a Derby County defender left him writhing on the Goldstone turf in agony. 'I was stretching for a ball around the centre circle and this guy went right over the top of me on purpose with both feet. Then he looks at me and goes "Penney, you won't be playing anymore today." I used to take the fact that I was targeted as a compliment but sometimes it went too far, and that was way too far. It was the worse tackle I ever got. Luckily he only broke the smaller bone in my foot, the non-weight baring bone rather than the main one, but my ankle ligaments had gone.'

He is not 100 percent certain – maybe 99.5 – but to this day Steve is convinced the man who caught him was none other than Steve McLaren, future boss of England.

Bad tackle though it was, it would be a year and two days before Steve appeared again in Albion's first team. The leg bone mended relatively quickly but the left knee had continued giving him grief. In the winger's absence Mullery had been replaced as manager by Barry Lloyd, who had been unable to prevent the club suffering the ignominy of a return to the old Third Division. Lloyd and Steve would suffer a fragmented relationship over the coming three years but were, for that moment in time, united in one common cause – making sure Brighton gained promotion back to Division Two at the first time of asking.

From October 1987 to March 1988 the Seagulls had been on the fringe of the promotion race, a tendency to draw too many games meaning they looked on course for a Play-off spot rather than one of the two automatic places. With the exception of Steve Gatting and Chris Hutchings (plus the either injured or out-of-favour Perry Digweed) the side now bore no resemblance to Steve's early days at the club. However, with talented performers on board such as goalkeeper John Keeley, defenders Keith Dublin and Doug Rougvie, midfielders Alan Curbishley and Dean Wilkins plus star centre-forward Garry Nelson, the club had exceeded many people's lowly expectations having finished bottom by a distance the previous season. Lloyd knew that if he could get Steve fit and anything like back to his former best, then Albion would have an outstanding chance of bagging promotion through the Play-offs (Sunderland and Notts County seemingly having wrapped up first and second place respectively).

Steve's first three games back in the fold were tentative to say the least. Short of match practice, he looked desperately off the pace. But Lloyd stuck with him. On 26 March he scored an absolute belter from outside the box in a 1–1 draw at Brentford. The following week he was on target again as Gillingham were sent packing 2–0 at the Goldstone. They say goals breed confidence and here was the living proof. Steve was flying once again, creating opportunities galore as Albion won six straight games during April to climb to third place.

'At that time playing for Barry was great. The two of us were getting on even though I always felt there was something not quite right between us. To be honest he had to play me because I strengthened the team and made a difference. I scored three or four during the run-in when we went unbeaten but made quite a few others for the likes of Dean [Wilkins] and Garry. I felt fine and the injuries all seemed to be behind me.'

In their penultimate game Brighton drew at Chester City having blown a 2–0 lead, yet ended up going second as the likes of Notts County, Walsall and Northampton continued dropping points. Barring a mathematical act of God, a win over Bristol Rovers at the Goldstone on 7 May would be enough to secure Second Division football the following season. On a warm day and in front of a packed house goals either side of half-time from Kevin Bremner and Nelson did the trick, Albion finishing as runners-up to Sunderland having come from nowhere over the final weeks. After five years at the club, Steve at last had an achievement to celebrate.

'When I came back from injuries I did the business for him [Lloyd] that season,' Steve says before pausing, and I immediately sense a 'but' coming. 'But when we started the following season I don't think some of the players were up to the standard we needed. I don't care what anybody says, they weren't the same quality. I'd been used to playing with guys like Jimmy Case, Steve Foster, Terry Connor, Danny Wilson. Now we were back up to the same level and the players he [Lloyd] brought in weren't as good. You can bring in the odd guy from non-League football – I was from non-League after all – but not five or six of them. Maybe that's what Barry was being told to do from upstairs, I don't know. It's just how I saw it. We suffered because we didn't have enough ability.'

Point taken. Albion lost eight of their opening nine League games during the 1988–89 season. Somehow they escaped relegation, but it was a year of few highlights, back-to-back wins over Crystal Palace (3–1) and Birmingham (4–0) between Christmas and New Year being the exception to the rule. Steve would be the first to admit that his form was patchy, though that didn't prevent Palace manager Steve Coppell from trying to buy him as 1988 made way for 1989.

The two clubs even got as far as talking figures. Albion valued him at £175,000, their rivals from up the A23 holding out for £50,000 less. If anything, his performance in the aforementioned 3–1 win only made Coppell even more determined to get his man.

And then the knee went and intervened big time.

'It had all started that season after I came back from the World Cup in Mexico. Being right footed, when I cross a ball I put all my weight on my left knee, and it was getting so painful. I had a simple problem involving the sack of fluid under the kneecap which is called the bursa. Bursitis is the swelling of this. Unfortunately it was ages, and I mean years, before it was properly diagnosed.'

To cut a long story short – and it really is a very long story – this is what happened. At the tail end of the 1986–87 season, and having recovered from the broken bone possibly suffered at the hands of Mr Steve McLaren, future England supremo, Steve went to see a surgeon who had a long-standing association with the Albion. The surgeon gave him several cortisone injections, but still the problem continued so a decision was taken to operate. Because Steve's bursitis only flared up after physical exercise, it was difficult to tell once his knee had been opened up what the problem was. Nevertheless, the surgeon decided to shave away bits of the patellar tendon which runs over the kneecap, thinking that might help solve things.

After two months in plaster, Steve set out on his long road to rehabilitation, the one that took him to the sharp end of the 1987–88 promotion season, but still the problem persisted. By January 1989 he could stand it no more. 'After half an hour playing it would start to flare up again. I'm thinking "What's going on here?" So I go back to the surgeon and he goes in and cuts more of the patellar tendon away. By now it's starting to get really serious, so I said to the club "Look, I know there's a tie-up with this guy, but I really need to see someone who knows what they're doing." So the club arranged for me to go up to Harley Street and see this Egyptian called Basil Helal, who had just operated on Tessa Sanderson's Achilles tendon. I took a weight up with me and sat there for an hour working my knee because I wanted to get it as sore as I could.

'So your man Helal opens me up and there's the bursitis showing up straight away. He whips it out, stitches me up, I get back on the training pitch, it's going well, then my whole knee suddenly feels like it's collapsing because the surgeon in Brighton had taken away so much of the patellar tendon. So I go back to Basil Helal. He takes out part of my hamstring, drills holes in my kneecap and puts my hamstring into my kneecap to replace my patella tendon. And to this day I've never had a problem since. All I needed was for

someone to diagnose right at the beginning that I was suffering from bursitis.'

All of which brings us round to 1991, by which time Steve and Barry Lloyd's precarious relationship had pretty much gone up in smoke. Lloyd has his regrets about how it all turned out, but maintains there were times when Steve seemed to put country above club. 'We did fall out once or twice because he was desperate to play for [Northern] Ireland,' says the former Albion boss. 'He'd play for them, then come back injured. That didn't please me. But it was a crying shame. He just wanted to play but was so plagued with injuries it was beyond belief. Coming in every day and not being able to train must have been soul destroying for him. And the doctors couldn't always seem to agree. You'd have one person saying he was fit, and another one saying he wasn't. In hindsight we'd have been better off shipping him out to America where they specialise in sports injuries. They're light years ahead of us. When Michael Owen injured himself in the [2006] World Cup, he was on a plane out there the next day.'

Steve remembers only too well reaching what for him was the point of no return with Lloyd. 'There was one time when Northern Ireland had a big international game on the Wednesday. The night before Billy Bingham pulled me in and asked how it was going at

Brighton. I said "Well I'm fit, but the team isn't doing so well." He then asked how I got on with Barry Lloyd. He [Lloyd] had brought me off 15 minutes from the end of our game on the Saturday, and it turned out afterwards had called Billy and said "If I was you I wouldn't play Steve Penney in the international." Billy had asked why not, and Barry replied "He didn't try an inch for me today." I might not have had my best game, but I'd never stopped running or trying. Billy says to him "Steve will be playing on Wednesday night because he's played 15 games for me and that's not his character." Once I heard about that, that was me and him [Lloyd] finished. Billy actually said to me afterwards "Steve, you need to get away from there." That was hard to take.'

Despite the Billy Bingham incident, Steve insists he never wanted to leave the club and was even prepared to continue playing under Lloyd when his contract came up for renewal in 1991. 'I just wanted to get playing again. I went to see Barry and said "I appreciate what this club has done for me, but I cost nothing. Just give me a contract for a year or two on the same wages and I'll prove to you I'm fit." He clearly thought I wasn't fit, so I said "Give me a free contract then. Let me go. I'll get myself another club." And he said "Alright, on you go, you'll not get a club." I didn't realise that being out of the game for two years is a long time. People forget about footballers after six

months, let alone two years. I remember thinking "Oh shit, I don't really want to leave Brighton, and now I have to."

'I have employees now and you don't like to think that someone is pulling the wool over your eyes and slacking. I appreciate the amount of pressure that's on a manager, so I can see it from Barry's point of view. It's understandable that he may have thought "He doesn't want to be part of this", but you don't go through what I went through for the fun of it, being in plaster for months watching your muscles disappear. I couldn't even bare to watch a match because it was too painful emotionally. If that's the case, he got my character wrong. The club had been good to me, looked after me and done everything they could, but on the other hand I'd done everything I could.'

For Steve, any personal upset at having to leave Brighton was offset by the fact that clubs did seem interested in signing him, providing he proved his fitness. It came down to a straight fight between Heart of Midlothian and Charlton Athletic for his signature, the latter managed by his former Albion teammate Alan Curbishley. Having already proved himself in Scotland over the course of a couple of trial games and with a contract on the table, he chose Hearts. Initially things went well in Edinburgh. Manager Joe Jordan had promised Steve a further year providing he played 15 first-team games during the 1991–92 season.

Pencilled in for a starting place, he suffered a minor groin strain and missed the start of the campaign. Hearts promptly went on a terrific run without him and led the Scottish Premier Division until February. Steve got to 14 appearances, but 'the tea lady had more chance of playing a 15th game than me'. He spent the rest of the season in the reserve team and then signed for Burnley on a free transfer in August 1992.

'I don't know how much you know about Burnley, but apparently it's the best supported club in the country when compared to the population of the town. To be honest there was very little going on up there compared to Brighton to keep people entertained, but it was still a big, big club with fanatical support. I went down for a week's trial, did well, signed a two-year contract and scored the winner in my opening game against Swansea. I got three or four more before Christmas when suddenly, out of the blue, my bloody Achilles started hurting. I'd never had Achilles problems in my life. I had to have a hot bath every morning because without it I could barely get up and down the stairs.'

Cue another operation, a successful one at that. Then his other Achilles went. This time the operation was unsuccessful. Burnley wanted him to have another one, but Steve didn't have the heart anymore. Enough was enough. His wife Valerie, a qualified optician, knew that the

Specsavers chain was looking for franchisees in Northern Ireland. It was time to go home. 'I hate to think what things would have been like if I'd been the sole breadwinner. Then we would have been in trouble, but my wife had a good job and good money coming in. I feel sorry for any professional sportsman that has to retire, but it was hard back then because the insurance wasn't so good or the wages. So that was the one positive thing – I knew we wouldn't struggle. And the business has gone from strength to strength because it's a good concept run by good staff.'

In one of those poetic coincidences that sport seems to specialise in, Steve's last-but-one game as a professional footballer came at the Goldstone when Burnley travelled south to face the Albion in English football's third tier. Named as a substitute, he took to the field for the final 20 minutes to a rousing and heartfelt reception from the home fans. 'I'll always remember that as long as I live. It was fantastic. Afterwards Jimmy [Mullen, Burnley's manager] said "Steve, you must have been a good player". I'm not a sentimental type of guy, but that did touch me."

As indeed did the sight of the Goldstone Ground being demolished in 1997 during one of Steve's return visits to Sussex. 'I really found that quite difficult. That's where my career started properly. On the one hand it was good to be back in

Steve Penney outside his home in Ballymena, 2007.

Brighton and on the other it hurt seeing something like that. You remember the warmth of the fans and the memories, things like this guy coming over on the first morning I was there to ask how I was settling in – and it was Ron Greenwood, the old England manager, who was a director then, asking me how I was! I still watch for their results first. I always will do.'

It seems almost pointless asking a man with such an injury-blighted career whether he has any regrets. Steve, it emerges, has two, neither of which are really to do with scalpels, swabs or operating tables. Number one: 'I wish I'd stayed 10 or 11 years [at Brighton] and had a testimonial than what I ended up doing. If you're not going to move clubs every two or three years that's the sensible thing to do. But I also wanted to play for somebody who really wanted me to stay and play for them.' And number two: 'I was very critical of myself. Some players only see the good things they do, but I was always worried about what I could've done better, the one cross I didn't get in rather than the eight or nine I did. That's not always a good way to be. I wish I'd had the confidence of Jack Nicklaus. There's a story about how he returned to play at a golf tournament where he'd once played a bad shot, and somebody asked him "What about that shot Jack?" And he said "I never hit a bad shot." He'd just blanked it out. As far as he was concerned it hadn't happened.'

And there lies a lesson to all of us who remember Steve Penney at his very best. Blank out the injuries. Think only of his flying runs down the right and the terrified look on Alan Kennedy's face that Sunday afternoon in January 1984. Priceless, just priceless.

Chapter Nine
Wardy

A story for you. Towards the end of December 2006 Peter Ward went into the University Community Hospital near his home in Tampa Bay to undergo surgery for a new right knee. The old one, by his own admission, was shot to pieces and had been since the closing chapters of his playing days back in the 1980s. It would be replaced by a new titanium knee which, all being well, would enable him to walk for the first time in years without a limp.

A week before the operation the amateur football team Peter has played for in Florida since his professional career ended had a fixture. The dodgy knee meant he had yet to make an appearance for the St Pete Kickers all season, but pressure was growing among friends and teammates for him to put in one final showing. With 30 minutes remaining, and the Kickers 1–0 down, Peter stepped off the substitutes' bench one last time to do what he has always done best – score goals. He bagged two, both with his left foot. One curled into the top-right corner, the other was dispatched with typical ruthlessness from level with the penalty spot. The Kickers ended up winning 2–1. Afterwards, a party was thrown in his honour, during which, you will not be surprised to hear, many beers were consumed.

That is what happens to people who, in the words of Ward's former Albion strike-partner Malcolm Poskett, are 'a complete one-off'.

A little over two months later and the knee 'is coming along very nicely' according to Peter. He has received get well cards and phone calls from Brighton fans all around the world – Malaysia, Hawaii, England, you name it. Some he knows (Albion supporters have been tracking Peter down to this corner of Florida for years), while others are complete strangers just concerned about his well-being. 'It's very flattering, almost humbling. They've never forgotten me. I was in hospital for four days and they kept coming. I had quite a few e-cards as well, you know those get well cards you can send on the internet. So it's nice to be remembered and it's nice to be able to walk properly again. Even when I was playing towards the end I was limping and walking funny. I was left-footed really because I was compensating so much for my right. Not being big-headed, but I was as good with my left so I didn't really suffer. It [the knee] is at 90 degrees now. Whether I'll get any more than that I don't know, but it

'A complete one-off' – Peter Ward in action.

feels okay. Well, as okay as having a piece of titanium in your body can.'

If anybody in my dream team can afford to be big-headed about his achievements in an Albion shirt, it is Peter Ward. That he is

not makes you warm to him even more. For five years spanning 1975 to 1980 it was Roy of the Rovers stuff for the lad from the Staffordshire town of Lichfield, as highlighted in the introduction to this book. Many would argue he is just as popular now as he was then, a touch of the old 'rose-tinted spectacles', plus the fact that no centre-forward since has managed to steal his crown. Some have come close – Garry Nelson and Bobby Zamora spring to mind – but 'Wardy' remains special, the golden boy of what proved to be a golden time for the club.

Like so many others who rose to prominence in the pre-academy days of British football, Peter David Ward cut his teeth not in a youth team but in the relatively hard surroundings of non-League soccer. He had left school a week before his 15th birthday and got a job as an apprentice engine fitter with Rolls-Royce in Derby, then, as it remains today, one of the city's largest employers. He combined his work with playing for the wonderfully-named Borrowash Victoria in the Derby Combination League before joining Burton Albion, still one of the superpowers of non-League football in the Midlands. However, although there was no doubting his ability, Peter, much like Brian Horton, was small for his age – at least too small to be deemed a professional footballer in the making.

'I had always played football, right the way through school and what have you. When I was coming up to leave I remember the careers advisor asking me what I wanted to do with my life and me saying "I want to be a footballer." He said "You've got no chance Ward. You're too small." A few

years later he sent me a letter asking if I would present trophies at an awards day ceremony. I told him to **** off! No, of course I didn't. I went. But, yes, I was small.

'Looking back I can't really believe how young I was when I went out to work, earning three pounds a week, which seemed a fortune in those days. I was 15 when I played for Borrowash, then moved on to Burton Albion where I wasn't getting any money to start with. They only signed me on a semi-professional contract after we won 4–1 at Tamworth one night and I scored a hat-trick. I was there one season before I went to Brighton for four and a half thousand pounds. I didn't do bad for that, did I?'

Peter signed in May 1975, just two months shy of his 20th birthday. He knew nothing about Brighton and nothing about any of the players in the squad at the time. The only reason he ended up in Sussex was Ken Gutteridge, a former manager at Burton Albion brought to the Goldstone in a coaching capacity by Albion boss Peter Taylor, a man about as familiar with the Midlands football scene as most of us are with our living rooms. The club installed Peter in digs in Rottingdean overlooking the sea, along with the former Spurs midfielder Phil Beal and Scottish centre-forward Neil Martin. It was, he recalls, 'the kind of place that makes you go "Jesus Christ!" It was just magnificent with an incredible view. I felt like some kind of god up there.'

'He shot, he scored, it must be Peter Ward'.

Over the next 10 months Peter played reserve-team football and scored several goals – he can't remember how many, only that there were a few. In March 1976 Peter Taylor reckoned he was ready for the first XI. As debuts go, it would take some beating. 'The night before I was coming down with a cold. I remember Glen Wilson [Albion's kit man] coming in with some whisky and saying "Here, have a drop of this." The following morning I went out for a walk, got back to the hotel for lunch and after that Peter [Taylor] just came right out with it. "Fred [Binney], you're not playing. Peter, you're playing." Fred was top scorer so I couldn't believe it. I was dead nervous and ended up having another shot of whisky before the game.'

Fifty seconds into that Third Division match against Hereford United at Edgar Street, Peter scored. 'It was a s**t goal to be honest. I turned the defender well and hit more of a cross shot. Sammy [Morgan] went in putting the 'keeper off and it crept into the corner. He even said he'd touched it so I didn't even know if it was mine. The unbelievable thing was that this all happened on *Match of the Day*. They only had one or two games on every show then but for some reason had decided to cover this one. We stopped the coach somewhere that night on the way back to have a drink and watch the game and it was proved it was my goal. That was it. I'd started. The last eight games I got something like six goals.'

Just two months after the last kick of the 1975–76 season, Wardy was brought crashing down to earth again following Peter Taylor's resignation. His immediate reaction was similar to that of Nobby Horton, a recent arrival from Port Vale who also now feared for his future under a new manager. 'I thought "S**t." I'd liked Pete. A couple of weeks after the season ended he called me into his office and gave me a nice pay rise and a bonus. Coming from Derby, not having any money or anything, all of a sudden someone had given me a few grand and a good pay packet. Then he left and Alan came in.'

Alan Mullery knew bits and pieces about some of the players he was inheriting from Peter Taylor at Brighton. Peter Ward was, however, a blank canvas. 'I hadn't heard of him at all,' says Mullery. 'He was just this skinny little kid who could do fantastic things with a football. I'll never forget the first team versus the reserves game we had on one of my first days there. Peter played for the reserves and scored three times in the first half. I swapped him over to the firsts at half-time and he scored three more. He was a bit raw, but he made everything look so simple and easy. The coaching staff told me what he had done towards the end of the season and that was it – I knew we had a striker to get us out of the Third Division.'

'It's funny what you remember,' says Peter. 'I can't remember s**t nowadays. My missus will tell me to go to the store to get three or four things and I'll have to call her when I get there because I can't remember what they are. But I can remember a lot of football stuff, like who played in the 1968 Manchester United European Cup-winning team. I'm not sure whether it was our first training session [under Mullery] but I do remember it, playing for the sort of reserve team, scoring a few goals and then switching teams. Alan must have liked what he saw and we just clicked from then.'

Peter's promotion to the first team under Mullery did not meet with everyone's approval. Fred Binney, popular with the supporters and Albion's leading scorer with 27 goals the previous season, was dropped a few games into the 1976–77 campaign when it became clear that the

two strikers' styles were very similar. From September 1976 Peter's forward partner would be former postman Ian Mellor, nicknamed 'Spider' because of his long legs. Mullery later claimed in his autobiography that Binney had offered him some advice following that first team versus reserves training match, which went along the lines of 'Ward's not strong enough for the Third Division – you should play me.' Nevertheless, Mullery remained convinced he had made the right decision.

Thirty-six League and Cup goals during the 1976–77 promotion-winning season to Division Two endorsed Mullery's stand. It was enough to put Peter at the top of the UK goalscoring charts that year, and no other Albion player has since managed to equal or conquer Wardy's total. Spider, it should be said, proved to be a more than adequate sidekick, weighing in with 15 goals. 'I didn't even take the penalties,' says Peter. 'Brian Horton did. I think I may have had one or two, but Nobby took the rest and we had quite a few. So if I'd had the pens I would've had even more. But you can't be greedy.'

'We joined at more or less the same time, although Wardy was already there when I arrived,' says Brian Horton. 'I didn't know him at all, never heard of him. He was this thin, scrawny little player that needed to learn the game, but his finishing was unbelievable, absolutely unbelievable. We steamrollered sides that year, and he was the man who got most of the goals. And because nobody knew anything about him nobody could work out how to play against him.'

'He was exceptional, there's no other way of putting it,' adds Peter O'Sullivan, who played in all bar three of the League games during the 1976–77 season. 'The thing I always remember about him was he had this long stride that just seemed to take him away from people. One step and he would be gone. Once he got goal-side of a player, that was it really – bang! Nobody ever seemed to be able to catch him, even in training.'

Four weeks into the 1977–78 season Peter's form won him a starting place in England's Under-21 side to play Norway at, irony of ironies, the Goldstone Ground. Like a page from a Hollywood movie script, he scored a hat-trick. 'The third one was the header, the first may have been in the box, and I put it in with my right foot, and the second was with my left foot. So one of each, the perfect hat-trick. On the morning of the game *The Argus* had run a headline saying "He's In", or something to that effect, meaning I'd been chosen to start. I hadn't been in the game five minutes and I'm making my Under-21 debut in front of a big crowd. Unbelievable, fantastic.

'The night before we'd all been to see *The Spy Who Loved Me* and then I go and score a hat-trick. Later on that same season we went to see it again when we played at Mansfield and I got another hat-trick. I should have gone to watch James Bond movies more often!'

Peter's success at club and Under-21 level for his country led to him being named in England's full squad for a World Cup qualifying game away to Luxembourg in October 1977. In the event he failed to win a place even on the bench as manager Ron Greenwood went with Birmingham City's Trevor Francis and Paul Mariner of Ipswich up front. The expected goal avalanche failed to materialise as England scraped through 2–0, one of the strikes coming in injury time. Greenwood's side would miss out on a place in the 1978 World Cup Finals to Italy, goal difference being the deciding factor. Would it have been any different had Peter Ward played against Luxembourg? More than a few Albion supporters certainly thought so.

'Jimmy Greaves said at the time "You've got to play him because he's on fire." I'd just scored two at Sunderland, I was playing well and the goals were going in. And he [Greenwood] never even put me on the bench. We won 2–0 and we needed about nine. You never know if playing me would have made a difference but when someone's in that form…'

Peter's voice trails off. Before I get the chance to change the subject he rather sheepishly makes a confession. 'I roomed with Trevor Brooking in Luxembourg, and I went out after the game with Brian

Greenhoff and a few other lads and got absolutely hammered. I was spewing in the room and everything, so he [Brooking] must have told Ron Greenwood "He's a bloody lunatic" or whatever. Ron didn't pick me for a long time after that.'

Not even finishing third behind Steve Coppell and Glenn Hoddle in a national poll to find the country's most popular footballer could compensate for missing out on promotion to the First Division in 1978. Like Brian Horton, Peter's main concern at being pipped to the post by Southampton and Spurs on the final day of the season ran along the lines of "What if we're not able to do it again?" The club had, after all, enjoyed two years of success and was, by the law of averages, due a poor run. That duly arrived during the opening weeks of the 1978–79 campaign as Albion lost five of their opening 12 League games, Peter retaining his goalscoring touch with six in the opening nine matches, including a brace away at Burnley in the League Cup. That did not prevent him from being dropped for the 13th League fixture of the season in favour of Malcolm Poskett, who scored in a 1–0 away win at Sheffield United with Teddy Maybank as his striking partner. Throughout the rest of the season the three forwards vied with each other for the two starting places. Wardy and Poskett in particular found the chop-and-change nature of Mullery's selections

hard to deal with, both feeling that a settled run in the team would benefit their respective form. In fact, Poskett asked for a transfer on several occasions, as indeed did Peter once the season had ended. By that time, of course, Albion were a Division One club.

The competition for places at the Goldstone did not prevent Poskett from being a huge admirer of Peter's abilities, even if the former found the latter hard to gel with whenever they were paired together in action. 'For around three or four seasons he just had the most amazing purple patch,' says Poskett. 'It was almost pointless involving him in team talks. He just did his own thing regardless of the formation we were playing. He was actually quite a frustrating player to play with because you never knew what he was going to do. With Teddy [Maybank] you knew what to expect, but with Peter anything could happen. But that also meant opposition players didn't have a clue either, which made him the player he was. He wasn't the brightest lad I've even known, but my god he could play!'

From the summer of 1979 until his departure from the club in October 1980, Peter was the subject of almost constant transfer speculation involving other First Division clubs. In November 1979, with Albion struggling at the foot of the table, Alan Mullery arranged a swap deal with Derby County for Gerry Daly (the player, rather than, as the old joke goes, the Irish newspaper). The move only fell through when Daly decided he did not want to come to Sussex. The same month Nottingham Forest, then the European Cup holders, made a bid of £600,000. Albion agreed to do business only for Brian Clough to withdraw the offer while Peter considered his future.

Through it all, Wardy's popularity in Sussex never failed to diminish. Everyone wanted a piece of him, whether it be a simple autograph or a personal appearance to open a new business venture. Cats and dogs the county over came running to the name 'Peter'. Parents even started calling their offspring after the striker. When my old school friend Simon Higgins announced the birth of his baby brother one morning at Warnham Primary School in 1980, it came as no surprise to hear that another Peter had entered the world. That was just the way it was.

So did all the interest – both from supporters and other clubs – ever have an adverse affect on the size of Peter's head? 'No, I don't think so,' he says. 'In fact, if it was today I'd probably have wanted away. That's the way a lot of players think these days. I mean Manchester United came in for me at one stage! Jesus Christ! The team I'd supported as a boy coming in for me! If it was now I'd go "I'm off!" But we were doing okay. We'd got to the top League. That first season [in Division One] we started badly but finished 16th, which was pretty decent. We had a great camaraderie. We always went out together. In fact, every season I was there every team got on well. It was a great place to live. And so on and so on. Why leave when there's so much going for you?'

The camaraderie around the Goldstone certainly had plenty to do with it. With hindsight you almost cringe at some of the things the players got up to. What was borderline acceptable in 1978 would almost certainly be a firing offence in the pasta-eating, one glass of wine with your meal environment of today's Premier League. Try this for example. On Friday 23 November 1979 Peter, together with Graham Moseley and Gerry Ryan, sneaked away from a hotel in Nottingham the night before Albion's crucial League game against Forest. They made for the pubs on the far side of the city where, Peter reckoned, nobody would have a clue who they were. On entering the first hostelry the trio were alarmed to discover the place was full of Brighton supporters. Once the shock had worn off they proceeded to sink four or five pints before heading back to the hotel. The following afternoon it was Peter who set up Ryan to score the only goal of the game as Albion recorded their first-ever away win in the top flight. As for Graham Moseley? Well, he kept a clean sheet and saved a penalty.

Peter's questionable by today's standards 'refuelling habits' ('We went to bed fine – we were athletes!') had little effect on his form as the 70s made way for the 80s and Albion began to get to grips with the First Division. Four days before Christmas he scored a hat-trick in a 3–1 win at Wolverhampton before hitting further goals in 3–0 and 4–1 victories over Crystal Palace and Manchester City respectively during the Christmas period. On 12 January 1980 he was on target twice as the Seagulls won away against Bolton Wanderers in front of the *Match of the Day* cameras. This goal rush once again sparked talk of an England call up. Four more during April (including another two against Wolves, giving him an overall season total of 18) finally convinced Ron Greenwood that Wardy was worth a try. He was selected to travel Down Under for an end of season match celebrating 100 years of football in Australia. It was only a friendly, not that Peter cared. Almost five years to the day after packing in Rolls-Royce to join Brighton, he was going to play for England.

Or was he? Peter was chosen as a substitute in Sydney. England led 2–0 at the break thanks to goals from Paul Mariner and Glenn Hoddle, but Australia pulled one back in the second half and began to look good for an equaliser. Would Greenwood dare blood a debutante in such circumstances? Finally, with nine minutes to go, the board went up for Wardy to replace Arsenal's Alan Sunderland, another international new boy. By the time the substitution took

place less than eight minutes remained. For only the second-time ever, one of Albion's very own was winning a full England cap (Tommy Cook having been the first in 1925). The game finished 2–1. Neither Peter nor Alan Sunderland ever wore their country's shirt in battle again.

'When I got up [off the bench] there was about 22 minutes to go but the board wouldn't go up. I kept on looking, as you would, but the thing just wouldn't go up. I still think it was more than eight minutes but hey – it was a great feeling to be putting on an England shirt. It doesn't happen to many players. Lots of good ones haven't got capped at all.' Does he still have the shirt? 'Course I have – and the blazer. They're going nowhere.'

Peter's forward partner at the Goldstone throughout the lion's share of the 1979–80 season was Ray Clarke, a Londoner who made his name scoring goals for fun while playing in Holland for Ajax. Unbeknown to just about everybody, including most of the Albion squad, Clarke had been struggling for months with severe post-match pains in both hips. They were, in effect, crumbling (Clarke told me in 2005 that he believed his transfer to Newcastle United in July 1980 came about as a result of Alan Mullery discovering the alarming extent of his ailments and that he was not insured). Clarke's replacement was the 22-year-old Michael Robinson, a hard-working bull of a centre-forward who had struggled to live up to expectations at Manchester City, having been transferred to Maine Road from Preston North End in July 1979 for a jaw-dropping £750,000. On paper the little and large pairing of Robinson and Wardy looked a potent one in a team that also now featured the creative talents of Gordon Smith, a new arrival from Glasgow Rangers who favoured playing in the hole between midfield and up front. In other words, goals looked to be on the agenda big time.

Although Robinson and Smith had an immediate effect, scoring 12 between them in the first dozen games of the 1980–81 season, Peter, by comparison, seemed strangely off-key. Come the middle of October he had just two goals to his name, one of those having come against Fourth Division strugglers Tranmere Rovers in the League Cup. This dip in form clearly failed to bother Brian Clough and Peter Taylor, long-term admirers of Peter. That month another offer came in from the City Ground for Albion's talismanic striker. Gary Birtles was on his way from Nottingham Forest to Manchester United and Clough and Taylor wanted Wardy to replace him.

This time there would be no red tape or last-minute hitches. Peter was sold for £450,000 just days after drawing a blank for the 12th time so far that season against, of all teams, Nottingham Forest. United's purchase of Birtles meant Andy Ritchie was in turn surplus to requirements at Old

Trafford, so the cash Albion received for Peter immediately went towards bringing him to Sussex. After 92 goals and 207 appearances spanning over five glorious years, Brighton & Hove Albion and Peter Ward appeared to have gone their separate ways for good.

'I was at a friend's house the evening it was announced that I was going to go. It came on the news – "Brighton have agreed a fee with Nottingham Forest for Peter Ward." That was the first I heard of it. I went "What?" I didn't want to go. I mean me and Mullers had the odd fight or two but that's going to happen after so many years. I remember [Terry] Venables calling me at the hotel while I was talking to Clough and Taylor saying "Whatever they give you, I'll give you more to go to QPR". I should've gone!'

Peter was not the first (and he certainly was not the last) player to experience a difficult relationship with Brian Clough. Wardy describes it as having been 'hot and cold', which at least betters the 'cold and cold' union some other less fortunates had with him. Clough expected his players to adhere to an almost 'seen and not heard' Victorian father and son style template. Those who failed to fit the mould were quickly left in no doubt as to what Cloughie thought of them. As someone who still prefers to speak his mind rather than suffer in silence, Peter soon became a victim of this school-mastery regime.

'One time we were driving back from Birmingham City on the team coach. He [Clough] hated Frank Worthington. We'd lost 2–0 and Frank had got both goals. So we're driving up the motorway and I go to the front of the bus and say to the driver "Albert, I'm getting off at Leicester Forest East services." He says "Okay." So he goes to pull over when we get to Leicester Forest East and Cloughie goes, "Albert, drive on." So he drives on! I'm thinking "What's going on here?" We must have gone another half-a-mile to a mile and he goes, "Albert, pull over." We pull over and he goes "Get out" to me. And as I step out into the pissing rain I hear him say "With a little bit of luck the **** might get run over!"'

On other occasions the knock-downs were a little more sugar-coated. 'We played at Sunderland once and won 3–2. I, we, had done well. Cloughie lived in Derby the same as me. We were all coming out of the showers and Cloughie goes "I need a lift to Derby. Who's going to take me?" Peter Taylor says "There's only Wardy" and he goes "Oh God, he'll drop me in the Trent!" So he got a lift with someone else. Another time I did actually give him a lift after training. I pulled up outside his house, stopped and he didn't do anything. He didn't move or get out. I said after a while "This is it, isn't it?" And he goes "Up the driveway." So I had to take him all the way up the driveway to the front door. Bizarre!'

For 18 months Peter struggled both with his manager's idiosyncrasies and to establish himself as a regular in the Forest side. There were good days, and there were bad days. 'Sometimes he would say "That's fantastic, you had a great game." Once against Valencia he chose me as Man of the Match. But at other times, well you just struggled to work out what was going on. I remember playing Paris St Germain and I had a horrible game. Afterwards he goes "That's the last time you're playing for me." Next game I was playing again. You never really knew what to expect.

'To be honest with you I had a great time at Forest. I got on well with the lads and had a laugh. It just came at a time when Cloughie had his heart murmur and that. He was going off to Spain every other week and Peter Taylor was picking the team. It got to the point where I'd start a game one week, then be on the bench the next when Clough came back. It was quite strange. But you can't argue with their record, can you? Just look what they achieved. Taylor was great, he really was, and funny with it. Cloughie would get you all panicky and then Taylor would come in and relax you ready to play. It really was a double act.'

In March 1982 Peter agreed to go on loan to the north west. Nope, not Liverpool but Seattle, or Seattle Sounders to be correct. He had been to the US before on tour with Brighton and warmed to the place. Over the next few months North America – or at least its soccer playing community – would in turn warm to him. Seattle finished as runners-up in what was known as the Soccer Bowl, with Peter winning the North American Soccer League's Player of the Year award. He wanted to stay stateside but complications arose over an acceptable fee, and he ended up returning to the Midlands that September. Peter came on as a substitute in Forest's 4–1 defeat at Spurs and played in the next couple of games, but it was clear Clough still had issues with his centre-forward. And vice-versa.

Within weeks Peter was farmed out on loan again, this time to somewhere slightly closer to home. By now Mike Bailey had taken over from Alan Mullery as manager at the Goldstone. With Albion struggling for goals up front in the old First Division and conceding like mad at the back, Bailey asked Clough whether Peter was available to buy. He received neither a 'yes' or 'no' answer but was told something temporary could be arranged. And so on 23 October 1982, Wardy (sporting a fine moustache) made his second debut for Brighton at home against top-of-the-table West Ham United. The attendance, unsurprisingly, was almost 7,000 up on the previous best for the season. He failed to score but played well as the Hammers were taken to the cleaners, goals by Steve Gatting, Michael Robinson and Gordon Smith giving Albion a win far more comfortable

than the 3–1 scoreline suggests. The king was back.

Three days later Brighton entertained Spurs at home in the first leg of a League Cup tie. With Wardy given the all-clear to play, the attendance rose yet again as some of the 'stay aways' from recent months returned to watch the golden boy in action. Albion lost 1–0 and again Peter failed to find the net. Four days on another blank was drawn against Liverpool. Had he lost his touch? Bailey did not think so and stuck with Peter for the home game against Manchester United on 6 November. It would prove to be a wise decision.

In the closing stages of a keenly fought and what had up until then been a scoreless match, Gerry Ryan hit a pass in the direction of Michael Robinson standing inside United's penalty area. 'Robbo' rose to meet the ball, which then fell kindly for Peter standing on the right-hand side of the goal around 15 yards out. He brought it under control with his chest, allowed it to drop and then propelled a shot past goalkeeper Gary Bailey's extended right arm into the top corner of the net. It proved to be the winner and remains to this day Peter's favourite goal of his entire career.

'It came against the team I have adored since I was about three years old. When I was a kid my bedroom walls were plastered with pictures of Law, Best and Charlton. I had a red ceiling with a white MU on it, which everyone in the street could see. Every time I played against United in my career I always got the match programme signed by their players. So yeah, I loved that goal. It was brilliant. I can still see Robbo going up for it – I think he may even have been fouled – and it coming my way, then chesting it down and volleying it right in the corner. I remember after that holding the ball up in one of the corners wasting time and Steve Coppell came in and absolutely hammered me. Once when I was back over in Brighton and he [Steve Coppell] was manager I went into his office to see him. He told me I was in most of his after-dinner speeches because he used to say "I got five yellow cards and the only one I ever deserved was when I kicked Peter Ward." He's done brilliantly as a manager, one of the finest in the country without a doubt.'

You would expect any victory against Manchester United to instil confidence in a team, sending it on to bigger and better things. Yet somehow Albion contrived to lose six of their next eight League games to slip into the relegation places at the foot of Division One. Peter had to wait until New Year's Day 1983 for the second goal of his loan spell, although in Wardy's defence the whole side was by that time playing poorly with scoring chances few and far between. On 12 January he grabbed another in an FA Cup third-round replay at Newcastle United, the game in which referee Trelford Mills

controversially disallowed two late United efforts. It proved to be the winner. Granted a regular starting place in Albion's XI, something denied him at the City Ground, his swagger was beginning to return.

Injury forced Peter to miss three games spanning the end of January and early February. He returned for what proved to be the shock of the season as Albion became the first club since 1974 to defeat Liverpool at Anfield in a Cup match, winning 2–1 in the FA Cup fifth round. Desperate to bolster the squad for the remainder of what was rapidly becoming a double-edged sword of a season – an increasingly desperate relegation struggle crossed with a surprise Cup run – Brighton asked Forest if they could extend Peter's loan period or even buy him. The reply was negative on both counts. On the evening of Saturday 26 February, after Albion's home game against Stoke City, Wardy flew home to the Midlands from Gatwick to face an uncertain future. All he knew was (a) he wanted to quit Forest for good and (b) he fancied a permanent move back to Brighton.

It was now that the relationship between Peter and Clough plunged to new depths. On returning to Nottingham the centre-forward told the manager that he would rather remain in Sussex playing an integral role in an FA Cup run than be a bit-part cast off around the City Ground. 'But he wasn't having any of it,' says Peter. 'This was before Forest had been to any FA Cup Finals. He said to me

"Son, I've never been to an FA Cup Final. Neither are you." Those were his exact words. That's when I said "**** off then, I'm leaving" and went back to the States. It was like he was doing it purely out of spite, the pillock.'

To add insult to injury Clough had no intention of playing Peter in Forest's first team. Instead, he was loaned almost immediately back to Seattle. On 21 May 1983 Wardy sat down in front of a television in Washington State to watch Albion take on Manchester United at Wembley, accompanied by some of the other British players who were at the club. 'Yeah, that was difficult,' he says with more than a hint of regret. 'I actually bet that Brighton would win. Smith should have scored. I'd have scored. I'll write a book one day – *Wardy Would Have Scored*. I'd have put it right in the corner with my left foot to [Gary] Bailey's right, depending maybe on how fast I was running. He stopped and I think he s**t his pants to be honest. But God, you can't blame him for that in the last minute of a Cup Final. I feel for him. He scored that day. Everyone forgets that.'

Towards the end of 1983 Nottingham Forest finally agreed to sell Peter Ward to Seattle's Canadian neighbours the Vancouver Whitecaps – for £20,000.

Besides a handful of games for Brian Horton's old club Hednesford Town during the autumn of 1990, Peter never returned to play football in Britain. In fact the remainder of his career resembled the route map of a Greyhound bus – Baltimore, Cleveland, Tacona, Wichita, Seattle again, and so on. He played in outdoor Leagues, he played in indoor Leagues, and he enjoyed just about every minute of it. In 1989 he joined Florida's Tampa Bay Rowdies and at the behest of the club's then player-coach, one Mr Mark Lawrenson. At the time of writing Peter still lives in the area and has no plans to up sticks and move on ('I mean the girls are lovely and it never drops below 80 degrees – would you?') He ran a bar in Tampa that for years became a Mecca for Albion fans visiting the sunshine state. The bar may have gone but supporters still track him down to ask for autographs, to sign memorabilia, to have a chat and simply pay homage.

In 2002 he married his second wife, Jacqueline. He has three daughters from his first marriage. The eldest is Rachael, who has no football connection whatsoever. The youngest is Louisa, who plays 'soccer' at Jacksonville University and is by all accounts a pretty decent defensive-midfielder ('She shot, she scored, it must be Louisa Ward!') The middle one is Rebekah, born around 7am on 18 August 1979 just hours before Albion's top-flight debut against Arsenal. As for Peter himself? Well, the hair may be receding but the moustache remains as does the Derbyshire accent, tainted only by the odd Americanism such as 'store',

(picture courtesy of Paul Hazlewood)

Peter Ward together with Albion supporter Norman Cook, aka 'Fat Boy Slim'.

'trash' and 'sidewalk'. Yep, besides the hair he looks pretty much the same as the Peter Ward of 1983.

How will history judge him? Undoubtedly as one of the Albion's most popular players ever, probably the most popular. The only dent in the fender is this: several of the players I spoke to during the writing of this book expressed regret that he didn't go on to better things. 'He was wasted a bit considering how good he was,' said one. 'The Forest move never really worked out for him and seemed to kill his career stone dead. He should really have built on what happened at Brighton, won honours, played regularly for England, that kind of thing. But it just never happened for him, which seemed a huge, huge shame.'

Nottingham Forest may have killed his career stone dead, at least as far as this country was concerned, but in the eyes of Albion fans young and old there is one corner of England where he remains a legend. 'I just loved my time at Brighton,' Peter says as we wrap up our chat. 'It's funny. Because I live in America I probably love it even more. When I go back everyone remembers you. If I lived there they would say "Hello" but it wouldn't be the same, you know what I mean? I thoroughly enjoy going over and seeing people, friends, the area. It's a special place in my heart. In a way I suppose I'm lucky in that they've been devoid of good teams since then, otherwise I'd be forgotten!'

Somehow I doubt that very much.

Chapter Ten
Not Shearer or Cole

At least 15 years have elapsed since I first started writing about sport for a living. In that time I have come to appreciate that the majority of British footballers fall into one of two categories. Category one is for retired players, full of stories (many of which are fabulously libellous) and loaded with opinions, who will happily talk to you for months on end about the game. Category two consists of those players still plying their trade, who, by and large, regard the press with disdain. When forced into doing an interview they will load their response to each question with the words 'gaffer', 'showed character' and 'the boys', giving off the impression throughout that they would rather forfeit a week's wages or fight a Bengal tiger than talk to a journalist.

I should say that not all footballers fall into these two brackets. You get your grouchy retired ones and the odd media-friendly professional. But, it pains me to admit, most do. Long gone are the days when players and sports writers would sit together in the buffet car of an express train on a Saturday night discussing the day's events over a dozen or so ales. One former Premier League striker once responded to my request for a quick chat with two words, the first containing four letters beginning with 'f', the second containing three beginning with 'o'. Around four years later that very same player, now retired, asked if I could help secure him some media work. Um, let me think about that…

One of the small band of professionals in the upper echelons of English football who bucks this category theory of mine is Bobby Zamora. Bobby does not tend to give many interviews. He is actually, especially by football's standards, very shy. However, when he does speak he is refreshingly honest and to the point. For example, days after I interviewed him for this book West Ham United played an away game at Blackburn Rovers. In the closing stages with the score delicately balanced at 1–1, Bobby was awarded a 'goal' that television replays showed had not in fact crossed the line (teammate Carlos Tevez, standing in an offside position, prevented it from doing so). Afterwards, a BBC reporter showed Bobby a re-run of the incident before asking how he felt about the error made by referee Howard Webb and his assistants. Other players in that situation would have run for cover, or not put themselves up for interview at all. 'It's just too bad for Blackburn,' said Bobby, straight faced without a hint of regret or any 'I didn't see it properly' nonsense. 'It's three points and we need them, and I don't think anybody is concerned about how we have got them.' Tell it like it is Bobby, tell it like it is.

There were many other players I could have gone for to partner Peter Ward up front in my Albion XI, heroes every one of them thanks to their uncanny ability to put the ball in the opposition's net. Take Michael Robinson for instance, the only man ever to have scored 20-plus goals for the club in a single season at the highest level. Then there is (in no particular order) Garry Nelson, Kit Napier, Fred Binney, Terry Connor, Mike Small, Adrian Thorne, Kurt Nogan, Arthur Attwood (75 goals in 104 appearances), Hugh Vallance, John Byrne, Tommy Cook…and so on. Bobby, on the other hand, was something else, an immensely-gifted player who almost single-handedly managed to put the club back on the football map after years in the doldrums. If I had a pound for every person (including my late grandmother) who from the years 2000 to 2003 asked me something akin to 'This Zamora, is he really that good?', I would have retired by now.

And on each occasion my response to that question was 'Yes he is.'

Robert Lester Zamora was born in Barking, East London, on 16 January 1981. The recently-deceased John Lennon was at number one in the charts with *Imagine*, while Albion, under the guidance of Alan

Mullery, were less than 24 hours from losing their third consecutive match in a row, this time by 2–0 to West Bromwich Albion at The Hawthorns. Bobby grew up in Manor Park deep in the heart of West Ham United territory and supported the Hammers as a kid. 'As long as I can remember I was always playing football,' he says over lunch in the restaurant at Upton Park. 'I'd come home from school in Barking and we'd set up goals between a couple of parked cars in the street and just play. There was loads of kids my age who used to play, and it was always football, football, football. We maybe used to play a bit of tennis when Wimbledon was on for about a week, and then it would be straight back to football. That's the way it was.'

As a young kid Bobby played for a team called Lake View, then for a side called Senrab. Over the years Senrab has become renowned as something of a production line for top talent. The name is actually 'Barnes' spelled backwards, giving rise to the theory that it was christened after John Barnes, the former Watford, Liverpool and England left-winger. I've always found this hard to believe, seeing as though Senrab was formed in 1961 when John Barnes was not even born. Another version is that it heralds from Senrab Street in Stepney, which is right next door to Barnes Street. Whatever the origins of its name, what is undisputed is that some darned-fine players have pulled on a Senrab shirt down the years, including Ray Wilkins, Alan

Curbishley, John Terry, Ledley King, Jermain Defoe, Jlloyd Samuel, Lee Bowyer, Paul Konchesky, Sol Campbell and Muzzy Izzet. Terry, Konchesky and Samuel were all in the same year as Bobby. 'It is remarkable really when you look at what everyone has gone on and done,' he admits. 'We had a good team and a good laugh as well, all being local East London lads. It was a good place to learn.'

When he was 15, Bobby's burgeoning reputation as a promising young player was temporarily put on hold. 'I developed "Osgood Slatters", which is a condition that affects some kids who play too much sport. Your bones grow a little bit too fast for your body. It makes you really sore and means you can't really play anything, so I had to have six months off football. All through that time Norwich were on the phone asking me "Can you come down here?" Eventually, when I'd recovered I did go down there because they seemed to be the most keen to take me. I was only little at the time, but I played half a season for the schoolboy team. At the end of that they said "We don't think you're going to grow. We can't offer you anything." A couple of days later I had phone calls from Bristol Rovers and Southend, both asking me to go and play a game for them.'

Bobby played 90 minutes for Southend United and less than half a match for Bristol Rovers. You would have thought that an East Londoner, proud of his roots, would have opted for the club down the A13 on the Essex coast rather than one deep in the west of England. However, Bobby had an uncle and cousins living in Bristol and knew the city relatively well. 'My best friend who had actually played at Norwich with me, Luke Williams, had also been released, and we both ended up going to Bristol Rovers and playing in the same game. They took us both off after about half an hour and said "Look, we want to offer you something." We said "We'll have a think about it and get back to you", acting all casual. But we were buzzing straight away. So we both decided to go there, away from London, for a bit of adventure.'

Bristol Rovers were then an ambitious third-tier club under the leadership of charismatic manager Ian Holloway, a proud Bristolian who had made almost 400 appearances as a player for the club. Bobby completed his two-year apprenticeship at the Memorial Ground and was offered a two-year professional contract by Holloway. He made a few substitute appearances for the first team but there was a catch – Rovers already had an array of striking talent in Barry Hayles, Jason Roberts, Jamie Cureton and Nathan Ellington.

Towards the end of 1999 Bobby was sent on loan by Rovers to their non-League neighbours Bath City. 'That was ideal for me because I just needed to be able to play some games,' recalls Bobby. 'I was only 18 at the time, but you're still looking ahead, and with Barry, Jason, Jamie and Nathan around there wasn't really much happening for me. I was there [Bath] about a month and scored something like eight goals in six games. I did really well for them, and they wanted me to stay, but I ended up going back to Bristol Rovers.'

Not for long, though. He may be wrong, but Bobby reckons either Micky Adams or Alan Cork, then manager and assistant manager of the Albion respectively, came to watch him play in a Rovers reserve-team match. At the time Brighton were enjoying their first season back in Sussex having spent two years in residency at Priestfield, home of Gillingham Football Club. The 1999–2000 campaign had started well with a 6–0 home win over Mansfield, followed up by a 2–1 victory at Leyton Orient, but a dip in form during the autumn meant that by December the club was marooned in the middle of Nationwide Division Three (the old Fourth Division). They were scoring goals, but they were also conceding them. The arrival of Danny Cullip would help patch things up in defence. Now Adams was on the lookout for a decent striker rather than having to rely on defenders and midfielders to bag the goals, the kind of bloke who would score in excess of 20 per season.

December 1999 had seen Adams manage to recruit Lorenzo Pinamonte on loan from Brentford. The Italian scored twice in a 4–2 win over Exeter City but not everyone (myself included) was convinced he had what it took to succeed

on the heavy pitches of England's Fourth Division. The deal expired and Pinamonte returned to Griffin Park to be replaced by yet another loan signing – none other than Bobby. Nobody besides Micky Adams and Alan Cork had heard of him. He had never even scored a goal in the Football League before. But that did not stop him from making an instant impression on the other Albion players during his first few days at the club.

'To be honest with you he was a normal lad, lanky and very, very shy, but on the training ground you could see he was something special,' remembers former Albion forward Darren Freeman. 'He did things like nutmegs that only the top players can do. He was very naturally gifted. He didn't run around launching himself into tackles. He was cleverer than that. He made it look easy. Everything flowed for him, but it wasn't luck, it was instinct. I never had that natural ability. The other thing that struck you was he wasn't a big-time Charlie. During that time he was with us on loan you could tell he wasn't the kind of player who would go off the rails. The football came first, not the parties or the showbiz side. I just wish I could have played with him more.'

The only thing Bobby knew about Brighton when he arrived on loan in February 2000 was that it was fairly close to London, somewhere he once again felt drawn towards following his spell in the west. During that first month at

(picture courtesy of Bennett Dean)

Bobby Zamora takes on Oldham Athletic at Withdean, October 2001.

Withdean he would embark on a crash course into the club's history – its struggle for survival, the Goldstone Ground, the 1983 FA Cup Final and so on. Gradually he began to feel rather attached to the place, no doubt helped by the fact he was scoring goals.

'It was a terrific performance by Bobby Zamora,' said Adams immediately after watching his loan signing get off the mark with a header against Plymouth Argyle at Withdean. 'I was very pleased with what he did. Everything that I was told about him he showed today.' But that was just the beginning. Two games later he scored a hat-trick away against Chester City, not just any hat-trick but a perfect hat-trick – a right-footer, a left-footer and a header.

'It was the scruffiest hat-trick imaginable,' says Paul Rogers, who scored goal number seven that day in a 7–1 mauling. 'The penalty even bounced over their 'keeper! But you could tell he got a lot of confidence from it and that means everything when you're a striker. He had never scored before he came to Brighton and suddenly they were going in left, right and centre.' Another brace followed at home to Halifax Town as Albion fought back from 1–0 down to win 2–1, making it six goals from four games for Bobby. He failed to score in the next couple of matches but an impression had certainly been made. And then suddenly the month was up. Back to Bristol he went.

Albion remained unbeaten throughout the rest of the season after Bobby's departure, although a few too many draws sank any hopes of making the Play-offs. Would it have been any different had he stayed? Yes, thought the manager. Yes, reckoned the supporters. 'It became a little bit frustrating towards the end because we genuinely thought we could sneak into the Play-offs with a striker that was capable of scoring goals on a regular basis,' said Adams at the time. 'We didn't have that. Having said that we still finished in the top-five teams in the Division in terms of scoring goals so we weren't too far away, but certainly losing Lorenzo to Brentford and for Bobby to go back to Bristol Rovers was disappointing. But it wasn't the be-all and end-all. We

were pleased with 11th place. If you'd asked me at the beginning of the season I genuinely thought we could get a top-10 finish. I maybe disappointed myself a little bit, but it was certainly a lot better than finishing 17th the previous season.'

Returning to the Memorial Ground and reserve-team football proved to be a massive anti-climax for Bobby. Albion's fans had taken him to their hearts. He had developed a scoring touch playing in a first team, one that was in the process of being rebuilt and appeared tantalisingly close to doing something. What happened now if his touch deserted him? 'Brighton had worked out superb for me. It was a new experience and a new challenge. I'd got to know all about the history of the place. I sort of kept in contact with Micky and Corky, and I knew they wanted to get me at the end of that season, but I also knew they had to go through all the right channels and speak to the club.

'I think they [Rovers] initially rejected a bid from Brighton. It was around then that I spoke to the youth-team manager down there at the time, a really nice guy called Phil Bater. He said "You're not going to get to play – go in and see Ian Holloway. I'll come in with you if you want." So we went in, sat down and I said "I want to go." He [Ian] said something along the lines of "I'm not going to let you go." Then Phil spoke up and said "Come on, that's not really fair. He wants to play football." And Ian said "Yeah, alright, fair enough." I'd worked hard for him so he was nice about it. And he let me go for £100,000, which was a lot of money for somebody who had only played a few first-team games, and definitely a lot of money for Brighton.'

You can say that again. Six goals in six games had given Albion fans a taste of what Bobby Zamora was capable of. But a six-figure sum for a centre-forward incapable of breaking into the Bristol Rovers first team? Sure enough, Bobby scored twice in the second game of the 2000–01 season at home to Rochdale. However, three defeats from the opening four League games (plus a League Cup loss to Millwall) had some fans calling for Adams's dismissal following a 2–0 reverse to Kidderminster at Withdean on 28 August. That 14-game unbeaten sequence at the end of the previous campaign had been enough for the bookies to install Albion as favourites for promotion. Bobby's return had only increased everyone's expectations. The time to deliver had come and was in danger of passing.

A few home truths were aired in private among the players following the Kidderminster game, with Adams organising a team-building session during the week to help boost morale. The following Saturday Albion thrashed Torquay United 6–2, with Bobby scoring a hat-trick. They would lose only one

more game between then and New Year's Day 2001, by which time Bobby's goal tally stood at 16, including a thunderbolt at home to Halifax Town on 2 December that he still rates as his finest for the club. The only spanner in the works (bar a sending-off in an FA Cup match at Scunthorpe) came when Alan Cork accepted an offer from his former Wimbledon mentor Sam Hammam to manage Cardiff City. No sooner had Cork arrived at Ninian Park than reports began to surface in the press linking the Welsh club with Bobby. The fee was reputed to be around £1.2 million. That £100,000 was already beginning to look like a bargain, but Adams insisted his prized striker was going nowhere.

Off the field Bobby was also settling in nicely. At first he commuted to Brighton from London by car for training sessions and matches. By the end of 2000 he had bought himself a place in Burgess Hill just down the road from Albion's new assistant coach Bob Booker, the man brought in by Adams to replace Cork. As the club's form improved, so too did the bond between the players. 'I already knew them of course because I had been down on loan, but it was different actually living there. You realise what a great bunch of lads and characters they really are, people like Charlie Oatway, 'Chippy' (Richard Carpenter) and Danny Cullip, all class players. So I absolutely loved it. Micky had also been there for a while and started bringing his players in and after a few games, with us doing well, I think we all began to realise we were in with a chance of doing something special.'

On 10 February 2001 a 15th-minute goal by Bobby was enough to give Albion all three points at home to Cardiff, one of half-a-dozen other clubs also chasing clear leaders Chesterfield for promotion. However, the Derbyshire outfit had a cloud hanging over its head in the shape of imminent punishment for financial irregularities resulting from the purchase of striker Luke Beckett. The nine-point deduction which followed, while far more lenient than many had expected, coincided with a collapse in form on the pitch around the same time as Albion began kicking for the finish line. On 14 April first-half goals by Paul Brooker and

Bobby saw Brighton win 2–0 at Plymouth Argyle to secure promotion, the club's first since 1988. Further goals against Darlington and Macclesfield Town saw Bobby finish the season with 31 goals to his name. On the evening of Tuesday 1 May Albion clinched the title thanks to a 1–0 win at home to, of all people, Chesterfield. Ultimately, that nine-point deduction was immaterial – Brighton would have won the League anyway. After the loss of the Goldstone Ground and years spent fighting to keep the club alive, it is hardly surprising that night remains a favourite moment of many supporters.

'Confidence is everything for a striker. If you're scoring goals, you're confident, and I was scoring lots of goals. But that was down to the running of a lot of other guys

Bobby Zamora, centre, celebrates winning the Nationwide Division Three Championship, 2001.

(picture courtesy of Bennett Dean)

in the team like Paul Brooker – "my bitches" I used to call them! They reckoned they deserved all the plaudits, and I do give them a lot of credit because they created a lot of goals for me. To be honest, I wasn't really aware of what it all meant to people. I was just young and enjoying my football. The people I'd grown up with like John [Terry] and Paul [Konchesky] had been playing regularly for Chelsea and Charlton since they were 17. No disrespect, but the Third Division didn't really seem that big a deal. Looking back on it now, it was massive. Just to be playing professional football was one thing, but to be doing it with a bunch of lads like that at a club like that was tremendous.'

Despite speculation regarding their futures, the 2001–02 season dawned with both Adams and Bobby still at Withdean. Some critics pointed out that scoring 31 goals a season in the fourth tier of English football was one thing. Doing it in the third would be another. Come Christmas 2001 Bobby already had 19 and Albion were looking good for a second successive promotion, albeit without Adams who by now had been prised away from Sussex to become assistant manager of Leicester City. His departure, though hardly unsurprising given what he had achieved at Withdean on limited resources, came as a huge blow to everyone connected with the club. Nevertheless, the identity of his replacement meant spirits were not down for long.

'Peter Taylor was a fantastic manager and him coming in was a real buzz for us,' says Bobby. 'I know people said it was Micky who built the team and everything, but Peter had his own ideas and was excellent to work with. It was great for me as well because there I was, having not been in the game that long, working with someone who knew the England set-up and had even managed the national side. It's funny. That season really was a strange one. We all thought it was going to be tough, but we just carried on where we left off. We played a few of the bigger teams in the division and did well against them so again you're thinking "We've got a chance here." And we just steamrollered through the League.'

Two of my own personal favourites from Bobby's canon came during the opening months of the 2001–02 season. The first was at Huddersfield just after Adams had resigned, a sharp turn followed by a simply-unstoppable left-foot rocket into the goalkeeper's top right-hand corner. The second came away at Bury six weeks later. 'Yeah, I remember that. I was sitting on the halfway line and I think it was 'Jonesy' [Nathan Jones] who put me through. I ran with it for a bit, saw their 'keeper off his line and managed to dink it over him. I enjoyed that one.'

Bobby's rich vein of form together with Albion's healthy position in the Nationwide Division Two table almost inevitably led to accusations of the one-man team variety. On 23 March, having scored his 31st goal of the campaign, he injured his shoulder in a home game against Notts County and had to be led from the field. If Brighton were going to be promoted it looked like they would have to do it without their talisman. The following Saturday Taylor's side won 4–1 at Colchester, dispelling the one-man team jibe for good, before seeing off Bristol City 2–1 at Withdean on Easter Monday. Other results that day went Albion's way. Suddenly, promotion was beginning to look inevitable.

On 6 April around 4,000 Brighton fans travelled to London Road, Peterborough, for what promised to be a promotion party in everything but name. Nobody expected Bobby to play. However, the striker had other ideas. 'I wanted the Golden Boot and 'Earnie' (Cardiff's Robert Earnshaw) was knocking on my door. He's a live wire, and we'd spoken a bit, developing a bit of a good-natured rivalry. I was lucky. I was only out for two weeks. I had a big brace fitted and managed to play with that on.' The gamble looked to have backfired when Bobby missed with a weakly-hit first-half penalty before fluffing a one-on-one with Peterborough goalkeeper Mark Tyler. But he persevered and sure enough hit the only goal of the game in the 63rd minute. Once again a familiar chant went up from the Brighton supporters packed behind Tyler's goal, sung to the tune of *That's*

Amore by Dean Martin. 'When the ball hits the goal, it's not Shearer or Cole, it's Zamora!' At the time of writing a version of this very same song greets on-hold callers to the Upton Park switchboard.

Bobby failed to find the net during the final two matches of the season but it did not matter. Albion were promoted in first place, and he won the Golden Boot for finishing as the League's top scorer. Like the proverbial London bus, Albion fans had waited years for a Championship, only for two to come along at once. 'I'm fortunate in that I've had four promotions as a manager and on each occasion I've had one of the best strikers in the League, if not the best striker,' says Peter Taylor. 'Bobby was and still is a tremendous finisher and a great forward. He could play on his own up front, with a big fella or with a little one. He was a very intelligent runner – people just couldn't read him – and his attitude was excellent. In training he only wanted to work on his right foot. He knew his left was good enough so it was his right all the time. That team as a whole was full of intelligent hardworking players, but having Bobby as our spearhead made us a real force to be reckoned with.'

'There's a certain ego trip to being a forward,' admits Lee Steele, one of Bobby's striking partners during Albion's back-to-back Championship-winning seasons. 'If you don't think you are the best, you can struggle. That first season when Bobby arrived I was doing okay, scoring goals, thinking "He's not that special." Then he started scoring. Before I knew it he had about 20 goals by February, and I was looking for excuses because I couldn't get back in the team. With all those goals came confidence, and he became more of a complete player. I was watching the video from that second promotion season recently and it's like the "Bobby Zamora Show." Some of them were just unbelievable. If you give Bobby Zamora chances, then he'll be in the top 10 percent of strikers in the Premier League. One hundred thousand pounds – that's got to be deal of the century.'

Zamora hit 63 goals in just two seasons, not including the six hit during his spell on loan from Bristol Rovers. By now it seemed every national sports writer was wondering how much longer Albion would be able to hang on to Bobby. The club had risen from the depths to the second tier of English football, but finances remained tight and facilities at Withdean prehistoric. No sooner had the 2001–02 season finished than Peter Taylor resigned, blaming lack of funds and the poor facilities for his decision. Given the circumstances, would the club really be able to turn down a sizeable seven-figure sum for their prolific goalscorer?

Bobby ran out at Burnley on the opening day of the 2002–03 season with three England Under-21 caps to his name, having been selected by then manager David Platt for the European Championships in Switzerland during May. He scored again at Turf Moor, ramming home Albion's third in a convincing 3–1 win and making it a memorable debut game in charge for Taylor's successor Martin Hinshelwood. 'It's going to be three in a row,' sang the travelling supporters, referring to the unlikely event of Brighton picking up a third successive Championship title. A 0–0 draw at home to Coventry City followed. And then the roof caved in. Bobby picked up a knee injury in the following match, a 2–0 defeat to Norwich City, keeping him out for the next six weeks. By the time he returned, Albion were bottom of the League and stuck in a 12-game losing streak that would ultimately cost Hinshelwood his job and lead to relegation.

'We won, then we drew, then we lost to Norwich, and I did my knee, which pissed me off massively. Then we just took a bit of a dive after that. Steve [Coppell] came in and we managed to get things back together, but in the end we just missed out and ended up going down on the last day of the season. We just lost too many games early on and were always playing catch up. You wonder whether things would have been different had I not been injured. It would have been nice to score a few more goals. We had a pretty good side as well, especially when Steve Sidwell came on loan. He's one of my best mates now. I see him all the time and he's done great things at Reading. I tell him I basically got him where he is today. He came for a month or two, played something like six games and scored three goals, so I tell him "You owe me!" He's a class player.'

Would it also have been different had Albion been playing in an arena fit for a second tier professional club rather than Withdean? 'Oh definitely! If you look up north the councils will give you land and money. Down here it's a fight to get even the smallest bit of land. The club has been fighting for year after year after year. They will get it in the end, but it's annoying it's taken so long.'

Albion's relegation in May 2003 following a 2–2 draw at Grimsby made Bobby's departure virtually inevitable. The speculation about which club he would be going to began before the team coach had even made it back to Sussex. 'In the early days it had been Cardiff who had offered an unbelievable amount of money for me, £1.2 million. Then it was Wigan, who offered about the same, but they never really interested me. They were in the same place as we were, trying to get up there, and I was happy where I was. Southampton's name came up and one or two other clubs. It was only the fact we went down and I just wanted to keep on progressing [that led to him leaving]. Steve Coppell said "I'm not going to stand in your way. I want you to progress as well." And I think most of the fans felt like that too.'

My own reaction when I heard Bobby was bound for Tottenham Hotspur was one of immense disappointment – not because he was leaving (he owed Albion nothing) but at his choice of destination. I was disappointed for two reasons. One, I wanted him to join a progressive top-flight club where he would improve as a player. And two, I wanted that club to pay the market value for a striker of immense talent, not try and rip us off. My opinion, for what it is worth, was that Spurs were not a progressive club. I also knew about their reputation for penny pinching when it came to signing players from the lower leagues, something that in 2000 had incurred the wrath of Peterborough manager Barry Fry when Tottenham were in negotiations for Matthew Etherington and Simon Davies, two of United's talented youngsters. Sure enough, the deal proved to be the wrong one on all fronts – for us (he was transferred for just £1.5 million, 30 percent of which went back to Bristol Rovers as a sell on fee), for Spurs and, worst of all, for Bobby, who endured a wretched time at White Hart Lane.

'Glenn Hoddle signed me. I played a few games under Glenn, he got fired, sacked, whatever. David Pleat came in and in any job I suppose if your face fits and you get on with the manager you're okay. Mine didn't. I sort of knew that I was never going to play so when West Ham came in I didn't have to think about it. Straight away, I was gone.' One month after turning 23 Bobby was back where he had come into this world, the East End of London. He had grown up a West Ham fan so the move made complete sense. The Hammers were then one rung down from the Premier League. Manager Alan Pardew knew that if Bobby could recapture the form that had brought him to everyone's attention with Brighton, then West Ham would be in with a good chance of promotion.

West Ham did make it through to the Play-off Final in Cardiff that May, taking on Crystal Palace the day before Albion faced Bristol City inside the Millennium Stadium looking for their third promotion in just four years. However, the Bobby Zamora that occasionally appeared in a Hammers shirt during the closing weeks of that campaign bore little resemblance to the one that had worn the blue and white stripes of Brighton. His confidence seemed shot to pieces by the Spurs experience. In a pub in Cardiff on the afternoon of West Ham's match against Crystal Palace, a group of around 50 Albion fans watched Bobby blow the kind of opportunity he would have put away blindfolded for Brighton. The ticketless Hammers supporters in the same pub openly cursed him for being, well, not very good. 'You're welcome to him,' one said to me after the final whistle had been blown on Palace's 1–0 victory. It was a sad moment, for me as well as the West Ham fan.

'It was a tough first season. Actually, it

was a tough first and second season. West Ham were my team, and it seemed like we were going to go back up, so losing in the Play-offs was heartbreaking. We had a good team at the time and really it was just a case of knuckling down after that, making sure we got it right the next time. I didn't really play too much that second season to be honest, for whatever reason, but then Teddy [Sheringham] got injured and I ended up playing the last few games and did well. Teddy got fit again for the [Play-off] semis, and I think he was going to play, but he [Sheringham] said "I told him [Pardew] that he's wrong and he should play you." For Teddy to say that was just amazing.'

In the Play-off semi-final against Ipswich Town Bobby scored twice in the first leg at Portman Road and once in the return at Upton Park as the Hammers progressed to the Final in Cardiff for the second season running. Bobby's second at Ipswich – a volley – was as eyecatching as anything he had scored for the Albion. 'Yeah, that was a really good finish, but I still wasn't sure if I was going to play in the Final or not. Alan eventually said he was going to go with me, and Teddy said "All the best – you're going to score today." That was really special. I look up to him massively. He's such a good player. And he was right. I scored the only goal [against Preston] and played really well. That day was perfect and meant we were back up in the top Division.'

Bobby's showing in Cardiff also meant he was back in the spotlight. In August 2005 Leo Beenhakker, coach of the Trinidad and Tobago national side, offered him the chance to play for them in a World Cup qualifying match against Guatemala (his father hailed from Trinidad). Bobby politely declined, deciding to concentrate instead on his club form. It proved to be a wise move. With the tireless Sheringham, Marlon Harewood and the recently-arrived Dean Ashton on the scene, Bobby again found first-team starts to be limited. He still managed to bag 10 goals from 20 games as West Ham finished mid-table in the Premiership and reached the FA Cup Final, losing to Liverpool on penalties following a thrilling 3–3 draw after extra-time (Sheringham was the sole Hammers player to score from the spot, with Bobby missing his kick). For both club and player, it appeared to be a case of onwards and upwards.

Unfortunately, it did not turn out that way. Bobby scored five times in West Ham's opening four League games of the 2006–07 season to become the Premiership's leading marksman. Then things began to go badly wrong. The defeats started to pile up, leading to Pardew's dismissal in December 2006. Two months later *The Observer* reported that 'a culture of reckless high-stakes gambling is causing division within West Ham and rupturing morale to such an extent that the first-team squad, already riven by cliques, is spiralling out of control.' One player spoke anonymously about unrest over different sized pay packets, tension between new boss Alan Curbishley and the dressing room, plus the widespread feeling that the club would be relegated. Alleged irregularities showed up in the signing of the Argentine players Javier Mascherano and Carlos Tevez. Defender Anton Ferdinand, already on charges of assault and violent disorder following a supposed brawl outside a London nightclub, disobeyed Curbishley's orders and headed for America to celebrate his birthday. There is more, but you get the picture.

The day Bobby and I met up, West Ham were bottom of the Premier League and seemingly just weeks away from being relegated. I did not press him about what had happened, much as I was tempted. He admitted only time would tell when it came to determining West Ham's fate, adding 'We've got to keep working hard and we'll see what happens. You want to play in the Premier League as long as you can. It was my dream to play in it and score goals. That will never change.'

Incredibly, the hard work paid off. The Hammers won seven of their remaining nine fixtures to stay up, with Bobby among the chief catalysts behind the escape (his spectacular strike at home to Everton in April 2007 was a contender for the Premier League's Goal of the Season). Another proved to be Tevez, who many argued should not have even been playing, with

Bobby Zamora in the claret and blue of West Ham United under the watchful eye of Albion centre-back Guy Butters.

West Ham somehow escaping an expected points deduction despite admitting the irregularities surrounding his transfer. Whatever the rights and wrongs of the matter, the Tevez affair left a sour taste in thousands of mouths nationwide over the London club's survival. Other clubs including Wigan clamoured for justice, having seen poor Sheffield United drop into the Championship on the final day of the season. Amid the furore some newspapers ran stories of a summer clearout at Upton Park. Harshly, perhaps, Bobby's name was mentioned as one of those destined for the axe.

No matter what the future may hold for Bobby Zamora, at least he (like Peter Ward) will always be regarded as a god in one corner of England, namely Sussex. 'I

thoroughly loved it down there, every minute. The stadium wasn't amazing or anything like that, but it was perfect, all the people, the fans, the managers I had there. They did everything for me. Micky took the gamble and gave me my break, which I thank him for massively. Peter Taylor opened the door for the England Under-21s. Steve Coppell said he wouldn't stand in my way, which I respect him for big time because he could have said no to me leaving. And the players! I still speak to 'Jonesy', Charlie [Oatway], 'Steely' [Lee Steele], all the boys. We met in London a few months back to have a drink and something to eat. They were a massive part of my life. I love them all – just don't tell them that!'

Chapter Eleven
Rivolino

And so we come to the final piece of the jigsaw, one that until the barking-mad squad system came along was always known as the number-11 shirt. Today the man on the left flank is just as likely to be wearing 14, 26 or even 42, something that just does not sit well with a traditionalist like me.

It is also time for your author to make a small confession. In 1978 my family moved to Sussex from London. I was nine years old and knew next to nothing about football. All the lads in our village bar one or two glory-seeking Liverpool fans supported Brighton. Keen to make new friends, it was not long before I started joining them on trips to the Goldstone. Over the course of those first few precious Albion home games, one player above all others grabbed my attention. That player was Peter O'Sullivan, or 'Sully' to his teammates and the thousands that used to fill the old ground.

Sully always seemed more like a character from *Butch Cassidy and the Sundance Kid* than a footballer. Or at least he did to me. He looked great in blue and white stripes, but I always got the feeling he was born to wear a beaten up jacket with tassels, Stetson perched nonchalantly on his head. Maybe it was

the moustache that did it, though if anything that made him more 'spaghetti western' than wild west. Whatever it was, Sully had the air of a maverick about him, and I quickly grew to worship the grass he so elegantly seemed to glide over. During lunchtime kickabouts at school or on the village green I tried to be him. I failed miserably of course, an inability to dribble even Ribena meaning my destiny lay between jumpers for goalposts doing imitations of Graham Moseley. But that did not change the fact that Sully was, and in many ways remains, my favourite Albion player of all time.

Peter Anthony O'Sullivan was born in March 1951 in the North Wales seaside resort of Colwyn Bay and spent his formative years in the picturesque Conwy Valley. Unlike South Wales, where rugby union remains the dominant sport, the northern half of the Principality is very much football country (or 'soccer' as they call it, to avoid confusion with rugby football). The nearest thing to a definitive explanation for this is that the main arteries in the Welsh transport system all tend to flow from east to west rather than north to south, making it far easier to get to north-west England from Sully's old stamping ground than, say, Cardiff. Kids

Peter O'Sullivan, Steyning, 2007.

in Denbighshire grow up dreaming of wearing the red shirts of Manchester United or Liverpool rather than the ones worn by the Welsh Rugby Union side. The young Peter was no exception.

'As soon as you're old enough to play football you're a Manchester United or a Liverpool fan,' explains Sully over the first of several early-morning coffees at his pad in Steyning. 'It might be a bit different for those who grow up close to Wrexham, which has its own team, but by and large United and Liverpool are the top dogs. That hasn't changed from when I was a boy. All my mates up there are still Manchester United or Liverpool. I worked very hard as a kid on my football, played for Wales Schoolboys and all those types of things and quite a few clubs came in for

me, including Manchester United, Leeds and Everton. And I made the fatal mistake of going to Manchester United.'

The fatal mistake? 'Well, I think it was a bridge too far for a 15-year-old coming out of a little village. It's like the old cliché now about the kids who go to Chelsea. They just don't get much of a chance to make any impression on the first team. The players Manchester United had then were established. Unless you were exceptional it was very difficult to break in. I think maybe for the position I played in at the time, which was more left-midfield than left-wing, I was also slightly too small.'

Still, at least Peter was getting to play in United's reserves, unlike the young Graham Moseley, desperately trying to gatecrash training sessions at the

Manchester Ship Canal Recreation Ground by sabotaging the iron bars surrounding the pitches. Yet it was far from a happy existence for the young Sully. 'On the one hand I was getting to train with these fantastic players like Bobby Charlton, Denis Law and George Best, because everyone at United always trained together. But on the other I was stagnating. To be honest I didn't really get on with Wilf McGuinness, who eventually took over as manager from Matt Busby. Wilf was my day to day contact because he looked after the reserves. I didn't really get to know Matt. The day I arrived he shook my hand and said "Good luck, I hope you make it", then four years down the line it was "You haven't made it, see you later." It just didn't happen for me.'

It was around this point that Bobby Charlton, the man responsible for giving Gary Williams his big break at Preston North End, once again sprang to the Albion's rescue. Transfer listed by United, Peter sifted through the list of interested parties before opting to spend a week training with Bristol City, then an ambitious club in the old Second Division. By coincidence the England team was also in town doing some work ahead of the 1970 World Cup Finals in Mexico. Spotting Sully on an adjacent pitch, Bobby wandered over to find out what he was doing there. 'He asked who else was after me and I ran through the list…Wrexham, Bury, Preston, Brighton. And he said "Ah, Brighton, Freddie Goodwin is manager there. He's a good lad. Go down there and try it." So I went back to Manchester where I had a girlfriend, spoke to Freddie and he arranged for me to go down.'

Charlton's connection with Goodwin went back to when they had both been 'Busby Babes', a remarkably-talented group of young players that progressed through the ranks at Manchester United during the 50s and 60s under the guidance of Matt Busby. Goodwin had initially played second fiddle to Duncan Edwards, arguably the most gifted of all the 'Babes'. When Edwards perished along with seven of his teammates in the Munich air crash, Goodwin was one of the players that stepped into the void as United's makeshift side finished runners-up in the 1958 FA Cup. Unbeknown to Peter, Goodwin was on the verge of becoming Birmingham City's manager when the two met face to face for the first time at Brighton railway station. They drove in an American Cadillac to Sussex University, where Goodwin showed his prospective player the training set-up before heading for a café in Saltdean to talk business. 'And to cut a very long story short I ended up here, but if it hadn't been for Bobby I'd have gone to Bristol City because they were a far better side in the Second Division at that time. I loved Bobby. He was, probably still is, a great

great man. When I was a kid at United he would train with you individually, taking the time to knock balls with you and showing you things. A gentleman. I owe him a lot.'

Peter might think that now, but the impressions he formed of Brighton over those first few months – the town as well as the football club – had him cursing Charlton's advice. For someone used to the hubbub of Manchester, his new home on the south coast seemed horribly quiet. 'There was one nightclub, possibly two, so it was completely different to how it is now. I was a young man but there didn't seem a lot to do. The football club was pretty grotty. We were in the bottom half of the Third Division playing crap football, with a lot of old pros just playing out their time and getting their wages. Everyone was out in the evenings all round the pubs – nothing wrong with that, except it was even happening on Friday nights. It was very, very amateurish.'

To make matters worse, Peter did not initially see eye to eye with Freddie Goodwin's successor, Pat Saward. 'I'm willing to admit I was naïve. In my first three or four games I'd be on the ball trying to beat four or five players. Pat would be getting hold of me saying "You don't play like that!" That was my first experience of being on the transfer list at Brighton. I was like "Bollocks to you, I don't like it down here anyhow." My

fiancée was still living up in Manchester and to tell you the truth I was dying to get back up there.'

Thankfully, Peter stuck at it despite the see-saw nature of his first three seasons at the club. He appeared 39 times in all competitions as Brighton fought successfully against relegation to Division Four during the 1970–71 campaign, cementing his position as a crowd favourite the following year as Saward's side finished runners-up in the League to Aston Villa and equalling the club record of 65 points set during the 1955–56 season in the process (under the two points for a win system). Twelve months later Albion were back in Division Three, a miserable run of 13 consecutive defeats making relegation inevitable. 'That second year I had a really good season but after that we fell apart. Again we had one or two players who were over the hill and Pat just lost the plot. It was grim. I wanted to get away at the time. I didn't want to go back to the Third Division. I've always been ambitious, otherwise I wouldn't have stuck it out in the game.'

One of the reasons Peter decided to stay was Mike Bamber, whose arrival on the board of directors in 1970 would be a pivotal moment in the Albion's history. Several clubs had made enquiries about his availability during the 1971–72 promotion season, and the calls kept coming the following year after Wales awarded him his first cap against Scotland

'Sully', Albion's Welsh wizard.

in March 1973. With one eye on the future following relegation, Bamber – by now chairman in his own right – gave Sully a pay rise to help keep his prized asset on the books.

But it was not all about money. In November 1973 came the news that Brian Clough, arguably the most sought after manager in Britain, was quitting Derby County and coming to the Goldstone.

This jaw-dropping coup represented a fantastic opportunity for Peter to work with a man at the top of his game. Clough would also be bringing his right-hand man Peter Taylor with him, someone revered in his own right as a coach. It was a ride everyone wanted to be on. For the time being at least there would be no more transfer talk for the Welshman.

'God, that was one hell of an experience,' remembers Sully. 'We got to meet him for the first time in a hotel in Lewes. We arrived on the Friday and stayed overnight before a game. We heard he'd got the job at the start of the week and every day in training we'd been mimicking his "Young man" thing. You remember? "Young man, it only takes a second to score a goal" and all that. Anyway, on the Friday he comes in and I'm sitting next to Barry Bridges who was a good laugh. I'm thinking "Oh no, I'm not gonna be able to keep a straight face here." He starts going round the room saying stuff like "You can get your hair cut, and you, and you." And I'm waiting for the young man bit because I know I'm going to die. In the end I don't think he actually said it, which is just as well because if he had I think it would've been the end for me.'

Clough's arrival heralded something resembling a nine-month media frenzy around the club, his first home match in charge adding 10,000 to the attendance. Unfortunately, some awful results only increased the newsworthiness of his appointment. In the FA Cup non-League Walton & Hersham came to the Goldstone and won 4–0, Bristol Rovers going four better in the League with a thumping 8–2 win on Sussex soil. Players were bought, dropped and recalled with the regularity of April showers, yet Clough and Taylor seemed to warm to Sully who went on to be ever present in the team throughout the 1973–74 season. Gradually results improved and relegation to Division Four was averted, but questions remained about what exactly Clough's intentions were. Was he in for the long haul or merely using Brighton as a convenient stopgap? He had, after all, just taken Derby to the semi-finals of the European Cup, having won the League Championship in 1972. Why bother with a struggling Third Division outfit when you are being tipped to become the next England manager?

'I think Cloughie was always too big for the club,' says Peter. 'Someone was always going to get hold of him, and I for one never thought he'd stay. When he arrived we were back to that scenario of being a bad Division Three side. It can be hard to adapt to the Third Division but, give him credit, he changed it to stop us going down again. Some of the players he brought in were good buys, like Peter Grummitt who was an excellent 'keeper. And he rated me because I played every game he was there, though obviously not enough to want to buy me afterwards! But he was better than all that and he knew it. Put it this way – I wasn't shocked to hear he was leaving.'

In July 1974 Clough surprised absolutely nobody by taking the Leeds United job that had been vacated by Don Revie. Albion issued a writ against the Yorkshire club but it seemed like a token gesture. No doubt about it – Clough had put Brighton on the map, but at what cost? 'I met John McGovern [captain of Nottingham Forest's 1979 and 1980 European Cup-winning sides] on holiday once and asked him his opinion of Clough,' says former Albion goalkeeper Brian Powney, released by the club that May ironically to make way for Grummitt. 'I think he would have probably run off Beachy Head for him. I didn't think like that. With all due respect, we were a stepping stone for him. Would it have worked if he'd stayed? I don't know. But we were never going to find out, were we? All the time he was down here he lived in a hotel. That says it all really.'

When the dust settled the common consensus among fans seemed to be that Albion had emerged from the whole Clough soap opera rather well. The club now had a public profile plus a half-decent side containing one or two names that probably wouldn't have come to Brighton had it not been for the manager. An added bonus was that the man behind most of the signings, Peter Taylor, had

decided to stay rather than jump ship for Leeds. So what if he seemed the model of a sourpuss? He liked the area, wanted to do a job with the team, and that, as far as most supporters were concerned, was all that mattered.

Sully, however, wasn't initially won over. That's because just one month into the 1974–75 season Taylor dropped him after an amazing run of 194 consecutive first-team appearances. Back on the transfer list at the Goldstone for the umpteenth time, Peter convinced himself the time had finally come to leave. Now 23 he'd had enough of Division Three, the managerial comings and goings and, yes, Sussex. He simply had to get out. Eight games later he was back in the side as if nothing had happened. 'I think I just decided to knuckle down and get on with it. Peter Taylor's heart was clearly in it, we'd got the basis of a fairly-good side and I thought to myself "Well, there are worse places I could be." We took a while getting going but eventually went on a push for promotion and ended up blowing it. I think Millwall came from out of nowhere to go up instead of us. But we were playing some good stuff.'

Having been restored to the team Peter went on to play in every game of the 1974–75 and 1975–76 seasons, missing out on promotion to the Second Division during the latter by just three points. Far from sulking about his inability to land a transfer, Sully seemed to revel in his role as the team's creative heartbeat. 'From a left-back's point of view he was excellent to play with,' remembers Harry Wilson, one of the new arrivals during Clough's brief spell at the club. 'We doubled up well down that side. He never hid and was always wanting the ball. But the really great thing about Sully was his crosses. You always knew with him that they were going to land where he wanted them to land. He was so precise, not like so many wingers who fail to get the ball past the first man or over-hit the thing. That's why he created so many goals for the likes of Fred Binney and Sammy Morgan.'

All seemed well when the players returned for pre-season training during the long hot summer of 1976, eager to erase the disappointment of the previous campaign by launching a full-on bid for promotion. And then from out of nowhere Peter Taylor resigned, citing the club's failure to make it into Division Two as the reason behind his decision. Within seven days he had resurfaced in Nottingham as Brian Clough's assistant at the City Ground. Albion were in limbo, their promotion hopes dealt the severest of blows before a ball had even been kicked. To his immense credit Mike Bamber acted quickly to appoint a successor. However, his choice of boss didn't meet with everyone's approval, including that of Peter.

'Peter Taylor, who had got the nucleus of that side together, left one day and all of a sudden Mullers was there the next. He comes in, spouting off even though he'd never been a manager before, giving it the large one about "I'm a winner" and that kind of thing. And I'm thinking "Oh no, here we go again." I'd been sitting next to Barry Bridges when Cloughie came and I was sitting beside Joe Kinnear when Mullers arrived. He had one of his medals round his neck and he's going "This is a winners' medal" and Joe whispers to me "I've got one of those." That's what he was like. That was his style. Give him his due, I think we went straight up that first season and the guy couldn't do any wrong. But it's interesting to think that had we got promotion under Peter Taylor, then would he have stayed? If he had, then there would've been no Mullers.'

Love/hate is probably a fair description of the relationship that existed between Sully and Alan Mullery. The pair fell out more times than Brighton's West Pier has burned down, yet there is no doubt the former Spurs captain managed to get the best out of his left-winger as the club began its steady ascent on the top flight. At the root of their frequently-volatile existence was Peter's willingness to speak his mind. If something had to be said, then he would say it. If Mullery didn't like what he heard, then tough. Of course, Mullery wasn't exactly backwards in coming forwards either. In 1973 while playing for Fulham against Brighton he had punched teammate Jimmy Dunne in the face for his lacklustre efforts in trying to prevent Ken Beamish from scoring. Mike Bamber remembered the incident vividly and, appreciating Mullery's will to win, appointed him as Peter Taylor's successor on the basis of it.

Mullery's arrival certainly didn't dampen Sully's appetite for the game, something that had steadily grown under Peter Taylor's regime. 'We'd been getting good crowds ever since Cloughie came but particularly during the time Peter was in charge, so it wasn't something that just took off when Mullers arrived. But we carried on playing the good football that we had during Peter's last year and that seemed to make even more people want to come. It was a great place to play. It got to the stage where you couldn't wait for Saturdays, which was a far cry from my early days at the club when we were crap and I'd be like "Oh God, not another Saturday." Everyone wanted to do well. We all had the same ambition. None of us I don't think had played in the top grade, and we all wanted to get there.'

It was around this time that Peter also acquired his nickname. The World Cup Finals of 1974 had thrown up a new star in a Brazilian by the name of Rivolino. Boasting a big moustache and a quite-devastating left foot which made him especially dangerous from set pieces, Rivolino is still regarded in his native country as one of the sport's most-graceful players ever. It wasn't long before

Peter's teammates noticed him adapting some of the Brazilian's traits, off the field as well as on it. And that was that. Sully became 'Rivolino' not just in the dressing room but also on the terraces.

'I think he began to base his whole life on Rivolino,' says Gary Williams. 'He had the moustache to match, he had Rivolino's walk even when he was off the pitch, he acted like him on the pitch with the step overs and he loved Brazil. He'd watch him on video and the next week he would come out and be doing the same things, which is no bad thing as Rivolino was one of the best players in the world.'

For the record, Peter fully admits the big influence Rivolino had on him, although he confesses the Brazilian was "about a million times better than me as a player". So was the moustache solely down to the influence of his South American namesake as well? 'Possibly, but I won't confirm it.' We will take that as a yes then.

Peter played in all bar three League games during Mullery's first year in charge as Albion won promotion to the Second Division. Yet his status as one of the first names on the team sheet along with Brian Horton and Peter Ward didn't prevent him from being dropped and once again transfer listed at the beginning of the 1977–78 season following, you've guessed it, a major bust up with the manager. 'I had loads of arguments with him, so many I can't even remember what that particular one was about. I'd like to think I certainly had my say. I wasn't like a lot of players who would sit on the fence and just take it. Most of it was about football rather than anything to do with lifestyle stuff. I remember playing games when I was injured, having cortisone injections and all that crap because I wasn't fit, playing on one leg because nobody else could play on the left. Then I'd be out for three or four weeks injured, recover and find I'd been dropped for someone else.

'Then again, if the team had won a couple of games in that period then I wasn't really entitled to come back, but I didn't see it like that. You always think "Hang on a minute, I'm better than him." Looking back now, if I was the manager I'd have done the same thing. But it's all about opinions. He's the manager so at the end of the day he's right, end of story. Nobody can argue with that, although I frequently did. Mullers was doing his job and as the most successful manager Brighton have ever had I can't knock him at all. I actually think he was quite a nice bloke.'

An admission that can't make the memory of Mullery and him grappling in the Goldstone tunnel following the manager's decision to substitute his number 11 a particularly nice one, Albion's kit man Glen Wilson having to separate the two of them before a proper fist was thrown. In the cold light of day

it's amazing Sully lasted as long as he did at the club, although the man himself has a take on that. 'I think every time I went on the transfer list perhaps they wanted too much money for me. I can remember Peter Taylor saying that John Bond at Norwich fancied me. Peter apparently said "That's what we want for him" and Bond said "He's not worth that!" In those days you didn't have an agent. It was up to the club to put your details about. Maybe they did, maybe they didn't. Maybe they knew me too well and waited until I'd calmed down. I'm certainly glad I never left.'

Whatever the facts surrounding the John Bond story, the naked truth during the second half of the 1970s was that Peter O'Sullivan was worth the money. Voted Player of the Season by supporters in May 1978, he continued to shine the following year as Albion finished runners-up in the Second Division to finally claim their place in the top flight. He only scored twice that term but created countless opportunities for Peter Ward, Malcolm Poskett and Teddy Maybank, something that made his ongoing failure to break into the Welsh international side all the more baffling. Perhaps his reputation for falling out with managers had something to do with it. Having first played for Wales way back in March 1973, Sully went on to win only two more caps throughout the rest of his career, a pitiful return for one so talented from a country with such a small pool of top players.

Peter puts his lack of international recognition partly down to the talented left-winger Leighton James, who played for Burnley and Swansea City, but admits he could have been worthy of a place playing on the left side of midfield, a position he always favoured. 'I'll always regard myself as more of an inside player than a left-winger. Even now I'll meet people in the street or a pub and they'll say "You were great on that left wing" and I feel like replying "I was bloody crap!" I know I wasn't – I had a good left foot – that's just the way I sometimes feel. But everyone remembers me as wide-left. Can't get out of that one!

'I played in the Welsh Under-23s, Youth team, the Schoolboys, I did the whole package but obviously not well enough. It just didn't really take off. I think some of the time it was because Brighton were in the Third Division. When we started doing well I should've been capped more but [Leighton] James was on the scene and other people. I was always regarded as a wide man so there wasn't a place for me. James was quicker than me. He could play well with his left or right foot, but towards the end even players like Mickey Thomas came in. I know Mickey. He's from just up the road from me in Wales, and I'm not being horrible but I was a better player than him. But it was a different situation – he played

for [Manchester] United, for Everton, big name clubs. I hit the post a few times so to speak, was quite unlucky, but that's life. You can't do anything about it.'

Peter's tendency to sometimes sell himself short ('I was bloody crap!') will come as a shock to many Albion supporters. It certainly did to me. Since interviewing him it has crossed my mind that maybe this had something to do with why people outside Sussex failed to fully appreciate his talent. 'I think he was definitely underrated,' admits Brian Horton. 'He was a Dapper Dan. He always had his new suits and liked the Italian restaurants around town. But he was a great player as well as a great lad, someone who gave the team tremendous balance. His passing and quality of crossing was simply excellent. We knew what he could do, but perhaps others didn't always see it even when we were up in the First Division.'

Sully played in the first 37 games of Albion's inaugural season in the top flight, only to lose his place with five matches left to go. He returned for a home win over Middlesbrough on 19 April 1980 and the following Friday travelled with the squad to Stoke for the final away fixture of the campaign. That evening he received a phone call from America. It was Robert Bell, owner of the San Diego Sockers. Did Peter fancy heading west to play a few games for the California outfit in the North American Soccer League?

The previous May the entire Albion squad had gone on a working holiday to the west coast of America as a pat on the back for winning promotion to the First Division. Their itinerary included a match against San Diego in which Peter scored a fantastic left-footed half volley from 25 yards. Afterwards, Sully had intimated to Bell that he would not mind coming out to play in America at some point. The phone call he received in Stoke was the invitation he had been waiting for.

'When we'd first been to San Diego there was no way I wanted to leave because we'd just been promoted and I wanted to play that season in Division One. But America had opened my eyes, no doubt about it. It was different class, a beautiful place. We travelled around a fair bit and I liked how things were done. George Best was out there, Franz Beckenbauer was out there, Johan Cruyff was out there, all those big players. That night up in Stoke Bob said "Do you fancy it? Mike [Bamber] will transfer you." After we'd talked a bit about money, I went to see Mike and we had a couple of beers. Mike said "Take the train back in the morning, get your bag packed, you can go." And I flew out on the Sunday. By Wednesday I was playing in Dallas on the astroturf where the Dallas Cowboys play. I blew up after 45 minutes. I'd been running round like you do in England in 100 degrees, and you just couldn't do that. Alex Stepney was in goal for them who I knew from my time at Manchester United.

He was going off shooting or something that weekend and he just said to me, "Enjoy it, it's a good lifestyle out here, the money's fine." And it was a great experience, one of the best parts of my life.'

San Diego reached the semi-finals of the NASL that summer. Afterwards, Peter had the option of either returning to the UK to find a club or remaining stateside to play in a winter indoor soccer League. Although Robert Bell and Mike Bamber were good friends, returning to Brighton – the club he had played for on 467 occasions – did not seem like an option, especially while Alan Mullery remained in charge. Portsmouth manager Frank Burrows, the man who would have such an influence on the young Steve Foster, offered him a season at Fratton Park, after which Sully would be free to return to America. The pair appeared to have struck a deal over lunch in Hayling Island. 'And then it all kicked off with Brighton when they got wind of the deal. They wanted me to come back to them because they still didn't have a left-sided player. I didn't have to sign but it seemed like the right thing to do, what with the relationship between Bob and Mike and me knowing all the lads there. So I had to phone Frank up and say I couldn't do it.'

On 22 October 1980 Peter made his second debut for Brighton, coming on as a substitute for Gary Williams away to Aston Villa. By the start of November he was back in the starting XI, Albion

187

winning six of their next 11 matches as Mullery's side fought desperately for points after a poor start to the season. He scored twice – one in a seven-goal thriller at Everton, the other at home to Crystal Palace in a 3–2 victory – and everything seemed once again to be right with the world. At least it did from the fans' perspective.

Yet behind the scenes trouble was once again brewing between the number 11 and his manager. On 28 February 1981 Sully was substituted at Norwich. He was not even on the bench for the following match at home to Coventry, or the one after that against Nottingham Forest. In fact, there was no sign of Peter until after that notoriously-bad 1–0 defeat at Middlesbrough on 11 April, the one that provoked Mullery into issuing his 'If I see any one of you crossing the street, I'll run you over' threat. With four matches left to go and Albion seemingly destined for Division Two, the Welshman was finally reinstated to the side.

Mullery's decision proved to be a masterstroke, albeit perhaps an unintentional one. By his own admission Peter had been 'a bit jaded' during January and February of 1981 – hardly surprising really, considering he had not had a proper break from the game since July 1979 thanks to his summer with San Diego. Peter's seven-week spell on the sidelines gave him the perfect opportunity to recharge his batteries.

Every player played his socks off as Albion won those final four games to stay in Division One, and Sully was no exception.

With Albion's top-flight status secured, Peter sat back and tried to decide what to do next. Should he return to America or consider offers from Charlton and Fulham? Then there was Brighton to think about, who still apparently wanted him. Now 30, he knew only too well that his next move could well be his last. That in mind, he wanted it to be a good one financially. Frank Burrows called again. Would he be interested in going to Portsmouth this time? Still, could be worse. At least he had options.

'Ken Craggs [Albion's assistant manager] said "Why don't you stay here?" I told him that I'd had enough, especially after he [Mullery] had left me out, then asked me to come back in and help them stay up. I wanted a clean break. I was after a pay day if I'm honest as well, if possible tax free. Charlton had offered me so much, Fulham had offered me so much and Pompey had offered me so much. I ended up letting Frank down again and called Mike Bailey, who was still Charlton's manager, to say I was going to Fulham. However, he'd gone on holiday. Charlton's assistant manager said "Don't sign anything. Mike will be back in a week. He'll give you what you want." It was very tempting but Malcolm [MacDonald, Fulham's manager] was pressing for an answer because they were going to Trinidad & Tobago and he wanted me out there with them. So I signed for Fulham.'

The very same month that Sully decided to quit Brighton, and in a classic case of synchronicity, Rivolino retired from first-class football.

Peter's 491st and last game for Brighton came on 2 May 1981 against Leeds United at the Goldstone. It would also prove to be the final curtain call for Brian Horton, John Gregory, Mark Lawrenson and, irony of ironies, Alan Mullery. 'I tell you what is bloody funny,' says Peter, struggling to keep a straight face. 'I signed for Fulham. A week later Alan gets the heave-ho at Brighton, Mike (Bailey) calls me up for Bamber's phone number, asks him for the Brighton job, gets it and Mullers goes to Charlton. If Mike had been in the country when I was deciding what to do next I would have probably signed for him and I'd have ended up working with Mullers again! Aaaggghhh! That would have been suicidal. You can only have so much of a manager.'

Peter's decision to join Fulham paid off in that the Cottagers won promotion from the Third Division during his first year at the club, although a bad knee saw him sidelined at the start of the following season. By the time he regained his fitness Malcolm MacDonald had bought a promising young midfielder by the name of Ray Houghton, who would go on to

star for Liverpool and the Republic of Ireland. Surplus to requirements at Craven Cottage, Sully agreed to go on loan to Charlton, Mullery having made way for Ken Craggs – his former assistant both at the Goldstone and the Valley. Further brief spells followed at Reading, Aldershot and in Hong Kong. By the end of 1983 his appetite for the game, at least at a professional level, had evaporated.

Over the next seven years or so Peter played for half-a-dozen non-League sides across Sussex, including Crawley Town, Worthing and Newhaven, clocking up several appearances for the county's amateur team along the way. The lure of a return to North Wales has occasionally been strong, but at the time of writing he has no immediate plans to quit his home in Steyning. Whether that changes or not could well depend on his Achilles heel, namely women. 'I left my wife and moved up here with another lady, then we split up and I moved back down to Hove and got hold of my last Mrs, then we split up again and I've come back here…and I'll probably stay until the next one arrives! I just seem to float on, but it's nice here. Everyone knows me because I've lived in Steyning off and on for 16 years. I like going down to Hove but it can be difficult escaping the football thing there. You know, every pub, "You used to be fantastic" and all that. Not that I'm complaining. I've done something reasonably good in my life and it's nice to be remembered for that, but sometimes you want to be around people who like to talk about something else, you know what I mean?'

No Sully, I do not. As a player I never came close to imitating Graham Moseley, let alone you. If I had made nine appearances shy of 500 for Brighton & Hove Albion, including 60 in what is now the Premier League, I'd bore people stupid about it until I'm six feet under. But I see what you are getting at.

'You make me sound like an ungrateful git!' says Peter, breaking into a laugh that falls halfway between Frank Bruno and Mutley from the cartoon Wacky Races. 'Seriously, it was a pleasure to play for Brighton. To be honest I think I was probably in the right place at the right time. I got to play for a club that went from being a rank bad one in Division Three to a semi-decent one in Division One. When I first went there even the Goldstone made Rochdale look like Wembley. But I stuck it out. You think of all those times I was on the transfer list. Can you believe that Cloughie was the only one who didn't put me on it!'

Come to think of it, I can. After all, Clough did once famously say 'If God had wanted us to play football in the clouds, he'd have put grass up there.' Peter O'Sullivan, lover of the green stuff and arguably the best dribbler the Albion have ever had, could not have put it better.

Chapter Twelve
The Bench

Forty-six. That is how many names I came up with the night I decided to sit down and work out my Albion dream team. Eleven were selected, one for each position, leaving 35 to fight it out for the five available substitute spots. If anything this proved to be far more testing than choosing who would be included in the team itself. Ultimately I tended to go for players capable of filling a variety of roles. They are:

Gerry Ryan – a loyal servant between the years 1978 and 1986, appearing in one short of 200 games and scoring 39 goals in the process. Played in midfield, on the wing and famously put in one performance at right-back in the 1983 FA Cup Final as substitute for the injured Chris Ramsey. He later returned to the club in a coaching capacity as manager Liam Brady's right-hand man.

Adam Virgo – that rarest of things in professional football, namely a public schoolboy. Equally at home in attack or defence, the former Ardingly pupil played a starring role in Albion's run to the Division Two (as it was then known) Play-off Final in 2004, scoring a dramatic diving header against Swindon Town at Withdean in the semi-finals.

Danny Wilson – a lovely bloke and a top player, not to mention a born leader. Took over the club captaincy from Jimmy Case during the 1984–85 season and never ceased to give 100 percent in his position as midfield general. Along with Peter O'Sullivan, possibly the best passer of a ball I can remember in an Albion shirt.

Gordon Smith – Albion fans appreciate there was far more to Gordon than one albeit high-profile miss. Appeared 125 times for the club between 1980 and 1984 both in midfield and up front, although by his own admission he preferred playing in the gap between the two positions. Famously described by Alan Mullery as the 'Trevor Brooking of Scottish football.'

Eric Steele – but it was a close call. Albion have had so many top-class 'keepers over the years but ultimately it came down to a toss up between Eric and the hugely-underrated Ben Roberts, an outstanding performer during the 2003–04 promotion season whose career was so cruelly cut short by injury. Eric may have left under something of a cloud (see Chapter One), but with his cat-like reflexes he will always be fondly remembered by those supporters who recall the heady days of the late 70s.

And that just leaves the manager, possibly the toughest call of all. Who do you go for? Charlie Webb, scorer of Albion's winning goal in the 1910 FA Charity Shield, who assembled entertaining teams between the years 1919 and 1947 despite not having two pennies to rub together? Peter Taylor, who during the mid-70s laid the foundations for the club's surge into the old First Division? Alan Mullery, the man who built on Taylor's foundations and achieved the seemingly impossible? Mike Bailey, who led the club to its highest-ever League position? Barry Lloyd, the so-called right man at the wrong time? Steve Gritt, saviour of Albion's League status? Micky Adams, another who overcame tight budgets and poor facilities to build a squad good enough to climb from the fourth to the second tier of English football?

In the end I plumped for a double act in selecting Micky Adams and Alan Mullery, with Adams taking on coaching responsibilities and Mullery assuming the role of overall manager. Besides a mix of old and new there is an element of 'good cop, bad cop' in this pairing, with Adams playing the 'good' to Mullery's 'bad'. As one former player said during the writing of this book, 'Anyone who thinks Alex Ferguson invented the hairdryer treatment clearly never worked with Alan Mullery!'